OXFORD POLITICAL THEORY

Series Editors: David Miller and Alan Ryan

———

ON NATIONALITY

OXFORD POLITICAL THEORY

Oxford Political Theory presents the best new work in contemporary political theory. It is intended to be broad in scope, including original contributions to political philosophy, and also work in applied political theory. The series will contain works of outstanding quality with no restriction as to approach or subject-matter.

ON NATIONALITY

DAVID MILLER

CLARENDON PRESS · OXFORD

Oxford University Press, Great Clarendon Street, Oxford OX2 6DP
Athens Auckland Bangkok Bogota Bombay
Buenos Aires Calcutta Cape Town Dar es Salaam
Delhi Florence Hong Kong Istanbul Karachi
Kuala Lumpur Madras Madrid Melbourne
Mexico City Nairobi Paris Singapore
Taipei Tokyo Toronto
and associated companies in
Berlin Ibadan

Oxford is a trade mark of Oxford University Press

Published in the United States
by Oxford University Press Inc., New York

British Library Cataloguing in Publication Data

Library of Congress Cataloging in Publication Data
Miller, David (David Leslie)
On nationality / David Miller.
(Oxford political theory)
Includes bibliographical references.
1. Nationalities, Principle of. 2. Self-determination, National.
3. Nationalism. I. Title. II. Series.
JC311.M475 1995 320.1'5—dc20 95–17966
ISBN 0–19–828047–5

3 5 7 9 10 8 6 4 2

Printed in Great Britain
on acid-free paper by
Biddles Ltd
Guildford & King's Lynn

For
MY FATHER,
and in memory of
MY MOTHER

ACKNOWLEDGEMENTS

To write this book, I have needed to seek the help and advice of many friends and colleagues. Some of their suggestions have been philosophical, some empirical, some what might be called political–prudential. I have tried to respond to all these suggestions, but (especially in the case of the third kind) not always in the way that my counsellors wished. So, despite my great indebtedness to them, they should not be held responsible for the views expressed here. It is impossible to say precisely how much each person contributed to the finished article, so let me simply divide them into two categories: those who read through and commented on the last-but-one version of the whole text, and those who read chapters, or bits of chapters, or simply gave advice when interrogated by me about particular issues. In the first category are Alan Ryan (the co-editor of the *Oxford Political Theory* series), Brian Barry and Will Kymlicka (the official readers for Oxford University Press), Simon Caney, Jerry Cohen, Jim Nickel, Wayne Norman, and Bhikhu Parekh. In the second category are David Archard, Harry Beran, Margaret Canovan, John Darwin, Avner De-Shalit, John Dunn, Andrew Hurrell, Chandran Kukathas, Christopher Lake, Meira Levinson, Andrew Mason, Tariq Modood, Brendan O'Leary, Joseph Raz, Fiona Robinson, Hans Roth, and Andrew Williams. To all of these my warmest thanks are due. I should also like to thank several institutions for providing settings in which certain of the ideas expressed in the book could be tried out before being committed to print: Nuffield College, and especially its Political Theory Workshop; the Society for Applied Philosophy; the Ethikon Foundation; the Fabian Society; the Commission for Racial Equality; the Faculty of Social and Political Sciences, University of Cambridge; the Department of Government, University of Uppsala; the Centre for Rationality and Interactive Decision Theory, Hebrew University, Jerusalem; the Centre for Practical Philosophy, Middlesex University.

I must thank my family—Sue, Sarah, Jamie, and Daniel—for their tolerance of an often distracted husband and father, and for their words of encouragement. Daniel, whose first experience of the whole business this was, has regularly asked 'Are you writing your book today?' followed somewhat more plaintively by 'Will it be finished tomorrow?' I have longed for the day when I could say 'Yes' to both questions, and now I can.

In writing the book, I have adapted some passages from the following articles, and I should like to thank the publishers for allowing me to do so:

'In Defence of Nationality', *Journal of Applied Philosophy*, 10 (1993): 3–16, reprinted in P. Gilbert and P. Gregory (eds.), *Nations, Cultures and Markets* (Aldershot, Avebury, 1994)

'The Nation-State: A Modest Defence', in C. Brown (ed.), *Political Restructuring in Europe: Ethical Perspectives* (London, Routledge, 1994)

'Reflections on British National Identity', *New Community*, 21 (1995): 153–66.

CONTENTS

In order that society should exist and, *a fortiori*, that a society should prosper, it is necessary that the minds of all the citizens should be rallied and held together by certain predominant ideas; and this cannot be the case unless each of them sometimes draws his opinions from the common source and consents to accept certain matters of belief already formed.

Alexis De Tocqueville, Democracy in America, ii, ed. P. Bradley
(New York, Vintage, 1945), 9

The reverence Callum Kerr had towards his own Scottishness came out in his speech, which held on to Scots usages in an accent barely Scots except to the ear attuned to the Borders bite at words. He also wanted to keep the past alive; though his intelligence suspected that much of the tradition owed itself to nineteenth-century invention and a wish in the Scots to be other than the Irish, his heart swelled in a way he could not stop at the old songs and stories. This access to something he could not describe but that filled his heart when he heard, for instance, the word 'Locheil' or the talking crackle of heather burning, he wanted to pass to his child. He supposed he wanted her to have those things he could not describe but knew he did possess, loyalty and a sense of place, as a father with faith might show the way to his child.

Candia McWilliam, Debatable Land
(London, Bloomsbury, 1994), 157–8

CHAPTER 1

———

Introduction

The claims of nationality have come to dominate politics in the last decade of the twentieth century. As the ideological contest between capitalism and communism has abated with the breakup of the Soviet Union and its satellite regions, so questions of national identity and national self-determination have come to the fore. It matters less, it seems, whether the state embraces the free market, or the planned economy, or something in between. It matters more where the boundaries of the state are drawn, who gets included and who gets excluded, what language is used, what religion endorsed, what culture promoted. Battles fought centuries ago suddenly assume new importance as they come to symbolize ethnic conflicts between groups who throughout recent history had lived side by side in apparent harmony. The ferocious civil war that has raged in Bosnia-Herzegovina during the time I have been writing this book has been taken by many observers to foreshadow the fate of several territories that once formed part of the Soviet empire. Meanwhile, in the West long-established nation-states are confronted by a variety of groups claiming that their identities are violated and their legitimate demands ignored by current national politics.

People of liberal disposition are left unsure how they should react to such events. They are likely to sympathize with the idea that separate nationalities should be able to govern themselves in the way that they prefer; but they are repulsed by the strident, sometimes almost racist, form that nationalism often takes in practice, and they will throw up their hands in despair when asked to resolve the practical problems that arise when populations are intermingled, or when two nationalities make claim to the same territory, as for instance in the case of the Jews and the Palestinians in Israel. Some of these problems may indeed prove to be insoluble; but in other cases careful reflection on the nature of nationality, and the legitimacy of the claims that it throws up, may help us to reach a defensible verdict. That is the aim of the present book. It neither celebrates nationalism nor writes it off as some kind of irrational monstrosity. It sets out to explore and defend what I shall refer to as 'the principle of nationality', a principle which I believe can offer us rational guidance when, as individuals or as citizens, we have to respond practically to some national question.

The questions of this kind that we confront appear to fall into four main categories. First, there are questions about boundaries, questions about how far, if at all, the borders of states, or of lesser political units, ought to be made to coincide with national divisions. Does every nationality have a right to its own state? When may a national grouping presently included in a large multinational state or empire legitimately secede and found a state of its own? May one state have a justified claim to incorporate territory that presently forms part of a neighbouring state on the grounds that the population in that territory shares the first state's nationality? (Might Hungary legitimately annex that part of Slovakia whose population is predominantly Hungarian?) These are the questions that are likely to spring first into our minds when we think about nationality and nationalism, and, as I have already observed, it is issues such as these that tend to produce the most tragic conflicts in practice. But nationality raises other questions that are no less momentous.

For, second, there are questions about national sovereignty. If we value national self-determination, we claim that each nation should enjoy political autonomy, which means that it must possess its own governing body. But how extensive a set of political rights must that governing body exercise? Does national self-determination imply that each nation should have its own sovereign state? If we assume for the moment that Britain does indeed qualify as a nation, which rights, if any, may Britain cede to super-national bodies such as the European Union (EU) without forfeiting the autonomy that its nationhood demands? Or, to take a different case, can Palestinian demands for national independence be properly satisfied only by the creation of a Palestinian state, or might a more limited form of self-government under Israeli protection fulfil whatever is legitimate in those demands? Given that, on the one hand, we are witnessing a growth of regional organizations of which the EU is possibly the prototype, while on the other hand there is also an upsurge of sub-state nationalism among groups such as the Scots in Britain, the Basques in Spain, and the Québécois in Canada, these questions too call out for a principled answer.

Third, there is the question of what nationality implies for the internal policy of a state. Many nation-states currently pursue policies designed to protect the particular identity and culture of their members, for instance by restricting the importation of foreign publications and television programmes. How far is it justifiable to impose limitations on individual freedom in the name of national identity? Is it legitimate, to take an extreme case, to enforce an official religion on the grounds that this is an essential component of national identity in the state in question? How far may cultural minorities be made to conform to the values and ways of life of the national majority? Should it be part of the purpose of education to instil in the rising generation a sense of their nationhood, and if so what does this imply for multicultural education of the kind which is currently practised in many liberal societies? How far may immigration policy legitimately be shaped by the demands of nationality? (For instance, is it permissible to set quotas and to give preference to those who are seen as already sharing important elements of national identity?) Since there is hardly to be found in the modern world a state that does not have a plurality of cultures within its borders, these questions, once again, are unavoidable.

Finally, there are questions about the ethical weight that we, as individuals, should give to the demands of nationality. At one extreme stands the view that the nation should be the supreme object of our loyalty, that every other claim should be set aside in its favour. At the other extreme stands the view that we are citizens of the world, members of a common humanity, and that we should pay no more regard to the claims of our co-nationals than to those of any other human beings regardless of where they happen to reside. Our answers to these questions will affect the view that we take about, for instance, programmes of foreign aid. But they assume a particularly poignant form when states come into conflict. Ought I to be willing to fight to defend my nation's interests just because it is my nation? Or may I fight only in the name of some more universal cause (which may, in a particular case, be promoted by the nation to which I belong)—the cause of human rights, for instance?

None of these questions can be answered without some understanding of what exactly we mean when we talk about national identities and national loyalties. Part of my task here will be to try to get these elusive entities into clearer perspective. In order to do this, I shall draw to some extent on the studies of nationalism in different times and places that historians and sociologists have composed. But my aim is different from theirs. I am not concerned to produce another 'theory of nationalism' in the sense of a general explanation of why national identities should have arisen or of the functions that they serve. I am concerned to establish how to think about nationalism, what practical attitude to adopt towards it. Of course the two concerns cannot be entirely separated. Some explanations of nationalism would virtually dictate our response to it. If nationalism is an ideology invented by the capitalist class to dupe the proletariat into submitting to its rule, then, unless we are especially tender to the claims of capital, we ought not to regard ourselves as obligated in any way by our *de facto* membership of this or that national community.[1] But few explanations are as crude as this one in reducing nationalism to a tool of sectional interests. Furthermore, most historical studies acknowledge that the role of national identities changes with time, that the demands and needs that first gave rise to national consciousness may give way to others without a radical rupture in the identity itself. I shall want to stress the openness of nationality, the extent to which national identities can be pressed into the service of different political programmes. (Nationalist ideas may, for instance, be appropriated and used in different ways by conservatives, liberals, and socialists, even within the political tradition of a single country.)

There is one way of understanding nationalism which I want to reject at the outset, a view that sees it as some kind of elemental force outside of human control, akin to natural phenomena like tidal

[1] 'The working men', Marx and Engels famously remarked, 'have no country.' But this sentence alone is very far from being an accurate guide to their thinking on questions of nationality and nationalism. Whatever may have been the case with their followers, Marx and Engels themselves subscribed to no simple form of reductivism on this issue. I am indebted here to Erica Benner's very perceptive treatment of this question in 'Marx and Engels on Nationalism and National Identity: A Reappraisal' (D.Phil. thesis, University of Oxford, 1992).

waves. An understanding of this sort can support two diametrically opposed responses to nationalism. One is outright rejection of all claims and demands with a national reference. Here nationalism is seen as essentially sub-human or primitive in character, a deformity with which no rational or civilized person would have anything to do. This view was epitomized by Albert Einstein when he described nationalism as an infantile disease, 'the measles of the human race'.[2] Friedrich Hayek took a similar view when he explained nationalism in terms of 'tribal sentiments': 'our emotions are still governed by the instincts appropriate to the small hunting band'; 'the savage in us still regards as good what was good in the small group'; and so forth.[3] If one takes this view, the only possible response to nationalism is to search for a means of inoculating humanity against the disease. We must try in every possible way to ensure that the rational and civilized part of human nature triumphs over the irrational and savage part. There is no point, from this perspective, in trying to understand national identities from the inside—in trying to see what meaning they have for those who share them. Nor is there any point in trying to distinguish acceptable from unacceptable forms of nationalism. Instead, we who are immune to the virus of national sentiments must try to persuade our less enlightened fellow-beings to abandon them, or else to find some mechanism—perhaps a reformed system of education—that will prevent the virus from taking hold in the first place.

Although I have presented this view in fairly stark form, I believe that something like it stands behind much liberal thinking about nationality. Isaiah Berlin has conjectured that the prevalence of such views among nineteenth-century philosophers of history may explain their virtually unanimous failure to predict the blossoming of nationalist ideologies.[4] The objections to it are twofold. First, it is empirically implausible. If nationalism is indeed the measles of mankind, then the human race shows no signs yet of passing beyond

[2] Cited in H. Dukas and B. Hoffman, *Albert Einstein: The Human Side* (Princeton, Princeton University Press, 1979).

[3] See F. A. Hayek, *Law, Legislation and Liberty, 2. The Mirage of Social Justice* (London, Routledge and Kegan Paul, 1976), ch. 11; 'The Atavism of Social Justice', in *New Studies in Philosophy, Politics, Economics and the History of Ideas* (London, Routledge and Kegan Paul, 1978).

[4] I. Berlin, 'Nationalism: Past Neglect and Present Power', in *Against the Current*, ed. H. Hardy (Oxford, Oxford University Press, 1981).

its infancy. National sentiments and demands may die down in one place only to spring up again with renewed vigour in somewhere else quite unexpected. Second, in seeing nationalism as, so to speak, something that happens to us rather than as something that we participate in creating, the view we are considering profoundly misunderstands its nature. Even if national allegiances have an instinctual basis, they cannot be *reduced* to instincts or emotions common to the human species. As I shall argue in the following chapter, ideas of nationality are the conscious creations of bodies of people, who have elaborated and revised them in order to make sense of their social and political surroundings, and we too are involved in this process. We cannot properly distance ourselves from it and treat nationalism as a force of nature that afflicts others but not ourselves.

A second variant of the nationalism-as-tidal-wave view is empirically more plausible, but from a philosophical standpoint equally misguided. This is the realistic perspective which counsels us to regard national identities and loyalties as inescapable parts of the modern human condition. For political purposes we should treat them as givens. Our aim must be to channel nationalist feelings and aspirations in the direction that causes least pain and suffering to others. The disease, so to speak, is ineradicable, and all that we can do is to make the lives of the patients as comfortable as possible. From this perspective, to ask whether a particular national identity is acceptable, or a particular nationalist demand is justifiable, is beside the point. For good sociological reasons—for instance people's need to have a secure identity in an open society where traditional 'stations' have lost their meaning—nationalism is a phenomenon that we must simply accept as a fact of life.

As I have already noted, this view is empirically better grounded than the first. The explanations its proponents offer for the appeal of nationalism are often plausible and suggestive, and may deepen our understanding of the arguments for and against different principles of nationality. It none the less suffers from the same defect as the first view, namely that it treats nationalism as something to be explained in terms of the subconscious needs of individuals, or perhaps more functionally in terms of the requirements of a modernizing society, rather than as something that is created and sustained by active processes of thought and interchange among the relevant body of people. Nationalism is still something that happens to you rather than something that we generate together. So this view, like the first, is not only false to our experience as participants in a long-drawn-out process of rethinking national identities, but discourages us from further intervention in that process. We are to ask, 'How can this volcanic force to which we are all subject be safely controlled?' not 'How are we to understand ourselves as members of this or that nation, and how in consequence should we behave towards one another and towards outsiders?'

In preferring the second question to the first, and repudiating the tidal-wave view of nationalism, I do not mean to pre-empt the conclusions we may reach about the validity of national identities and loyalties. It may indeed turn out that such identities are fatally flawed and that there is nothing of value in the allegiances we customarily feel to our fellow-nationals. But this is a conclusion to be reached by critical reflection on our beliefs and sentiments, not one that is foreordained by the adoption of a wholly external approach to nationality.

In introducing the subject of this book and the perspective from which I mean to approach it, I have so far been deliberately casual in my use of terms such as 'nationality' and 'nationalism', and I now want to pay some attention to this question. These terms do not have fixed meanings, but each has its own particular resonance, and these nuances influence the way in which those who write from different perspectives about nationality and nationalism present their views. 'Nationalism' is often thought to have a range of unwelcome connotations which can be avoided by using some other term, such as 'patriotism' or 'national consciousness' for the defensible position, and abandoning 'nationalism' to the opposition. Berlin, for instance, contrasts nationalism with 'mere national consciousness—the sense of belonging to a nation',[5] and then proceeds to pack a great deal into the definition of nationalism proper. It involves, he says, four essential beliefs: first, that the characters of human beings are profoundly shaped by the groups to which they belong; second, that such groupings are quasi-organic in nature, such that the ends of their individual members cannot be dissociated from the good of the whole; third, that the ultimate ends that individuals pursue are to be interpreted as the values of one specific national grouping, rather

[5] I. Berlin, 'Nationalism: Past Neglect and Present Power', in *Against the Current*, ed. H. Hardy (Oxford, Oxford University Press, 1981), 346.

than as having a universal and transcendent status; fourth, that the interests of the nation are to be regarded as supreme, and nothing is to be allowed to obstruct its pursuit of these interests.[6] Here nationalism is identified by reference to doctrines that are characteristic of one particularly strong version of it: that species of nineteenth-century nationalism whose roots lay in German romanticism, in its organic view of society and its cultural relativism. Clearly, to say of someone in ordinary parlance that he is a nationalist is not necessarily to impute to him all (or any) of these beliefs; it may mean no more than that he is involved in a campaign for the independence of his nation.

Yet, although Berlin's characterization might be criticized for taking the species for the genus, he does, I think, bring out what it is about the idea of nationalism that makes many people shy away and look for some other term to express their commitment to nationality. 'Nationalism' conjures up the idea of nations as organic wholes, whose constituent parts may properly be made to subordinate their aims to common purposes, and the idea that there are no ethical limits to what nations may do in pursuit of their aims, that in particular they are justified in using force to promote national interests at the expense of other peoples. Nationalism then appears both an illiberal and a belligerent doctrine, and people of a liberal and pacific disposition who nevertheless attach value to national allegiances will search for some other term to describe what they believe in.

Not everyone has taken this way out. An alternative is to draw distinctions between different kinds of nationalism, and then to argue that one of these is defensible while the other or others are not. In this vein it is common to contrast a desirable 'Western' form of nationalism with an undesirable 'Eastern' form, although different writers make this distinction in different ways, and draw the line between East and West in different places. For Hans Kohn, for instance, Western nationalism was rational and liberal in character, looking forward to a future in which all should enjoy the rights of man, whereas Eastern nationalism was backward-looking and mystical, basing itself on an exclusive, quasi-tribal understanding of nationality.[7] For John Plamenatz, Western nationalism was the

---

[6] I. Berlin, 'Nationalism: Past Neglect and Present Power', in *Against the Current*, ed. H. Hardy (Oxford, Oxford University Press, 1981), 341–5.

[7] H. Kohn, *The Idea of Nationalism* (New York, Macmillan, 1944), ch. 8.

nationalism of peoples with strong cultural identities capable of competing on equal terms with those of existing nation-states (for instance the Germans and the Italians in the nineteenth century), whereas Eastern nationalism was the nationalism of peoples whose native culture is relatively primitive and who must create a new identity for themselves if they are to compete successfully in the modern world (for instance the Slavs).[8] For Anthony Smith, Western nationalism is 'civic–territorial', based upon the idea of a people who share a common territory, are subject to a common set of laws, and participate in a common civic culture; whereas Eastern nationalism is 'ethnic–genealogical', based upon the idea of a people bound together by common descent and a shared ancestral culture.[9] In each case, the distinction is used to make the point that 'Western' nationalism is at least compatible with a liberal state if not positively conducive to such a state, whereas 'Eastern' nationalism leads more or less inevitably to authoritarianism and cultural repression.

A different kind of distinction is frequently drawn by those who write about nationalism from the perspective of political philosophy. This is the distinction between a nationalism that proclaims the superiority of one particular nation, and asserts that nation's right to trample upon others in pursuit of its vital interests, and a nationalism that recognizes the equal rights of all nations to protect their cultures and pursue their interests. Let me again cite three examples. Neil MacCormick distinguishes a generic concept of nationalism as 'the principle that those who belong to distinct nations ought to have distinct governments based upon their own distinctive laws and customs' from a particular nineteenth-century conception which held that the nation is the highest form of human association, having claims on its members which override all other claims, and leading to the view that 'nations in turn may be ranked in hierarchical order, superior nations having rights of domination over inferior ones', a conception that MacCormick describes as 'morally intolerable'.[10] Stephen Nathanson, using a different vocabulary, contrasts 'moderate patriotism', which involves recognizing moral constraints on the

---

[8] J. P. Plamenatz, 'Two Types of Nationalism', in E. Kamenka (ed.), *Nationalism: the Nature and Evolution of an Idea* (London, Edward Arnold, 1976).
[9] A. D. Smith, *National Identity* (Harmondsworth, Penguin, 1991), ch. 1.
[10] N. MacCormick, 'Nation and Nationalism', in *Legal Right and Social Democracy* (Oxford, Clarendon Press, 1982), 260, 254.

pursuit of national goals, with 'extreme patriotism', which entails exclusive concern for one's own country, a desire that it should dominate others, etc.[11] Michael Walzer draws a distinction between 'covering-law universalism', which affirms the rightness of a particular way of life, and sees one nation as the bearer of that way of life, and 'reiterative universalism', which recognizes that, subject to certain minimal constraints imposed on all, there are a number of radically different and valuable forms of life which flourish in different places; the first outlook sanctions imperialism and the exploitation of 'base' nations by 'noble' nations, the second demands that we show equal respect for cultures other than our own.[12]

Both sets of distinctions are very pertinent to our enquiry and we shall return to the issues they raise at various points in the course of it. But I am not persuaded that it is either possible or desirable to try to sanitize the idea of nationalism by means of them—by defending a nationalism that is 'Western', and also 'moderate' in the sense that it recognizes the equal claims of other nationalities. The idea evokes too strongly beliefs and passions that cannot be assimilated to the sanitized version. I prefer, therefore, to use the term 'nationality' for the position I want to explore and finally defend, following here in the footsteps of (among others) John Stuart Mill, who employed the term in a similar sense to mine in chapter 16 of *Considerations on Representative Government*.[13] To be more specific, I shall explore and defend an idea of nationality which I take to encompass the following three interconnected propositions.

The first concerns national identity, and claims that it may properly be part of someone's identity that they belong to this or that national grouping. This claim in turn subdivides into two: that nations really exist, i.e. they are not purely fictitious entities, so that someone who believes that they belong to one is not simply the victim of error; and that, in making our nationality an essential part of our identity, we are not doing something that is rationally indefensible. A person who in answer to the question 'Who are you?' says 'I

[11] S. Nathanson, *Patriotism, Morality and Peace* (Lanham, Rowman and Littlefield, 1993), ch. 3.

[12] M. Walzer, 'Nation and Universe' in G. B. Petersen (ed.), *The Tanner Lectures on Human Values*, xi (Salt Lake City, University of Utah Press, 1990).

[13] Since, however, 'nationality' has no separate adjectival form, I shall occasionally use 'nationalist' for this purpose without intending to imply anything beyond support for the idea of nationality as explained below.

am Swedish' or 'I am Italian' (and doubtless much more besides) is not saying something that is irrelevant or bizarre in the same way as, say, someone who claims without good evidence that she is the illegitimate grandchild of Tsar Nicholas II. This proposition is a fairly modest one: it does not say that we are rationally *required* to make our nationality a constitutive part of our personal identity, or that having a national identity excludes having collective identities of other kinds. Nor does it say that a person's national allegiances must always have a single object: it does not exclude a person's identifying herself as both Jamaican and British or (a different case) as both Québécois and Canadian. It says simply that identifying with a nation, feeling yourself inextricably part of it, is a legitimate way of understanding your place in the world.

The second proposition is ethical, and claims that nations are ethical communities. They are contour lines in the ethical landscape. The duties we owe to our fellow-nationals are different from, and more extensive than, the duties we owe to human beings as such. This is not to say that we owe *no* duties to humans as such; nor is it to deny that there may be other, perhaps smaller and more intense, communities to whose members we owe duties that are more stringent still than those we owe to Britons, Swedes, etc., at large. But it is to claim that a proper account of ethics should give weight to national boundaries, and that in particular there is no objection in principle to institutional schemes—such as welfare states—that are designed to deliver benefits exclusively to those who fall within the same boundaries as ourselves.

The third proposition is political, and states that people who form a national community in a particular territory have a good claim to political self-determination; there ought to be put in place an institutional structure that enables them to decide collectively matters that concern primarily their own community. Notice that once again I have phrased this cautiously, and have not asserted that the institution must be that of a sovereign state. Historically, the sovereign state has been the main vehicle through which claims to national self-determination have been realized, and this is not just an accident. Nevertheless national self-determination *can* be realized in other ways, and as we shall see there are cases where it must be realized other than through a sovereign state, precisely to meet the equally good claims of other nationalities.

I want to stress that the three propositions I have outlined—about national identity, about bounded duties and about political self-determination—are linked together in such a way that it is difficult to feel the force of any one of them without acknowledging the others. It is not hard to see how a common identity can support both the idea of the nation as an ethical community and the claim to self-determination, but what is more subtle—and I shall try to bring this out as I go along—is the way in which the political claim can reinforce both the claim about identity and the ethical claim. The fact that the community in question is either actually or potentially self-determining strengthens its claims on us both as a source of identity and as a source of obligation. This interlinking of propositions may at times seem circular; and the fact that the case for nationality cannot be spelt out in neat linear form may make us suspicious of it. But I believe that, if we are to understand the power of nationality as an idea in the modern world—the appeal of national identity to the modern self—we must try to understand its inner logic.

The idea of nationality as I have outlined it makes fairly modest claims, certainly by comparison with Berlin-style full-blooded nationalism as described above. Even so, it remains controversial, and many people of liberal or progressive disposition would be inclined to challenge it. Challenges to the idea of nationality are mainly of two kinds (they may be combined). One, more philosophical, alleges that the idea itself cannot withstand critical examination. National identities are indeed fictitious, and we can show this by asking questions about how nations are supposed to be constituted, what distinguishes one nation from another, why the boundaries run here rather than there, and so forth. Moreover, the idea that our moral obligations should be defined by national borders is rationally indefensible; it represents the triumph of sentiment over genuine morality. A critically reflective person must adhere to some form of cosmopolitanism.

The second, more political, challenge focuses on the practical consequences of national allegiances. Among the main charges levelled here against the idea of nationality is the claim that it lends support to political authoritarianism. The emotional ties of nationhood can be invoked to persuade people to support leaders and policies that diminish their liberty or exploit them economically. Acts of international aggression are justified by appeal to vital national interests.[14] If we could persuade people to discard ideas of nationality and to regard themselves simply as members of the human race, perhaps with cultural affiliations to a particular group but nothing more than this, the world would be a freer and more peaceful place. This is the internationalist ideal which has been embraced by much progressive opinion in the present century.[15]

These are some of the challenges that must be confronted if we are to embrace the idea of nationality. My aim here is to examine more closely the three propositions which that idea encompasses, and at the same time to assess the main criticisms that can be brought against them. There is, though, one general difficulty which anyone writing in this area must at some stage confront. Is there not something deeply incongruous in trying to describe and justify nationality in the abstract, as something transcending the experience of particular people in particular places? Our thinking about national questions seems to vary quite substantially in two ways. There are great variations *between societies*, both in the strength of their national allegiances and in the content of those allegiances. If you were to ask representative groups of citizens of, say, the United States, France, and Serbia 'What does it mean to be an American (French, Serbian)?' and 'How much does it mean to you to be American (French, Serbian)?' the answers would differ in ways that might seem to throw into doubt the project of describing and assessing nationality in general. Equally, there are great variations *between individuals*, even among those of a similar social background. To some people, national loyalties seem to matter a lot; others express indifference when asked about their national allegiances. We can see these differences expressed in attitudes to emigration: there are some for whom exile from their homeland would be a personal tragedy, only to be contemplated in the most extreme circumstances; at the

[14] These charges can be found expressed in their strongest form in Leo Tolstoy's essay 'On Patriotism' in *Essays and Letters* (London, Henry Frowde, 1903). For discussion of Tolstoy, see Nathanson, *Patriotism*, chs. 1–2.

[15] In the Oxford branch of the Body Shop (and doubtless in the branches in Paris, Tokyo, and elsewhere) you can buy a lapel badge that quotes H. G. Wells: 'Our true nationality is mankind.' H. G. Wells and the Body Shop in tandem epitomize the modern idea of progress, whose disciples were described by George Orwell in such a wonderfully acid way: 'all that dreary tribe of high-minded women and sandal-wearers and bearded fruit-juice drinkers who come flocking towards the smell of "progress" like bluebottles to a dead cat' (G. Orwell, *The Road to Wigan Pier*, Harmondsworth, Penguin, 1962, 160).

other extreme there are those who view the world as a kind of giant supermarket, where place of residence is to be decided by the particular basket of goods (jobs, amenities, climate, etc.) available there. Again, general propositions might seem redundant here. To claim, for instance, that national identities are important elements in people's understanding of who they are will simply induce incredulity in those who take the giant supermarket view.

So can one do more than articulate a personal perspective on nationality? It is currently fashionable to try to illuminate abstract topics by drawing upon the subjective experience of the author ('How the world looks to me coming from where I am'), but it is not clear to me why anyone else should pay attention to insights arrived at in this way, except in so far as they are collecting *mentalités* in the way that others might collect exotic species of plants. Unless my claims and arguments find a resonance in the experience of my readers, they are barely worth making. So if national identities, and the demands that they give rise to, were indeed merely matters of subjective sentiment, as my foregoing remarks seem to suggest, I for one would find this profoundly discouraging. But perhaps the evidence can be looked at in a different way.

There are good reasons why nationality may seem to play a relatively peripheral role in the lives of people in the advanced liberal societies. There are few occasions on which national allegiances are directly evoked and displayed. It may take some exceptional event to call these allegiances out of the back room of the mind into full consciousness. Such events may in one sense be trivial. A friend recounts that he was quite unaware how much importance he attached to being Dutch until a night in June 1988, when the Dutch football team defeated the German team in the European Cup, provoking a mass celebration on the streets of Amsterdam. More often it is events that are genuinely momentous that have this effect: armed conflicts provide the most obvious examples, but other causes, such as natural disasters, may have something of the same result. These are the occasions on which we are suddenly confronted with the ties that bind us to our fellow nationals, ties which in everyday life remain hidden from view. What I am claiming, then, is that even those who profess their indifference to nationality under ordinary circumstances are very likely to find that, at those exceptional moments when the fate of the whole nation is determined collectively, their sense of identity is such that they see their own well-being as closely bound up with that of the community. Simply to give an accurate account of people's experiences requires us to give due weight to these mainly subterranean loyalties.

Another reason why national identities may appear to us to have less significance than in fact they do is that many people consciously repress the sentiments associated with such identities. They do so for what seem to be good reasons. They are repelled by the raucous form that nationalism often takes in countries that are less developed and less liberal—the military parades, the contrived displays of national solidarity, the pompous speeches of the national leaders—and they think it a mark of civilization not to be affected by the vulgar emotions that nationality evokes. For people whose politics are left-of-centre, there is also the sense that to give in to nationalist sentiments is to betray one's political ideals, for reasons that I have already touched upon. If national loyalty is linked to political authoritarianism, then progressives ought to try to extirpate any such sentiments that they find lingering inside them. So the sentiments may be there, but people will deny that they have them or, if they concede that they do, regard them as an unwanted relic from a more primitive age, rather than as an integral part of their personal makeup.

No abstract and general argument such as the one I shall offer here can persuade people to affirm a national identity if they do not already have one. If this is not already clear, it will become abundantly so when we explore, in the following chapter, what it means to see oneself as belonging to a nation. What such an argument can do is to establish how far it is legitimate to express and act upon pre-existing national identities. It may perhaps turn out that the reasons people have for playing down the significance of such identities are bad ones, in which case this will have important implications both for personal ethics and for politics. What I have been suggesting in the last few paragraphs is that people may vary less in the extent to which nationality is an important part of their identity than in how far they see it as legitimate to acknowledge that fact about themselves. The nationalist celebrates his attachment to an historic community; the progressive liberal concedes it with reluctance and shame. We want to know which of them has the better reason on his or her side.

The chapters that follow explore the three propositions that compose the idea of nationality as I understand it. Chapter 2 looks more closely at what it means to have a national identity, and considers whether such identities are rationally defensible. Chapter 3 examines the claim that nationality has ethical significance in determining the duties we owe to people inside and outside the boundaries of our own nation. Chapters 4 and 5 explore the political significance of nationality: the former considers the questions of self-determination, sovereignty and secession, while the latter confronts the possible conflict between nationality and cultural pluralism within the state, and asks what policies towards cultural minorities the principle of nationality mandates. Finally, Chapter 6 takes up the idea that national identities are eroding in Western democracies, using the vicissitudes of British nationality as an example. I conclude with the question: how should embracing the principle of nationality alter the way we think politically?

CHAPTER 2

National Identity

I

To understand what we mean when we talk of someone's having a national identity, we must first get clear about what nations are. This is not entirely straightforward, and a good deal of the later discussion will depend on my answer to this question. It should be obvious right away that nations are not things that exist in the world independently of the beliefs people have about them, in the way that, say, volcanoes and elephants do. In the case of volcanoes and elephants, once we know the criteria for something's being one, it becomes a fairly simple matter of observation to decide whether a given object is an elephant or a volcano, or to settle how many elephants (or volcanoes) there now are in a particular region of the earth. Asking the analogous question about nations involves us in difficulties of a different order. It is not merely that the criteria are more complex; it is also that people's own beliefs about their nationhood enter into the definition. So if we say of a set of people that they compose a nation, we are not merely saying something about their physical characteristics or their behaviour, we are also saying something about how they conceive of themselves. And this may be controversial inside the group as well as outside it.

It may help us to grasp the point if we take a parallel case that raises fewer emotive issues. Consider what is involved in a set of people forming a team. When we describe a group of people in this way, we imply that they work or play in close proximity to one another. But we also imply more than this: we imply that they see themselves as co-operating to achieve some end, that they regard one another as having obligations to the team. These two parts of the definition can pull apart. For instance, we might say 'The England cricket team isn't really a team at all; they're just a bunch of individuals.' We call them a team because they act together in certain ways—they go out on the field together, they throw the ball to one another, and so on— but we deny that they're a team because we believe that each is motivated by personal ambition rather than team spirit. (And this will of course have some consequences for the way that they behave; bowlers will be unwilling to bowl at the most aggressive batsmen, and so forth.) We can imagine two participants arguing about such a claim, one seeing individualism where the other sees co-operation, and we could see that it would not be easy to decide who is right.

Nations are like teams in this respect. There can legitimately be disagreement about whether a particular group of people, say the Scots or the Québécois, form a nation or not, and this is not just a matter of the vagueness or complexity of the criteria for being one. It is also a matter of interpreting what people believe about themselves. As I suggested at the end of the last chapter, the problem is further complicated by the fact that the attitudes and beliefs that constitute nationality are very often hidden away in the deeper recesses of the mind, brought to full consciousness only by some dramatic event. So simple empiricism isn't going to settle the issue, not even empiricism of the kind that surveys people's beliefs about their place in the world. You cannot resolve the issue of Scottish nationhood by asking a representative sample of Scots, 'Do you see yourself as belonging to a distinct Scottish nation?' This is relevant evidence, certainly, but it has to take its place alongside evidence of other kinds before a final judgement is made.

To gain a fuller understanding of what nationhood involves, it may be helpful to clear away two common misunderstandings that bedevil this question.[1] The first is the confusion of 'nation' and 'state'. In ordinary speech 'nation' is sometimes used as a synonym for state: when someone refers to 'the newly emerging nations of the Third World', it is very likely that they are really talking about newly created *states*. This usage is not likely to be helpful if we are trying to

---

[1] These confusions were both nailed down with force and precision in B. Barry, 'Self-Government Revisited', in D. Miller and L. Siedentop (eds.), *The Nature of Political Theory* (Oxford, Clarendon Press, 1983), reprinted in B. Barry, *Democracy, Power and Justice* (Oxford, Clarendon Press, 1989), but they continue to flourish and so it seems necessary to make these points once more.

clarify the principle of nationality, since one of the main issues we have to consider is precisely the relationship between nations and states, and in particular the question whether each nation has a right to its own state. When this question is posed, 'nation' must refer to a community of people with an *aspiration* to be politically self-determining, and 'state' must refer to the set of political institutions that they may aspire to possess for themselves. Let us say, following Weber, that a state is a body that successfully claims a monopoly of legitimate force in a particular territory.[2] We count states by seeing how many such bodies there are. Some of these states will be multi-national, in the sense that they exercise their rule over several discrete nations. The Soviet Union was such a state; rather unusually, it openly conceded that the peoples it governed were of different nationalities. (More than one hundred were recognized.) Rather less common is the case where a single nation is for historical reasons divided between two states. This was the case for the Germans before the reunification of 1990, and is still the case for the Chinese and Koreans today. A third case occurs where people of a single nationality are scattered as minorities in a number of states—the position today of the Kurds and the Palestinians. None of this would make sense if we did not understand 'nation' and 'state' in such a way as to make it an empirical question whether those who compose a nation are all united politically within a single state.

The confusion of nation and state is an elementary error, albeit one that is encouraged by everyday usage. The confusion of nationality and ethnicity is more understandable, because here we are dealing with phenomena that are indeed of the same general type. Both nations and ethnic groups are bodies of people bound together by common cultural characteristics and mutual recognition; moreover, there is no sharp dividing line between them. Let us say, again somewhat stipulatively, that an ethnic group is a community formed by common descent and sharing cultural features (language, religion, etc.) that mark it off from neighbouring communities. Two points must then be conceded at once. The first is that, in order to understand the national identities of various peoples in the world today, we need to examine their ethnic origins. Typically, though not always, a nation emerges from an ethnic community that furnishes it

[2] M. Weber, 'Politics as a Vocation', in H. H. Gerth and C. W. Mills (eds.), *From Max Weber* (London, Routledge and Kegan Paul, 1970), 78.

with its distinct identity.[3] The second is that ethnicity continues to be a possible source of new national identities. Indeed, one could put this more strongly: where an ethnic group finds its identity being threatened or its legitimate political aspirations being denied, it would be quite surprising if it did not begin to think of itself as a nation and to express those aspirations in nationalist terms.[4]

But having conceded these points, we must also insist on their contraries. Even nations that originally had an exclusive ethnic character may come, over time, to embrace a multitude of different ethnicities. The clearest example of this is the American nation originally ethnically Anglo-Saxon, but now incorporating Irish-Americans, Italian-Americans, and many other such hyphenated groups.[5] This example also reveals the limits of the second point. We have no reason to think that Italian-Americans, an ethnic group, will develop a national identity separate from that of other Americans. I

[3] For a detailed exploration of this point, see A. D. Smith, *The Ethnic Origins of Nations* (Oxford, Blackwell, 1986).

[4] For a recent example, consider the emergence of Tamil nationalism in Sri Lanka. (I draw here upon R. N. Kearney, 'Ethnic Conflict and the Tamil Separatist Movement in Sri Lanka', *Asian Survey*, 25 (1985), 898–917.) Ethnic conflict between the minority Tamil community and the majority Sinhalese community began to appear shortly after independence in 1948. The Tamils felt that both their religion and their language were under threat from the Sinhalese, and they also feared the effects of government-sponsored migration into traditional Tamil homelands. After two decades in which the Tamils attempted to secure political protection for their community through a federal constitution, a nationalist movement emerged in the 1970s. 'Immediate precipitating factors were said to include the adoption in 1972 of a new constitution that contained no elements of federalism, on which Tamil leaders had insisted, and that reiterated the exclusive position of Sinhalese as the official language. Further, the constitution conferred a special status on Buddhism as the religion of the majority, dealing another symbolic blow to the Tamil community (p. 905). In 1976 the Tamil United Liberation Front was formed, an organization which claimed that an independent Tamil state 'has become inevitable in order to safeguard the very existence of the Tamil Nation in this country'. The ensuing political violence has been widely reported.

[5] In saying this I do not mean to imply that all sub-communities in America have found adopting an American national identity as comparatively straightforward as have the immigrant Irish and Italians. American Indians have typically had a sense of their identity and a desire for political autonomy that sets them at odds with the larger community. In the case of blacks, the problem is not so much one of a competing national identity as a difficulty in wholeheartedly adopting a national identity whose principles—equal rights, equality of opportunity—have been flouted in their own case. I use American examples to show how ethnic and national identities can co-exist, without supposing that the group identities of all Americans have the same relatively harmonious shape.

seems perfectly possible for ethnicity and nationality to co-exist, neither threatening to drive out the other. Everything will depend on whether the ethnic group feels secure and comfortable with its national identity and the political institutions that correspond to it. So to say that the boundary between nationality and ethnicity is a porous one is not to say that the two phenomena should be conflated. Overlooking the distinction has got a good deal of discussion of nationality off to a false start.[6] Ernest Gellner, for instance, defines nationalism as 'a theory of political legitimacy which requires that ethnic boundaries should not cut across political ones', and he quickly draws from this the inference that, since 'there is a very large number of potential nations on earth', but there is only room for a smaller number of political units, 'not all nationalisms can be satisfied, at any rate at the same time'.[7] The fault here lies with the premiss, which assumes that a nation must be understood as an ethnically homogeneous community. Once we recognize that there can be multi-ethnic nations, the inference can no longer be made. Of course in a purely hypothetical sense any ethnic group can be regarded as a 'potential nation', in so far as we can envisage circumstances which lead it to have national aspirations. But we should interest ourselves in what is likely to happen, not in what merely *could* happen. Gellner's critical claim about nationalism may be no more damaging than the observation that the telephone system would grind to a halt if every subscriber chose to make a call at the same time.[8]

II

Having now drawn preliminary distinctions between nationality and statehood on the one hand, and nationality and ethnicity on the other, let us look more directly at what distinguishes national identities from other identities, what is implied by describing a

---

[6] Further examples can be found in Barry, 'Self-Government Revisited'.

[7] E. Gellner, *Nations and Nationalism* (Oxford, Blackwell, 1983), 1–2.

[8] Gellner does not in fact think that every 'potential nation' is likely to make nationalist demands; indeed, he calculates that we find at the very most one 'effective' nation for every ten potential ones. But he estimates the number of potential nations by counting languages, making the assumption that having a distinct language is sufficient to make a group into a 'potential nation'. Once again, this blurs the distinction between ethnicity and nationality.

particular community of people as a nation. For the moment I want to bracket off the critical questions that we shall need to ask later, and try to understand nationality from the inside, to say what is involved in thinking of oneself as a member of a national community. There are at least five aspects that deserve our attention.

The first noteworthy point, acknowledged very widely among those who have thought seriously about the subject, is that national communities are constituted by belief: nations exist when their members recognize one another as compatriots, and believe that they share characteristics of the relevant kind—which shared characteristics are relevant will be apparent shortly. So it is a mistake to begin from the position of an outside observer trying to identify nations by looking to see which people have common attributes such as race or language. On the one hand, we may find people who share one or more such attributes, and yet do not constitute a nation because they do not think of themselves as forming one (Austrians and Germans, for instance). On the other hand, if we take those peoples who do by the test of mutual recognition and shared beliefs form nations, there is no one characteristic (such as race or religion) that each of them has in common. This becomes clear as soon as one looks at the candidates that have been put forward as objective criteria of nationhood, as Ernest Renan did in his famous lecture on the subject:[9] to every criterion that has been proposed there are clear empirical counter-examples.[10]

The conclusion one quickly reaches is that a nation is, in Renan's

[9] E. Renan, 'What is a Nation?' in A. Zimmern (ed.), *Modern Political Doctrines* (London, Oxford University Press, 1939). Renan wrote as a liberal nationalist who opposed the aggrandizing element in German nationalism, and especially the annexation of Alsace-Lorraine. By insisting that nations were constituted by the beliefs of their members rather than by objective criteria such as race or language, he sought to counteract such ambitions.

[10] The most plausible of these criteria is language. Most nations possess a single public language (which may co-exist with a number of private languages spoken by the members of particular groups), and this is not an accident. If nations require a common public culture, as I shall later argue, then this is most easily expressed through a national language that everyone can speak. Moreover, political unity is easier to sustain when communication between members of the polity is not hampered by linguistic divisions. But it is not hard to find examples of nations with two or more official languages: Switzerland is perhaps the most prominent. In these cases we may expect most nationals to be bi- or tri-lingual. One might try to salvage the language criterion, therefore, by saying that a nation must either speak one (public) language, or else, by common agreement, give public accreditation to two or

memorable phrase, 'a daily plebiscite'; its existence depends on a shared belief that its members belong together, and a shared wish to continue their life in common. So when I identify myself as belonging to a particular nation, I imply that those whom I include as my co-nationals share my beliefs and reciprocate my commitments. The claim I make may be a false one; I may see myself as belonging to a distinct Cornish nation, say, but if other Cornish men and women do not regard their Cornish identity in this way, then I am simply mistaken. More generally, one may argue that all national identities are fictitious: this is an issue we shall return to shortly. These possibilities stem directly from the fact that nations are not aggregates of people distinguished by their physical or cultural traits, but communities whose very existence depends upon mutual recognition.

The second feature of nationality is that it is an identity that embodies historical continuity. Nations stretch backwards into the past, and indeed in most cases their origins are conveniently lost in the mists of time. In the course of this history, various significant events have occurred, and we can identify with the actual people who acted at those moments, reappropriating their deeds as our own. Often these events involve military victories and defeats: we imagine ourselves filling the breach at Harfleur or reading the signal hoisted at Trafalgar. Renan thinks that historical tragedies matter more than historical glories. I am inclined to see in this an understandable French bias, but the point he connects to it is a good one: sorrows have greater value than victories; for they impose duties and demand common effort'.[11] The historic national community is a community of obligation. Because our forebears have toiled and spilt their blood to build and defend the nation, we who are born into it inherit an obligation to continue their work, which we discharge partly towards our contemporaries and partly towards our descendants. The historical community stretches forward into the future too. This then means that, if we are going to speak of the nation as an ethical community, we are talking not merely about

more. Notice, however, that this amended criterion makes essential reference to the way people regard their languages, not merely which languages they speak, so it is not 'objective' in any straightforward sense. On this question see also R. Quirk, Language and Nationhood', in C. MacLean (ed.), *The Crown and the Thistle* Edinburgh, Scottish Academic Press, 1979). I defend the claim that the Swiss are a nation despite their linguistic diversity in Ch. 4 below.

[11] Ibid. 203.

community of the kind that exists between a group of contemporaries who practise mutual aid among themselves, and that would
dissolve at the point at which such practice ceased; but about a com
munity that, because it stretches back and forward across the gener
ations, is not one that the present generation can renounce. Here we
begin to see what sets national communities apart from other group
to which we may give our allegiance, groups that may, from another
point of view, appear more 'real' or solid because they are based on
face-to-face contact between the members—sports teams or profes
sional associations, for instance.

The third distinguishing aspect of national identity is that it is ar
active identity. Nations are communities that do things together
take decisions, achieve results, and so forth. Of course this cannot be
literally so: we rely on proxies who are seen as embodying th
national will—statesmen, soldiers, sportsmen, etc. But this mean
that the link between past and future that I noted above is not merely
a causal link. The nation becomes what it is by the decisions that i
takes—some of which we may now regard as thoroughly bad, a
cause of national shame. Whether this active identity is a valuabl
aspect of nationality or, as some critics would allege, merely a dam
aging fantasy, it clearly does mark out nations from other kinds of
grouping, for instance churches or religious sects, whose identity i
essentially a passive one in so far as the church is seen as responding
to the promptings of God; here the group's purpose is not to do o
decide things, but to interpret as best it can the messages and com
mands of an external source.

The fourth aspect of a national identity is that it connects a group
of people to a particular geographical place, and here again there is
clear contrast with most other group identities that people affirm
For example, ethnic or religious identities often have sacred sites o
places of origin, but it is not an essential part of having the identity
that you should permanently occupy that place; if you are a good
Muslim you should make a pilgrimage to Mecca at least once, but
you need not set up house there. A nation, in contrast, must have
homeland. This may of course be a source of great difficulties, a
point I shall return to when considering the politics of nationality
but it also helps to explain why a national community must be (in
aspiration if not yet in fact) a political community. We have seen
already that nations are groups that act; we see now that the action

they aspire to perform must include that of controlling a chunk of the earth's surface. It is this territorial element that has forged the connection between nations and states, since as we have already noted a state is precisely a body that claims legitimate authority over a geographical area.

Finally, a national identity requires that the people who share it should have something in common, a set of characteristics that in the past was often referred to as a 'national character', but which I prefer to describe as a common public culture. It is incompatible with nationality to think of the members of the nation as people who merely happen to have been thrown together in one place and forced to share a common fate, in the way that the occupants of a lifeboat, say, have been accidentally thrown together. There must be a sense that the people belong together by virtue of the characteristics that they share. It is not so easy, however, to pin down precisely what this entails. Let me at this stage at least try to guard against certain elementary errors. One is that the shared characteristics must be based on biological descent, that our fellow-nationals must be our 'kith and kin', a view that leads directly to racism. If what matters to nationality is that people should share a common public culture, then this is quite compatible with their belonging to a diversity of ethnic groups. Indeed, it is possible to regard ethnic mixing as the source of the nation's distinctive character, as Defoe did in his satirical description of the English:

> While ev'ry nation that her powers reduced,
> Their languages and manners introduced;
> From whose mix'd relics our compounded breed;
> By spurious generation does succeed;
> Making a race uncertain and uneven,
> Derived from all the nations under heaven.[12]

All that matters is that the melding together of different 'races' should have produced a people with a distinct and common character of its own. Equally, although every nation must have a homeland, it is by no means essential that every member should have been born

[12] D. Defoe, *The True-Born Englishman* in *Works*, v (London, Bell and Daldy, 1871), 437. More acerbically still (p. 439):

> We have been Europe's sink, the jakes, where she
> Voids all her offal out-cast progeny.

there. So immigration need not pose problems, provided only that the immigrants come to share in a common national identity, to which they may contribute their own distinctive ingredients. Indeed, it has proved possible in some instances to regard immigration as itself a formative experience, calling forth qualities of resourcefulness and mutual aid that then constitute the national character—I am thinking of the settler cultures of the New World such as the American and the Australian. To arrive with nothing and then to make good in the new society is to show that you are made of the right stuff. As everyone knows, there is nothing more illustrious for an Australian today than to have an ancestor who was carried over in chains by the First Fleet.

Another error is to suppose that the common public culture required for a national identity must be monolithic and all-embracing. A public culture may be seen as a set of understandings about how a group of people is to conduct its life together. This will include political principles such as a belief in democracy or the rule of law, but it reaches more widely than this. It extends to social norms such as honesty in filling in your tax return or queueing as a way of deciding who gets on to the bus first. It may also embrace certain cultural ideals, for instance religious beliefs or a commitment to preserve the purity of the national language. Its range will vary from case to case, but it will leave room for different private cultures within the nation.[13] Thus, the food one chooses to eat, how one dresses, the music one listens to, are not normally part of the public culture that defines nationality. The boundary between public and private culture will often be subject to controversy: I shall return to look at this issue in some detail in Chapter 5. Let us for the moment remind ourselves that national identities are not all-embracing, and that the common public culture that they require may leave room for many private cultures to flourish within the borders of the nation.

It is equally wrong to suppose that 'national character' consists in a set of features that everyone who belongs to the nation must display in equal measure. Hume remarked that the vulgar think that

[13] This is an empirical generalization, since plainly some national identities are more inclusive than others, and at the extreme one can envisage a public culture that left little room for private diversity. It is also intended as an indication of what a public culture *needs* to contain in order to serve its unifying function—one can argue, as I do in Ch. 5, that a public culture should not be so all-embracing as to obliterate private subcultures.

everyone who belongs to a nation displays its distinctive traits, whereas 'men of sense' allow for exceptions; nevertheless, aggregate differences undoubtedly exist.[14] This is surely correct. Instead of believing that for any given nation there is a set of necessary and sufficient conditions for belonging to that nation, we should think in terms of Wittgenstein's metaphor of a thread whose strength 'does not reside in the fact that some one fibre runs through its whole length, but in the overlapping of many fibres'.[15] Most Poles are Catholics, but you do not have to be Catholic in order legitimately to identify yourself as Polish. It is also worth noting that people may be hard pressed to say explicitly what the national character of their people consists in, and yet may have an intuitive sense, when confronted with foreigners, of where the differences lie.[16] National identities can remain unarticulated, and yet still exercise a pervasive influence on people's behaviour.

III

These five elements together—a community (1) constituted by shared belief and mutual commitment, (2) extended in history, (3) active in character, (4) connected to a particular territory, and (5) marked off from other communities by its distinct public culture—serve to distinguish nationality from other collective sources of personal identity. This gives rise to a further question over which theorists of nationality and nationalism have divided rather sharply: is national identity a distinctively *modern* phenomenon, something specific to post-Renaissance or perhaps even post-Enlightenment societies, or is it simply a continuation of tribal and other such loyalties which are coeval with the human species? Each of these perspectives may in turn be combined with a positive or negative attitude to nationality itself. Thus, those who see it as a modern phenomenon may on the one hand see it as performing necessary functions in industrial societies, as allied to notions of democracy,

---

[14] D. Hume, 'Of National Characters', in *Essays Moral, Political, and Literary*, ed. E. Miller (Indianapolis, Liberty Classics, 1985), 197–8.

[15] L. Wittgenstein, *Philosophical Investigations* (Oxford, Blackwell, 1963), 32.

[16] 'It is only when you meet someone of a different culture from yourself that you begin to realize what your own beliefs really are' (G. Orwell, *The Road to Wigan Pier*, Harmondsworth, Penguin, 1962, 145).

etc.; on the other hand, they may regard it as, say, a pernicious invention of late eighteenth- and early nineteenth-century ideologues, to be contrasted with the benign rationalism of the Enlightenment proper.[17] Equally, those who see it as a continuation of older loyalties may regard it as a cement that holds societies together, inspires mutual concern between members, etc.; or else they may see it as a relic left over from a more barbaric period of human history, which we should strive to overcome as far as we can.[18]

We might hope to throw some light on this question by examining the history of the concept of 'nation' itself. Those who adhere to the modernist interpretation of nationalism often claim by way of supporting evidence that the concept in its present meaning is also of relatively recent origin.[19] Unfortunately, the story appears to take a rather different form in different European languages. Originally the term was used for kin groups, and by extension for groups of foreigners regarded as having a common place of origin. In this sense it was used to classify students in medieval universities by country of origin—'the nation of France', etc. However, in English at least it is also possible to find early uses of the term to refer to people of common stock and customs which distinguish them from their neighbours, encompassing what we would today recognize as separate nationalities. Thus, the *OED* cites a passage from Fortescue's *Absolute and Limited Monarchy* (*c.*1460) in which he describes the Scots, the Spaniards, and other such peoples as 'nations'.[20] In the debates arising from the Union of the Scottish and English Crowns in 1603, the Scots and the English are commonly referred to as two distinct nations.[21] In Defoe's poem of 1701 cited above, 'nation' is repeatedly applied to Romans, Saxons, Danes, Normans and the many other peoples who are identified as having contributed to 'that heterogeneous thing, an Englishman'. In France, we find 'nation' widely used alongside 'patrie' in political debates throughout the eighteenth century; characteristically, both king and *Parlements*

[17] This is the view of E. Kedourie in *Nationalism* (London, Hutchinson, 1966).
[18] In the previous chapter I cited Hayek as an example of someone who took this latter view.
[19] See e.g. E. J. Hobsbawm, *Nations and Nationalism since 1780* (Cambridge, Cambridge University Press, 1990), ch. 1.
[20] *Oxford English Dictionary*, x (Clarendon Press, Oxford, 1989), 231.
[21] For examples see A. V. Dicey and R. S. Rait, *Thoughts on the Union between England and Scotland* (London, Macmillan, 1920).

appealed to it to justify their authority.[22] We cannot then say that the concept of nation entered political discourse only with the rise of nineteenth-century nationalism; it is already recognizably in place at least a century earlier in French, and a good deal before that in English.

There may none the less have been a small but subtle shift in its meaning. One indication of this is that appeals to 'nation' appear to increase in their intensity at moments when traditional structures of authority are being challenged. Kohn has pointed out the frequent invocation of the concept by seventeenth-century anti-royalists such as Milton and Cromwell.[23] During the French Revolution we again find constant appeals to the idea. As the Abbé Sieyès wrote, in his great revolutionary tract, 'The nation is prior to everything. It is the source of everything. Its will is always legal; indeed it is the law itself.'[24] What this suggests is that, where structures of authority can no longer be taken for granted, the source of authority has to be found in something more fundamental, and the nation provides such a source. Kings and parliaments could each claim that they represented the nation more authentically than the other.[25] But for these appeals to make sense, the nation must be conceived as an entity capable of acting on its own behalf and expressing its will. So what is added to the older idea of a nation as a people united by place, descent, and customs is the idea of common agency—the third element in the account of nationhood that I offered above.

To put this slightly differently, there seems to be a connection between the idea of nationality as it emerged in the seventeenth and

---

[22] See R. R. Palmer, 'French Nationalism Before the Revolution', *Journal of the History of Ideas*, 1 (1940), 95–111; L. Greenfeld, *Nationalism: Five Roads to Modernity* (Cambridge, Mass., Harvard University Press, 1992), 154–88.

[23] H. Kohn, *The Idea of Nationalism* (New York, Macmillan, 1944), ch. 4.

[24] E. J. Sieyès, *What is the Third Estate?* (London, Pall Mall Press, 1963), 124. Note also that Sieyès, in direct opposition to the royalist position cited below, *identifies* the nation with the Third Estate; 'it is impossible to find what place to assign to the caste of nobles among all the elements of a nation' (p. 57).

[25] Thus in 1766 Louis XV remonstrated with the Parlement de Paris, claiming that no nationwide body of *parlements* could be 'the organ of the Nation, the protector of the Nation's liberty, interests and rights'. Those who took this view forgot 'that public order in its entirety emanates from me, and that the rights and interests of the nation, which some would make a body separate from the monarch, are necessarily joined with mine, and rest entirely in my hands' (Palmer, 'French Nationalism', 104).

eighteenth centuries and the idea of popular sovereignty.[26] By the latter I do not mean the idea that the people should rule in any direct way, but the idea that they are the ultimate source of political author- ity. Although this idea was more congenial to liberal and radical opponents of the *ancien régime* than to its supporters—monarchists would prefer to find the principle of political unity in the monarchy itself—once it became a staple of political argument, it could be invoked by all parties. In later periods it was taken up by democrats proper. If we are going to say that all power stems ultimately from the people, we need to have some conception of who 'the people' are, what binds them together into a single body. With the activist ele- ment added, nationality does this for us: 'the nation' conveys the idea of a circumscribed body of people bound together by common cus- toms and capable of being represented by a prince or a parliament.

We are now better placed to see in what sense nationality is a mod- ern idea. Three of its constituent elements can readily be discovered in pre-modern cultures, for instance in the Greek and Roman peri- ods:[27] the idea that peoples are marked off from one another by dis- tinct characteristics, so that a line can be drawn between compatriots and foreigners (e.g. between Greeks and barbarians); the idea that each people has its own homeland, for which they should rightly feel a special affection; and the idea that the nation is a fitting object of loyalty, and service to it is a virtue. These ideas are sufficient to ground the claim that rule by foreigners is a form of oppression which may rightly be resisted, so it would be wrong to suggest that this older proto-nationalism has no political implications. (Thus, we find Scottish writers of the sixteenth century listing the distinctive national traits of the Scots and the English as grounds for resisting the Union of the Crowns.[28]) But what is missing here, and is new and distinctive in modern ideas of nation and nationality, is the idea of a body of people capable of acting collectively and in particular of conferring authority on political institutions.

It seems, then, that those who see nationality as an exclusively modern phenomenon and those who see it as the continuation of

---

[26] See E. Kamenka, 'Political Nationalism: The Evolution of the Idea', in E. Kamenka (ed.), *Nationalism* (London, Edward Arnold, 1976).

[27] This is borne out in Kohn, *Idea of Nationalism*, chs. 1–2.

[28] See N. MacCormick, 'Nation and Nationalism', in *Legal Right and Social Democracy* (Oxford, Clarendon Press, 1982).

ancient tribalism are both half right. There was no sudden concep-
tual break, no invention of a radically new way of thinking about
human communities. Ideas of national character and so forth were
of long-standing. What was new was the belief that nations could be
regarded as active political agents, the bearers of the ultimate powers of sovereignty. This in turn was connected to a new way of thinking about politics, the idea that institutions and policies could be
seen as somehow expressing a popular or national will. I have
pointed out that there is no necessary link between nationalism and
democracy, but equally, it is no surprise that the activist element in
nationality should be anathema to a certain kind of conservative.
Those who view politics as a practical activity best left in the hands
of an élite who have been educated in the relevant political tradition
are bound to view with distaste the activist idea of a people collectively determining its own destiny. Two of the most swingeing of
recent attacks on nationalism have come from acolytes of Michael
Oakeshott, Elie Kedourie and Kenneth Minogue.[29] Minogue
regards nationalism as essentially a revolutionary theory and 'therefore a direct enemy of conservative politics'. He offers a reductive
psychological explanation of its appeal: 'Nationalist theories may
thus be understood as distortions of reality which allow men to cope
with situations which they might otherwise find unbearable.'[30]

IV

The politics of nationality will occupy us later. The point I have been
making here is that, when conservatives of Oakeshottian stripe
deplore nationalism, they are reacting precisely to the element that
distinguishes modern ideas of nationality and nationalism from pre-
modern ideas. But now I want to consider another respect in which
nationality may be considered a distinctively modern phenomenon,
an aspect that leads us directly to the question that will occupy the
rest of this chapter: are national identities *defensible* parts of personal identity? This aspect is the dependence of national identities
on media of mass communication.

Such dependence arises for the fairly obvious reason that nations

[29] Kedourie, *Nationalism*; K. Minogue, *Nationalism* (London, Batsford, 1967).
[30] Minogue, *Nationalism*, 148.

cannot be communities in the most straightforward sense of that term. Unlike, say, monastic communities, they are not based on face-to-face relationships with each member having direct personal knowledge of the identity and character of the others. Nor are they bound together in the way that tribes, clans, and other kinship groups are, where each member is indirectly linked to every other by ties of marriage and descent, so that, although I may not personally know my clansman, I can if need be trace out the lines that affiliate us. What holds nations together are beliefs, as I have already emphasized, but these beliefs cannot be transmitted except through cultural artefacts which are available to everyone who belongs—books, newspapers, pamphlets, and more recently the electronic media. This is the basis of Benedict Anderson's claim that nations are 'imagined communities', by which he means not that they are wholly spurious inventions, but that they depend for their existence on collective acts of imagining which find their expression through such media.[31] How do I know what it means to be British, what the British nation is supposed to be like? I find out from newspaper editorials, or history books, or films, or songs—and I take it for granted that what I am ingesting is also being ingested by millions of other Britons whom I will never meet. So nations cannot exist unless there are available the means of communication to make such collective imagining feasible.

As noted earlier, this gives us another sense in which nationality is a distinctively modern phenomenon. But it seems also to reveal what is intellectually suspect about it. If nations are imagined in this way, why are they not indeed wholly spurious inventions? We might describe the process as follows. A number of people find themselves tied together politically, either because they are subjects of the same state or because it is in their interests to acquire a state of their own. In either case, it is helpful for them to conceive of themselves as forming a community with its own distinct national character, traditions, and so forth. There is an incentive both to produce and consume a literature that defines such a common identity. But we have no reason to think that the identity so defined corresponds to anything real in the world; that is to say, there is nothing that marks off this group of people from those around them other than their *wish*

---

[31] B. Anderson, *Imagined Communities*, rev. edn. (London, Verso, 1991).

to think of themselves as forming a distinct community. National identities are, in a strong and destructive sense, mythical.

It may be helpful to flesh this story out with some examples. Consider two elements that are frequently central to national identity: language and a common history. If we examine the formation of national identities in the nineteenth century especially, we often discover that as part of this process a national language had to be created. In some cases this might involve transforming a spoken dialect into a print-language by compiling dictionaries and so forth. In Bohemia, for instance, Czech was spoken only by peasants, while the nobility and middle classes spoke German. Integral to the emergence of a distinct Czech nation was the elevation of Czech into a literary language, involving among other things the compilation of a grammar, a history of the language, and a Czech–German dictionary. Two manuscripts purporting to contain Czech poetry from the Middle Ages were discovered. These were later shown to be forgeries,[32] but meanwhile they performed an important role in fostering the illusion that the Czech language—and by implication the Czech people—had deep historical roots.

In other cases, the language itself was in reasonably good shape, but was used by only a proportion of those who were to be included in the nation. This case is exemplified by Hungary, where Magyar was spoken by rather more or rather less than half of the population, depending on how inclusively Hungarian territory is defined. From the middle of the nineteenth century onwards, a policy of enforced Magyarization was pursued, with Magyar used exclusively in government and administration, Magyar made compulsory for all children in primary schools, and harassment of newspapers appearing in non-Magyar languages.[33] This policy did not in the end succeed, but once again it underlines the importance attached to a common national language in most national identities. In cases of either kind—the artificial creation of a written language, or the imposition of such a language on minority groups—someone who later appeals to common language as a feature marking off one particular national community from its neighbours will be obliged to draw a veil over the actual process whereby the language gained its current status.

---

[32] See H. Seton-Watson, *Nations and States* (London, Methuen, 1977), ch. 4.
[33] Ibid. ch. 4; Anderson, *Imagined Communities*, ch. 6.

Veil-drawing is also required in the case of national history. Renan remarked that 'to forget and—I will venture to say—to get one's history wrong, are essential factors in the making of a nation'.[34] One main reason for this is that the contingencies of power politics have always played a large part in the formation of national units. States have been created by force, and over time their subject peoples have come to think of themselves as compatriots. But no one wants to think of himself as roped together to a set of people merely because the territorial ambitions of some dynastic lord in the thirteenth century ran thus far and no further. Nor indeed is this the right way to think about the matter, because the effect of the ruler's conquests may have been, over time, to have produced a people with real cultural unity; nevertheless, because of the historical dimension of the nation, together with the idea that each nation has its own distinct character, it is uncomfortable to be reminded of the forced nature of one's national genesis.

As a result, various stories are concocted about the past history of the people who inhabited the territory now defined as national. Personal characteristics presently seen as constitutive of national identity are projected back on to these distant forebears. Consider one of the examples chosen by Schama to illustrate the consolidation of a Dutch national identity at the beginning of the eighteenth century, de Hooghe's eulogy of the Dutch Republic:

Romeyn de Hooghe disposed of the whole problem of *when* the Dutch became Dutch by following much earlier chroniclers in attributing to the Batavians of antiquity most of the characteristics he liked to imagine embodied in his contemporaries. Thus the first dwellers in the bog-lands or hol-lands of the nether Rhine exhibited the perseverance, simplicity, hatred of imperial tyranny that was to emerge in their Netherlandish descendants seventeen hundred years later. This imaginary historical continuity was to have great force and endurance, keeping the fable of burghers in bearskins at the back of the popular imagination when it considered its remote national origins.[35]

Sometimes the back-projection had a more explicitly political character. A staple of English political thought in the seventeenth century was the idea of an 'ancient constitution' which found the

---

[34]   Renan, 'What is a Nation?' 190.
[35]   S. Schama, *The Embarrassment of Riches* (London, Fontana, 1991), 54.

source of the rights and liberties of Englishmen in a common law whose origins lay in the distant past beyond the Norman invasion.[36] Defenders of the status quo against royal absolutism saw an essential continuity between the ancient constitution and the present one; radicals (such as the Levellers) saw the Norman Conquest as introducing a rupture, and on this basis sought to reclaim what they took to be their ancestral rights against the present political establishment.[37] Both sides needed to mythologize the past. As Pocock says of the common lawyers, they 'supposed that the common law was the only law their land had ever known, and this by itself encouraged them to interpret the past as if it had been governed by the law of their own day . . .'[38] Here, then, what is projected back is not a set of personal traits, but a set of institutions which is portrayed as the unique and treasured possession of the people in question.

V

These examples show that national identities typically contain a considerable element of myth. The nation is conceived as a community extended in history and with a distinct character that is natural to its members. Dispassionate research is likely to reveal considerable discontinuity, both in the character of the people who have occupied a given territory, and in their customs and practices. It is also likely to reveal that many things now regarded as primordial features of the nation in question are in fact artificial inventions—indeed, very often deliberate inventions made to serve a political purpose. It appears, therefore, that national identities cannot survive critical reflection. If one applies to them normal canons of rationality, they are revealed to be fraudulent. It seems to follow that there can be no justification for giving national loyalties any role in our ethical and political thinking.

But this conclusion is too quick. Rather than dismissing nationality out of hand once we discover that national identities contain

---

[36] See J. G. A. Pocock, *The Ancient Constitution and the Feudal Law* (Cambridge, Cambridge University Press, 1957).

[37] This is to simplify a complicated picture. See C. Hill, 'The Norman Yoke', in *Puritanism and Revolution* (London, Mercury, 1962) for a far more detailed analysis.

[38] Pocock, *Ancient Constitution*, 30–1.

elements of myth, we should ask what part these myths play in building and sustaining nations. For it may not be rational to discard beliefs, even if they are, strictly speaking, false, when they can be shown to contribute significantly to the support of valuable social relations.[39] So what purposes do myths of the kind described above serve in the constitution of national identity? Two purposes at least: they provide reassurance that the national community of which one now forms part is solidly based in history, that it embodies a real continuity between generations; and they perform a moralizing role, by holding up before us the virtues of our ancestors and encouraging us to live up to them. Now these may be valuable functions. If we accept for the moment the idea of nations as ethical communities—this is a question to be explored in the following chapter—it seems very likely that their ethical character will be strengthened by the acceptance of such myths. People's sense of solidarity with and obligation to their compatriots will be increased.

Consider, as an example of a salutary myth, the evocation of the 'Dunkirk spirit' in post-war Britain. At Dunkirk in 1940 the British Expeditionary Force had been evacuated under German fire by a flotilla of small boats crossing the Channel. The symbolic importance of this event was quickly appreciated. It was taken to show, on the one hand, the instinctive solidarity of the British people in the face of a national crisis; on the other hand, it revealed something distinctive about their character: their ability to improvise a solution to a problem without being ordered to do so by some higher-up (in implicit contrast to their German opponents). Shortly after the event, Orwell drew his lesson:

... there can be moments when the whole nation suddenly swings together and does the same thing, like a herd of cattle facing a wolf. There was such a moment, unmistakably, at the time of the disaster in France. After eight months of vaguely wondering what the war was about, the people suddenly knew what they had got to do: first, to get the army away from Dunkirk, and secondly to prevent invasion. It was like the awakening of a giant.

---

[39] In an earlier discussion of this point, I gave the example of a happy and loving family which is supported by the (false) belief that all the children are the biological offspring of the parents; see D. Miller, *Market, State and Community* (Oxford, Clarendon Press, 1989), 243.

Quick! Danger! The Philistines be upon thee, Samson! And then the swift unanimous action—and then, alas, the prompt relapse into sleep.[40]

This image, of a people whose patriotism was usually dormant but who were capable of pulling together in an improvised way when the need arose, served as a salutary myth in the years that followed. Naturally enough, it was invoked by politicians: most banally, perhaps, by Harold Wilson, who at the end of 1964 launched a 'Spirit of Dunkirk' campaign in an attempt to ward off the sterling crisis that was destroying the economic policy of the Labour government.[41] Probably a close study of the evacuation of Dunkirk would reveal many aspects—incompetence, cowardice—that the myth overlooks.[42] But it was surely no bad thing for the British to have the story of Dunkirk in their collective memory of the years that followed. It reminded them of what they were capable of, and served as a kind of moral example. Orwell himself put the general point very nicely in a later essay. 'The belief that we resemble our ancestors—that Shakespeare, say, is more like a modern Englishman than a modern Frenchman or German—may be unreasonable, but by existing it influences conduct. Myths which are believed in tend to become true, because they set up a type or "persona", which the average person will do his best to resemble.'[43]

But what if the myth runs directly counter to what we know to be historical fact? This is an unusual case. Normally the imagined history fills in blanks where no direct evidence is (or even could be) available: we shall never be in a position to know very much about

[40] G. Orwell, 'The Lion and the Unicorn', *The Collected Essays, Journalism and Letters of George Orwell*, ii, ed. S. Orwell and I. Angus (Harmondsworth, Penguin, 1970), 86.

[41] 'I believe that our people will respond to this challenge because our history shows that they misjudge us who underrate our ability to move, and to move decisively, when the need arises. They misjudged our temper after Dunkirk, but we so mobilised our talent and untapped strength that apparent defeat was turned into a great victory. I believe that the spirit of Dunkirk will once again carry us through to success' (cited in P. Foot, *The Politics of Harold Wilson*, Harmondsworth, Penguin, 1968, 155). It should be said that Wilson, who had previously deplored appeals to the Dunkirk spirit, later tried to pass this off as a temporary lapse.

[42] I learn from David Archard that this exercise has indeed been carried out—see N. Harman, *Dunkirk: The Necessary Myth* (London, Hodder and Stoughton, 1980).

[43] G. Orwell, 'The English People', *The Collected Essays, Journalism and Letters of George Orwell*, iii, ed. S. Orwell and I. Angus (Harmondsworth, Penguin, 1970), 20–1.

the real moral qualities of the primitive Batavians. Or else it places a particular interpretation on events whose occurrence at a sufficiently basic level is not in dispute: no one in seventeenth-century England denied that William I had sailed to England with his troops and defeated Harold in battle; but, whereas one party talked about the Norman Conquest, implying a radical break in the nation's legal constitution, the other party refused to apply that description to the event. (William 'acquisivit, non conquisivit Angliam', wrote Spelman.[44]) Equally, it is not in dispute that the *Mayflower* landed somewhere in the vicinity of what was to become Plymouth in 1620, but to what extent the landing represented a decisive moment in the colonizing of America (the Pilgrims were approached shortly after they arrived by an Indian who already spoke English), or whether the country's liberalism can be traced back to the ideas expressed in the *Mayflower Compact*—these are much more contestable questions.

National histories contain elements of myth in so far as they interpret events in a particular way, and also in so far as they amplify the significance of some events and diminish the significance of others. Renan remarked, again with characteristic insight, that 'it is of the essence of the nation that all individuals should have much in common, and further that they should all have forgotten much . . . every French citizen must have forgotten the massacre of St. Bartholemew's and the massacres in the South in the thirteenth century.'[45] Anderson draws attention to the curious character of this last phrase.[46] The events referred to were religious pogroms, directed against the Huguenots in the first case and the Albigensians in the second. 'Must have forgotten' implies both that the events were remembered and that the memory was deliberately suppressed. Renan's meaning, I take it, was that no Frenchman could recognize as his forebears those who had carried out the massacres. It is not denied that the events occurred, but they do not form part of the story that the nation tells itself.

Where the occurrence of certain events is explicitly denied, this is likely to signal a nation gripped by a monolithic ideology. The obliteration of Trotsky from the historical record of the Bolshevik

---

[44] Cited in Pocock, *Ancient Constitution*, 112.
[45] Renan, 'What is a Nation?' 191.
[46] Anderson, *Imagined Communities*, 199–201.

revolution by Stalin and his successors is a case in point. It was well nigh impossible for a regime whose legitimacy depended upon acceptance of an official ideology to concede that its most famous critic had also played a leading role in bringing the regime into existence. Here, then, we find a stark contradiction between the official history imposed on the peoples of the Soviet Union by the Communist regime, and the facts as any impartial historian would recount them. But this, fortunately, is a comparatively unusual case. More often, national myths involve telling stories about events whose occurrence is not in doubt, and different factions inside the nation will offer competing interpretations of these events along the lines of the English dispute about the Norman invasion. In this respect the political disputes that arise over national identity may not be so different from the disputes that arise between historians themselves whenever they go beyond the simple recording of fact to offer general explanations of the events they are describing.

If this is so, the crucial line of division may lie not between the truth of 'real' history and the falsehood of 'national' history, but between national identities that emerge through open processes of debate and discussion to which everyone is potentially a contributor, and identities that are authoritatively imposed by repression and indoctrination.[47] In the former case the collective sense of national identity may be expected to change over time, and, although at any moment some of its components may be mythical in the sense I have indicated, they are very unlikely indeed to involve the outright denial of historical fact. Identities that are authoritatively imposed, by contrast, serve a narrower range of interests, and it may be imperative to falsify the historical record at certain points in a fairly blatant way. (This will be so, for instance, whenever the current regime's title to authority rests on some alleged historical event such as the abdication of a king or the revolutionary overthrow of the previous regime.)

Should we say that national identities are more valuable the more accurately they reflect the real historical record? Leaving aside questions about the sense in which we can call any historical narrative true or false, the historical accuracy of national stories seems to

[47] For a fuller discussion of this issue, and of national myths more generally, see D. Archard, 'Myths, Lies and Historical Truth: a Defence of Nationalism', *Political Studies*, 43 (1995), 472–81.

matter less in its own right than for the effect it has on the nation's present self-understanding. For instance, we think that Germans should not deceive themselves about what went on during the Holocaust; but this, I think, is less because we think it intrinsically valuable for present-day Germans to have true beliefs about what their fathers did[48] than because we think they are less likely to succumb to racism once again if they understand how the Holocaust came about. (This example also shows us the limits of Renan's remark about the importance of forgetting.) Very often, where national identities are freely debated, there is a healthy struggle between those who want to hold up a bowdlerized version of the nation's history as an extended moral exemplar in Orwell's sense and those who draw attention to lapses and shortcomings: injustices inflicted on minorities, acts of treachery, acts of cowardice, and so forth. The first group remind us of how we aspire to behave; the second group point to defects in our practices and institutions that have allowed us to fall short.

Let us recall, therefore, that the aim of this book is by no means to offer a blanket defence of nationalism, but to discriminate between defensible and indefensible versions of the principle of nationality. We have discovered that, when assessing national identities, we need to look not only at what the identity presently consists in—what people believe it means to be Italian or Japanese—but at the process by which it has arisen. To the extent that the process involves inputs from all sections of the community, with groups openly competing to imprint the common identity with their own particular image, we may justifiably regard the identity that emerges as an authentic one. No national identity will ever be pristine, but there is still a large difference between those that have evolved more or less spontaneously, and those that are mainly the result of political imposition. Compare, for example, the emergence of a national identity in eighteenth- and early nineteenth-century Britain, which involved competition between a number of groups—tradesmen, women, the Welsh and Scots, as well as the English aristocracy—each seeking to establish themselves as citizens, and offering contrasting images of

---

[48] Except in so far as we think it an insult to the survivors of the Holocaust to have the truth about it distorted or suppressed. This may matter less when those survivors have themselves died.

British identity to support their claims,[49] with the Chinese cultural revolution of the 1960s, where an attempt was made by a small political clique to impose a uniform definition of Chinese identity upon the mass of the people, involving a deliberate attempt to destroy traditional Confucian moral values and replace them with Maoist ideology. Although in both cases we can find mythical elements in the final product, the *quality* of the myth will be very different in the two cases.

But, still, why succumb to myths at all? Why not simply acknowledge that national identities are fictitious and start one's practical thinking somewhere else? To revert to a metaphor that I used above, why *shouldn't* I regard myself as having been thrown together with my fellow-citizens in the same random way as the occupants of a lifeboat have been thrown together? The occupants of a lifeboat, after all, must establish relationships among themselves. They must treat one another decently, they must work together to keep their craft afloat, and so forth. It seems no handicap that they can all recognize that it is the merest chance that has brought them together. In the same way, people who live together under a common set of institutions are obliged to respect and co-operate with one another, and it is not obvious why, in order to do this, they must think of themselves as bearers of a common historical identity.

The answer to this question comes in two parts, of which the second will be treated more fully in the following chapter. The lifeboat model is badly misleading as an account of social relationships in a national community. For in such a community people are held together not merely by physical necessity, but by a dense web of customs, practices, implicit understandings, and so forth. There is a shared way of life, which is not to say that everyone follows exactly the same conventions or adheres to the same cultural values, but that there is a substantial degree of overlap in forms of life. One can't detach this way of life from the national identity of the people in question. Even the physical landscape bears the imprint of the historical development of the community: roads may meander round fields in deference to the property rights of landowners, or they may be driven in straight lines to serve the needs of the state and its

---

[49] See the account in L. Colley, *Britons: Forging the Nation 1707–1837* (New Haven, Yale University Press, 1992). I return to consider the formation of British identity in greater detail in Ch. 6 below.

armies. Language, social customs, holidays and festivals, are all equally the sediment of a historical process which is national in character. So one is forced to bear a national identity regardless of choice, simply by virtue of participating in this way of life. Of course, one may react violently against the current interpretation, struggle by every available means to change it. But it misrepresents the position completely to suppose that we are starting out with a blank sheet in the way that the occupants of the lifeboat have to do.

In national communities people are more tightly bound to the past than the denizens of our imaginary lifeboat. This limits the choices they can make in various ways, but it also gives them resources on which they can capitalize. As I noted earlier, their obligations to one another do not arise simply from the present fact of their co-operation; they can appeal to their historic identity, to sacrifices made in the past by one section of the community on behalf of others, to back up the claims they make on one another now. No one can reasonably complain if a lifeboater jumps across to the first piece of wreckage that floats by, preferring to take his chances alone, whereas in a national community a case can be made out for unconditional obligations to other members that arise simply by virtue of the fact that one has been born and raised in that particular community.[50]

The implications of this last point will be spelt out more fully in later chapters. What I have tried to indicate here is what we would lose if, in hyper-sceptical vein, we were to regard national identities as wholly fictitious merely because we find that they embody shared myths. There is one last issue that I want to address before concluding the present chapter. So far I have been focusing on the 'national' in 'national identity', trying to get clear about what distinguishes nationality from other kinds of collective identity, and trying to see what follows from the fact that nations are 'imagined communities' in Anderson's phrase. The final question is this: how far is it defensible to regard as a constituent of personal identity our unchosen membership of an historic community?

[50] We do of course recognize the right of individuals to emigrate, which is the equivalent in this context to jumping boat. But it may be that the aspect of personal liberty that is protected by this right is seen as so important that it overrides an obligation to the community which nevertheless continues in force. We are surely prepared to disapprove of people who desert their country in its hour of need merely in order to enjoy a more comfortable life.

Behind this question lies the idea that a person's identity should be something that he works out for himself, reflecting his choices as to what is really valuable to him. To say this is not necessarily to sub-scribe to a shallow form of individualism; this view can accommo-date the person who decides to identify with a group or an institution—an ethnic group, say, or a political party—because that group or institution embodies the values that on reflection she sub-scribes to. The trouble with nationality, however, is precisely that it is something for the most part unchosen and unreflectively acquired. Of course, sometimes people do choose their nationality—for example when they emigrate with the intention of becoming American or British. But we should think of these cases as necessar-ily being exceptions to the general rule—you could not have national identities in a world where everyone chose their 'nation'—and so they do not confute the general point. Valid identities are those that are freely chosen, and nationality (normally) fails this test.

I believe that this view rests on an equivocation over the sense in which one's identity ought to be a matter of choice. Let us accept for the sake of argument that there is something wrong with a person's having an identity that is inherited uncritically and simply taken for granted.[51] We want people to be self-reflective and self-critical, to think for themselves about which relationships and affiliations really matter to them and which are of secondary importance. But this does not tell in favour of identities that one chooses at a certain moment to adopt, for instance by enlisting as a member of a partic-ular group. With inherited identities, too, there is normally consid-erable scope for critical reflection. If one is born a Jew, there is a sense in which one has no option but to be the bearer of a Jewish identity in one form or another. But there is still much to decide: whether to be practising or non-practising; if practising whether to be orthodox or liberal, etc.; in general, how much importance to attach to one's Jewishness, whether to make it a central feature of

---

[51] This would of course be challenged by a certain kind of conservative, but I assume that the reader is likely to share a commitment to personal autonomy of the kind expressed by John Stuart Mill when he wrote that 'he who lets the world, or his own portion of it, choose his plan of life for him, has no need of any other faculty than the ape-like one of imitation' (*On Liberty*, in J. S. Mill, *Utilitarianism; On Liberty; Representative Government*, ed. H. B. Acton, London, Dent, 1972, 117).

one's identity, or only a minor aspect.[52] Answers to these questions are worked out partly by reflection on the identity itself ('What does it mean to be Jewish in today's world?') and partly by deciding how best to integrate that identity with other identities one bears (one's nationality, one's political commitments, one's position as spouse or parent, etc.). The case is similar with nationality: one interprets the identity, weighs it against other aspects of personal identity, and so forth. There is no predetermined outcome to this process. Note in particular that it may involve a radical rejection of the political status quo. 'Being a good German' may involve one in trying to overthrow the present regime, as in a case that Alasdair MacIntyre has discussed, that of Adam von Trott.[53] Or, to take another example, 'being a good South African' has been taken to mean uncompromising opposition to white minority rule and apartheid.[54]

The claim that only freely chosen identities are acceptable ones is likely to derive from a misguided picture of what is going on when one chooses an identity. This picture, which we might call the radical chooser view, supposes that a person can arrive by abstract reasoning at a conception of what is personally valuable to him or her, and then can look around to find concrete embodiments of those values in groups, communities, churches, political movements, etc. We start with a blank sheet, so to speak, inscribe on it our freely worked out view of what is intrinsically valuable, and from that perspective decide what identity to adopt, including which affiliations to recognize. The radical chooser view makes the task of forming a distinct personal identity an impossibly demanding one.[55] A more reasonable picture recognizes that we always begin from values that have been inculcated in us by the communities and institutions to which we belong; family, school, church, and so forth. As we come to

---

[52] In some circumstances there may be little choice about this. Hannah Arendt, for instance, who generally regarded her Jewish identity simply as one aspect of herself among others, found herself obliged to emphasize it during the Nazi period and its immediate aftermath. 'When one is attacked as a Jew, one must defend oneself *as a Jew*' (cited in E. Young-Bruehl, *Hannah Arendt: For Love of the World*, New Haven, Yale University Press, 1982, 109).

[53] A. MacIntyre, 'Is Patriotism a Virtue?' Lindley Lecture (University of Kansas, 1984). Trott took part in the plot to assassinate Hitler in 1944.

[54] See Michael Walzer's discussion of Breyten Breytenbach as a 'connected critic' of Afrikanerdom in *The Company of Critics* (London, Peter Halban, 1989), ch. 12.

[55] It may also be philosophically incoherent, but this is not an issue I can pursue here.

reflect on these values, we find we can no longer adhere to some, we find tensions and contradictions between others, and so forth. Finally, we reach a point where we have balanced the competing demands upon us and established our own scale of priorities between the different values. At that point we have worked out our own distinct identity. Of course, the identity is always a provisional one, and new events, or further critical thought, may cause us to revise it. But we now have an independent vantage point from which we can define our relationship to the various communities and other sources from which our values were first taken.[56]

There is no reason why nationality should be excluded from this process, and no reason why a person's final identity should not have national identity as one constituent. There would be an incompatibility only if national identities were so tightly defined as to leave no room for selective endorsement—e.g. if being French meant having to adhere unconditionally to a whole string of beliefs and attitudes— or if these identities had necessarily to be regarded as overriding— e.g. if seeing oneself as French entailed giving *that* commitment absolute priority over all the other commitments one might have. The analysis I have given in this chapter shows why the first worry is groundless. The very fluidity of national identities, which, as we have seen, gives rise to the suspicion in some quarters that they are essentially fictitious, also entails that in maintaining them people do not commit themselves rigidly to a particular set of values. Recognizing one's French identity still leaves a great deal open as to the *kind* of Frenchman or Frenchwoman one is going to be.

As to the second worry, it is certainly true that nationalist doctrine often *proclaims* the absolute precedence of national allegiances over allegiances of other kinds.[57] But to have a national identity, one does

---

[56] For an account of personal autonomy that is close to the one sketched here, see S. Benn, *A Theory of Freedom* (Cambridge, Cambridge University Press, 1988), ch. 9. Although I agree with Benn that the search for consistency among one's beliefs and commitments is essential to becoming autonomous, I am not convinced that a person achieves autonomy only when the quest is successful. An autonomous person may simply have learned to live with incoherence, acknowledging different identities and commitments which do not fit together in one neat pattern. See my review in *Government and Opposition*, 24 (1989), 244–8 for an elaboration of this point.

[57] For instance, if we accept Fichte's claim that the nation is the individual's only passport to eternity, then it follows that anyone of high ideals 'will sacrifice himself for his people . . . In order to save his nation he must be ready even to die that it may

not have to be a nationalist in this doctrinaire sense. Indeed, it would be an extreme and unusual case to find someone whose nationality always took precedence over every other source of identity. Sartre's famous example, of the young man deliberating whether to go off to fight for his country or to stay behind to look after his sick mother,[58] would make no sense if national identities necessarily trumped all others, for in that case, in recognizing his duty to fight—a duty of patriotism—he would also be recognizing its absolute priority over other duties. The fact that the dilemma appears to us a real one shows that we typically regard our nationality as a constituent of our identity on a par with other constituents, and the obligations that flow from it as competing with obligations arising from other sources.

A different case occurs when people identify with two nations, and may then be forced to decide which should be given their primary allegiance on a particular occasion. Once again, nationalist doctrines may attempt to pre-empt this by insisting that membership is an all-or-nothing affair. American immigrants take an oath of allegiance requiring them to 'renounce and abjure absolutely and entirely all allegiance and fidelity to any foreign prince, potentate, state or sovereignty', but they and their descendants have often in practice retained dual loyalties.[59] Some Jewish Americans, for example, have thought of both Israel and America as their national homes and acted accordingly, and parallels can be found among other ethnic groups such as the Irish. The point is that national identities are not in practice treated as exclusive and overriding by their bearers, whatever certain nationalist theories may claim.

In this chapter I have been demolishing various barriers to the recognition of national identities. I have sought to bring out what is

live, and that he may live in it the only life for which he has ever wished' (J. G. Fichte, *Addresses to the German Nation*, Chicago, Open Court, 1922, 136). But the claim is extravagant, and certainly not entailed by the idea of nationality itself.

[58] J. P. Sartre, *Existentialism and Humanism* (London, Methuen, 1948), 35–6. Consider also the case of conscientious objectors such as the Mennonites who fled across the border from America rather than violate their religious principles by accepting the draft.

[59] See M. Harrington, 'Loyalties: Dual and Divided' in S. Thernstrom (ed.), *The Harvard Encyclopaedia of American Ethnic Groups* (Cambridge, Mass., Harvard University Press, 1980). For an illuminating discussion of the loyalty oath, see S. Levinson, *Constitutional Faith* (Princeton, Princeton University Press, 1988), ch. 3.

distinctive about such identities, and have hinted that this may give them a special kind of value. I have tried to pin down the sense in which we might describe such identities as mythical, and to argue that this is not a fatally damaging feature. I have also shown why acknowledging the importance of one's nationality is consistent with choosing one's own plan of life in Mill's sense. I have not, however, looked in any depth at the *ethical* significance of nationality, at the extent to which national identity may legitimately affect the way we understand our moral commitments to other human beings. This is the subject of the following chapter.

CHAPTER 3

————

The Ethics of Nationality

I

The second proposition contained in the idea of nationality is that nations are ethical communities. In acknowledging a national identity, I am also acknowledging that I owe special obligations to fellow members of my nation which I do not owe to other human beings. This proposition is a contentious one, for it seems to cut against a powerful humanitarian sentiment which can be expressed by saying that every human being should matter equally to us. Each person can feel happiness and pain, each person can feel respected when his or her claims are recognized and demeaned when they are not, so how can it be right to give priority or special treatment to some human beings just because they are tied to us by the kind of bonds identified in the last chapter? From an ethical point of view, nationality may seem to give our feelings for our compatriots a role in our practical reasoning that is rationally indefensible.

To get a grip on the issues here, I am going to begin by distinguishing between ethical universalism and ethical particularism. These are two competing accounts of the structure of ethical thought, and I shall argue that it makes a big difference to our understanding of nationality which account we accept. The division between them is not, however, rigid: it is possible to start from a universalist position and then to move some considerable distance to accommodate particularist concerns, and vice versa. It is also important not to confuse this question of the structure of an ethical theory with the question of its content. Someone who subscribes to ethical universalism might, for instance, be a utilitarian or on the other hand a defender of natural rights. How far the division between universalism and particularism coincides with substantive differences over the content of ethics is not an issue I can address here.

So where does the distinction lie? Ethical universalism gives us a certain picture of what ethics is about, the elements of which are individuals with their generic human capacities, considered for these purposes as standing apart from and prior to their relationships to other individuals. Each person is an agent capable of making choices surrounded by a universe of other such agents, and the principles of ethics specify what he must do towards them, and what he may claim in return from them. Because the principles are to be universal in form, only general facts about other individuals can serve to determine my duties towards them. Thus, a principle that might figure in a universalist ethics might be 'Relieve the needy', and then it would be relevant fact, in working out what I owe to Tom, that he is in need and that I have resources which could be used to allay his need. On the other hand, what we might call relational facts about Tom, facts about some relationship in which he already stands to me, cannot enter the picture at this fundamental level. So the fact that Tom is my brother or my neighbour cannot, on a universalist view of ethics, count in determining my duty towards him *at the basic level*. Now as we shall see shortly, an ethical universalist may well want to argue that at a less fundamental level facts such as these should count in determining my duty towards Tom. But these have to be brought in by means of an argument showing why, in the light of the fundamental principles, it may be justifiable to act on the basis of such relational facts. No ethical universalist can allow 'because he is my brother' to stand as a basic reason for action.

Ethical particularism is simply the opposite of this. It holds that relations between persons are part of the basic subject-matter of ethics, so that fundamental principles may be attached directly to these relations. It invokes a different picture of the ethical universe, in which agents are already encumbered with a variety of ties and commitments to particular other agents, or to groups or collectivities, and they begin their ethical reasoning from those commitments. Different forms of ethical particularism will portray these ties in different ways, and attach significance to different relational facts. Moreover, to say that we must begin our ethical reasoning by taking account of the various relationships in which we stand to others is not to say that we must conclude by endorsing the moral demands that conventionally attach to those relationships. 'Because he is my brother' can count as a basic reason for the particularist, but this does not mean that I am bound to behave towards him as convention dictates that brothers should behave towards one another.

Now it seems that both ethical universalism and ethical particularism have strong arguments in their favour. On the one hand, there is little doubt that we do feel a sense of responsibility to other human beings considered merely as such. On the other hand, in our everyday life we decide what to do primarily by considering what our relationships to others, and our memberships of various groups, demand of us. So it seems natural to look for some compromise view that would do justice to both of these powerful intuitions.[1] How, starting from a universalist perspective, might we try to explain and justify particular ethical commitments?

There are two broad avenues that we might follow. (Which we choose will depend in part on the *content* of our universalist ethics.) First, we might argue that, in order to realize the values that lie at the base of our ethical theory most effectively, it makes sense for each agent to pursue those values in relation to particular other agents rather than the whole universe of agents. There is, so to speak, a parcelling out of the basic duties so that I am given a relatively concrete set of duties to carry out in my day-to-day existence.[2] Thus, to take the example given earlier, suppose that one of our basic principles is 'relieve the needy'. It may be that this principle is discharged most effectively if each of us takes care of the needy in our immediate environment. Why is this? Well, first of all, there are many possible relievers and many people in need, so there is a problem of co-ordination. We want to ensure that everyone in need gets taken care

---

[1] Alternatively, members of either camp may try to tough it out, holding on to simple and rigorous forms of universalism and particularism respectively. The best example of a tough-minded universalist is perhaps William Godwin, well known for his rejection of special relationships of all kinds, including family relationships, as carrying any ethical weight. On the other side, one could cite extreme forms of nationalism such as that advocated by Fichte (see Ch. 2, fn. 57), in which the nation is presented as the supreme object of loyalty and duty.

[2] This avenue is followed in R. Goodin, *Protecting the Vulnerable* (Chicago, University of Chicago Press, 1985), especially chs. 4–5. Goodin assigns duties to B according to how far the interests of others are vulnerable to his choices. 'If A's interests are vulnerable to B's actions and choices, B has a special responsibility to protect A's interests; the strength of the responsibility depends strictly upon the degree to which B can affect A's interests' (p. 118).

of, and that as far as possible there is no duplication of the relief. If we say that each person should look after their own family first, next their immediate neighbours, then after that other members of their local community, and so forth, we may hope to achieve these two desiderata. Second, I am likely to be far better placed to relieve the needs of some people than others, partly because it is simply more feasible for me to transfer the necessary resources, and partly because I will know more about what is actually needed by the particular people in question.[3] I am likely to know *in detail* what members of my family need, and I can get resources to them easily. So, we require conventions to decide who is to discharge duties such as this in particular cases, and it is easy to see that the most effective conventions will be ones that take account of relationships like those we find in families. Let us call this the 'useful convention' method of getting from universal duties to particular ones. The idea is that, if everyone acts on the convention in question ('Help members of your family first', etc.), all of us together will end up better discharging a duty that is universal in form.

The second avenue involves arguing that, from the universal perspective, each of us is empowered to create special relationships of various kinds, establishing particular sets of rights and obligations.[4] The simplest case would be a promise or contract: by making a promise or entering a contract, we confer special rights on our partners in agreement, and undertake special duties towards them. This is justified from a universalist perspective because it is seen as valuable for people to have the moral power to enter such agreements. (It promotes their well-being, it is an essential part of their freedom, etc.) The argument can be extended to relationships within the family and to membership of other groups by portraying these groups as voluntary associations: I am entitled freely to enter such associations, and once I have become a member I am subject to the rules and obligations of membership. (It is implicit in the story that I cannot enter *any* such association, but at the very least only those associations whose purpose does not contravene the basic principles of uni-

[3] This is the line of argument used by Peter Singer to explain special responsibilities in 'Reconsidering the Famine Relief Argument', in P. G. Brown and H. Shue (eds.), *Food Policy* (New York, Free Press, 1977), 44.
[4] For an example of this approach, see A. Gewirth, 'Ethical Universalism and Particularism', *Journal of Philosophy*, 85 (1988), 283–302.

versal ethics.) Let us call this the 'voluntary creation' route from universal duties to particular ones. The general idea, to summarize, is that it is valuable from a universal point of view for people to have the moral power to bind themselves into special relationships with ethical content.

If these are the ways in which universalists typically try to accommodate our sense that special relationships and special loyalties matter to us ethically, how do particularists try to account for universal duties? The picture of ethical life favoured by particularists tends to be pluralistic. That is, we are tied in to many different relationships—families, work groups, voluntary associations, religious and other such communities, nations—each of which makes demands on us, and there is no single overarching perspective from which we can order or rank these demands. In case of conflict—say, where I have to decide whether to use my resources to help my brother or my colleague at work—I simply have to weigh their respective claims, reflecting both on the nature of my relationship to the two individuals and on the benefits that each would get from the help I can give. Given a picture of this kind, it is relatively straightforward to include the claim that I owe something to my fellow human beings considered merely as such. The relationships in which I stand vary considerably in their complexity and closeness. There is nothing in particularism which prevents me from recognizing that I stand in *some* relationship to all other human beings by virtue of our common humanity and our sharing of a single world. The problem is rather to decide on what ethical demands stem from this relationship, and to weigh it against other more specific loyalties.

Despite these conciliatory manœuvres made to incorporate the moral intuitions appealed to by the other side, there still remains a fundamental gulf between ethical universalism and particularism. One way of expressing this, which I shall try to show is misleading, is that universalists believe in ethical *impartiality*, whereas particularists believe in ethical *partiality*. This may seem to be an accurate way of describing the contrast because, from a universalist point of view, what the particularist is advocating is naturally referred to as 'favouring your own family' or 'showing preference for your own community', and this appears to be a case of 'showing partiality', whereas 'favouring everyone equally' looks like 'being impartial'. But in fact this is wrong. 'Impartiality' always gains its meaning from a specific context, and it means something like 'applying the rules and the criteria appropriate to that context in a uniform way, and in particular without allowing personal prejudice or interest to interfere'.[5] So a judge is being impartial when she applies the rule of law even-handedly to the cases that come before her, not taking bribes or allowing racial prejudice, say, to influence her verdicts. But she need be impartial only towards the cases that come before her, and she is not being partial because the rules she applies require her to punish crimes more leniently than the equivalent crimes are punished in some other jurisdiction. Equally, a father may deal impartially with his children, but this doesn't require him to dole out the same treatment to his neighbour's children as he gives to his own.[6]

The ethical particularist is not an advocate of partiality. He will agree that ethical conduct must be impartial, but he will simply deny that impartiality consists in taking up a universalist perspective. Thus, if I am a member of group G, then I must act towards all the other members of group G in certain ways, and that will require me to be impartial even if I happen to like Elizabeth more than John; and so forth. But I am not required to act in the same way towards people who are not members of G, and in refusing them what I would be obliged to give to people who are members, I am not displaying partiality.[7] Partiality (in the morally relevant sense) means treating someone (possibly yourself) favourably in defiance of ethically sanctioned rules and procedures, so we don't know what it consists in until we know what those rules and procedures are in a given case.

Describing the contrast between universalism and particularism in terms of a contrast between impartiality and partiality muddles up a question about the structure of ethics with a different question. This second question has to do with how far ethical demands, *however construed*, may justifiably constrain individuals' pursuit of their own

---

[5] At least, this is the meaning of impartiality in its morally relevant sense. There may perhaps also be a morally neutral sense in which any discrimination in the way that I treat people can be called partiality.

[6] Cf. here the analysis of impartiality in J. Cottingham, 'Ethics and Impartiality', *Philosophical Studies*, 43 (1983), 83–99.

[7] The argument here runs parallel to that made in A. Oldenquist, 'Loyalties', *Journal of Philosophy*, 79 (1982), 173–93. Oldenquist argues that the demand for 'impartiality' always in reality amounts to the demand that we should consider equally the interests of a wider 'tribe' of people than the present objects of our concern.

projects and goals. Several recent authors, most notably perhaps Bernard Williams and Thomas Nagel, have explored the conflicts that arise between impersonal morality and what Nagel calls 'the personal standpoint'—the agent's view of himself as someone with particular concerns and interests whose satisfaction is vitally important to him.[8] This may indeed legitimately be presented as a conflict between impartiality and partiality, since what goes into the scales against impersonal morality is the agent's concern that his own life should go well. It is important to see that the conflict between personal and impersonal standpoints can be just as severe when 'impartial morality' is construed in particularist terms—for instance, when a person has to choose between pursuing his own ambitions and doing what his profession or his country requires of him. Both Williams and Nagel veil this point to some extent, by thinking of impartiality in universalist terms. So the picture they present is of an agent with his own projects confronted with the demands of some global principle such as utility or equality.[9] But the position is really much more complex than that. What constrains the pursuit of individual projects is typically a whole raft of demands and obligations, stemming from someone's commitments, memberships, and allegiances, as well as from the rights or needs of humanity as such. All of these, I have argued, can best be seen as (possibly conflicting) requirements of impartiality.

How, then, *should* we understand what is at stake in the contest between universalism and particularism in ethics? We can get a better grasp of it by seeing what the universalist will identify as the main weakness in particularism, and conversely what the particularist will

---

[8] See B. Williams, 'Persons, Character and Morality', in *Moral Luck* (Cambridge, Cambridge University Press, 1981); T. Nagel, *Equality and Partiality* (New York, Oxford University Press, 1991).

[9] This point is made in criticism of Williams in A. MacIntyre, 'The Magic in the Pronoun "My"', *Ethics*, 94 (1983–4), 113–25. It bears especially upon Williams's discussion in 'Persons, Character and Morality', and it may be worth adding that, in providing a general characterization of ethics in *Ethics and the Limits of Philosophy* (London, Fontana, 1985), Williams makes it very clear that he does not identify the ethical standpoint with universalism. Nagel is also somewhat inconsistent on this question: when explaining the general distinction between impartiality and partiality, he treats national solidarity as a form of partiality, but in other places he focuses on the tension between the pursuit of private interests and the responsibilities people have to other members of their political community as an instance of the conflict between personal and impersonal standpoints.

regard as the main weakness in universalism. To begin with the first of these, to the universalist, particularism appears as the capitulation of reason before sentiment, prejudice, convention, and other such rationally dubious factors. By allowing existing commitments, relationships, and loyalties to enter our ethical thinking at a basic level, the particularist signally fails to subject these bonds to rational scrutiny. And this exposes him immediately to two dangers. One is moral conservatism, the sanctification of merely traditional ethical relations, based perhaps on the interests of dominant social groups, on outmoded philosophies, or perhaps on sheer ignorance. The other is incoherence, where the ethical demands that stem from relationships of different kinds are not brought into any rational relation with one another, so that a person who follows a particularistic ethics would receive no guidance in cases where he was pulled in one direction by one set of obligations and in the opposite direction by a second set—the position, for instance, of Sartre's young Frenchman referred to at the end of the last chapter. Indeed, because different aspects of the situation might appear salient on different occasions, such a person might act inconsistently—and inconsistent behaviour would seem to be the epitome of irrationality.

The ethical universalist aspires instead to a model of the following sort: rational reflection on the foundations of ethics will lead us to a single basic principle, or else to an ordered set of principles, with universal scope—for instance to the principle of utility, or a principle of basic human rights, or some version of the principle of equality. In the light of this basic principle, we will then be able to scrutinize our more specific ethical intuitions (say, about our familial obligations), accepting some, rejecting others, modifying yet others, and assigning them consistent weights to be used in cases of conflict. We would then have something that deserved the name of an ethical *system*, a set of principles and rules of varying scope that together would guide our conduct consistently, and that could resolve moral dilemmas such as the one described above. Of course, adopting a universalist perspective does not entail discovering such a system—it may turn out that there is simply an irreducible plurality of basic ethical principles—but the idea that we should at least *try* to devise such a system seems to me to provide a good deal of the motive force behind universalism.

Let me now turn the question around and ask what particularist are likely to see as the main defect of ethical universalism. The answer, I think, is that in two respects at least universalism relies upon an implausible picture of moral agency, of the person who is to be the bearer of responsibilities and duties. It draws a sharp line between moral agency and personal identity on the one hand, and between moral agency and personal motivation on the other. According to the universalist, we discover what our duties are by abstract reflection on the human condition and on what others can legitimately ask of us. When we act morally, we act out of a regard for these purely rational considerations; for instance, having decided that the basis of ethics is the general happiness, we resolve to act according to those rules of conduct that are best calculated to promote that objective. But, the particularist will argue, this involves driving a wedge between ethical duty and personal identity. No considerations about who I am, where I have come from, or which communities I see myself as attached to are to be allowed to influence my ethical reasoning. As Alasdair MacIntyre has put the point, a position of this kind:

requires of me to assume an abstract and artificial—perhaps even an impossible—stance, that of a rational being as such, responding to the requirements of morality not *qua* parent or farmer or quarterback, but *qua* rational agent who has abstracted him or herself from all social particularity, who has become not merely Adam Smith's impartial spectator, but a correspondingly impartial actor, and one who in his impartiality is doomed to rootlessness, to be a citizen of nowhere. How can I justify to myself performing this act of abstraction and detachment?[10]

Equally, the particularist will claim, universalism rests upon an implausible account of ethical motivation. When I act on moral principle, I am supposed to act simply out of a rational conviction that I am doing what morality requires of me. I am not to be influenced by my sentiments towards the objects of my duty, nor am I to allow the reactions of those around me in my community to guide my behaviour. So, for instance, thoughts such as 'I'd be letting down my family if I did that' or 'This is not how a good Christian should behave' have to be seen as extraneous to ethics proper. But it seems unlikely that rational conviction can carry the weight required

[10] A. MacIntyre, *Is Patriotism a Virtue?*, Lindley Lecture (University of Kansas, 1984), 12.

of it, except perhaps in the case of a small number of heroic individuals who are genuinely able to govern their lives by considerations of pure principle. For the mass of mankind, ethical life must be a social institution whose principles must accommodate natural sentiments towards relatives, colleagues, and so forth, and which must rely on a complex set of motives to get people to comply with its requirements—motives such as love, pride, and shame as well as purely rational conviction.[11]

II

These arguments and counter-arguments could be spelt out at much greater length than is possible here, but my aim has simply been to identify what is at stake in the contest between universalism and particularism in ethics. The universalist sees in particularism a failure of rationality; the particularist sees in universalism a commitment to abstract rationality that exceeds the capacities of ordinary human beings. These are the main charges that each side has to rebut if it is to provide a convincing account of ethical life. So let us now turn our attention back to nationality and ask about its ethical significance. It should be clear from what has been said that national allegiances could have intrinsic significance only if we adopt some form of ethical particularism. If we begin from a universalist position, then the fact that Elizabeth is my compatriot cannot justify my having special obligations towards her at the basic level. On the other hand, it is no

---

[11] One way of putting this is to say that the view of ethics invoked by particularists is Humean rather than Kantian. Hume saw that morality had to be understood in relation to natural sentiments, so that the judgements we make about others must reflect their (and our) natural preferences for kinsmen and associates. 'When experience has once given us a competent knowledge of human affairs, and has taught us the proportion they bear to human passion, we perceive, that the generosity of men is very limited, and that it seldom extends beyond their friends and family, or, at most, beyond their native country. Being thus acquainted with the nature of man, we expect not any impossibilities from him; but confine our view to that narrow circle, in which any person moves, in order to form a judgement of his moral character. When the natural tendency of his passions leads him to be serviceable and useful within his sphere, we approve of his character, and love his person by a sympathy with the sentiments of those, who have a more particular connexion with him' (D. Hume, *A Treatise of Human Nature*, ed. L. A. Selby-Bigge, rev. P. H. Nidditch, Oxford, Clarendon Press, 1978, 602). I have discussed Hume's account of morality more extensively in D. Miller, *Philosophy and Ideology in Hume's Political Thought* (Oxford, Clarendon Press, 1981), especially chs. 2 and 5.

so clear that nationality must be devoid of ethical significance at a less basic level. Perhaps special obligations to compatriots can be derived by universalists in one of the ways in which they seek to derive limited obligations generally. So let us see how an ethical universalist might try to do this.

In this investigation we must guard against one possible source of confusion. We have on the one hand groups of people who share a national identity, in the sense that I tried to explain in the last chapter. On the other hand we have people who are involved in common schemes of political co-operation, in the sense that they are subject to the same set of laws, contribute to one another's welfare through schemes of taxation, and so forth; the most familiar case is those who are citizens of the same state. Now of course relationships of these two kinds may coincide, as they do when we have genuine nation-states in which all citizens share a common nationality. But equally, as we have already seen, there can be groups of compatriots who are not (now) involved in common schemes of political co-operation (e.g. are citizens of different states), and people may share a common citizenship even though they are the bearers of separate national identities. So we need to be clear whether we are trying to assess the ethical significance of nationality as such, or instead the ethical significance of membership in a scheme of political co-operation. The importance of this will shortly be apparent.

How, then, might an ethical universalist try to justify special obligations among compatriots? We have seen that there are two broad strategies that he might follow. Consider first the 'voluntary creation' strategy. This would seek to portray a nation as a voluntary association which someone might choose to join, and would argue that the special rights and obligations attached to nationality are justified in roughly the same way as the rights and obligations of more immediate associations such as families and sports clubs. Such an argument runs into difficulties immediately. We have seen already how misleading it is to suppose that nationality could be interpreted on the model of a voluntary association. Bearing a national identity means seeing oneself as part of a historic community which in part makes one the person that one is: to regard membership as something one has chosen is to give way to an untenable form of social atomism which first abstracts the individual from his or her social relationships and then supposes that those relationships can be

explained as the voluntary choices of the individual thus abstracted.
Now admittedly, it is possible to renounce one's nationality, in the
sense of removing oneself from the society in question, making no
further claims against it, and acknowledging no further obligations.
But for this renunciation to be genuine, one or other identity—the
person's or the nation's—must have changed in such a radical way
that the person in question could no longer see herself as a member
of that nation—the position, for instance, of a Jew in Hitler's
Germany. The fact that in certain circumstances membership must
be renounced does not make continuing acknowledgement of one's
nationality a matter of voluntary choice.

Even if this difficulty could be surmounted, there would be the
further question whether nations *qua* voluntary associations are the
kind of things one could *legitimately* join according to universalist
principles. What, positively, are the moral gains, or the gains in personal welfare, that flow from membership of large agglomerations of
people such as nations usually are? It is very difficult to see how the
arguments deployed by universalists to justify obligation-creating
practices such as promises and contracts which involve small numbers of individuals could be extended to these more extensive communities. And indeed, if we look at the arguments actually used by
universalists in this area, we find that they are targeted not on nations
as such but on schemes of political co-operation, or, more
specifically, states. What the arguments actually try to justify are the
special rights and obligations one has as citizen of this or that state.

To take a familiar instance of this argument, assume that our universal obligation is to secure the basic rights of everyone else—rights
to life, liberty, and so forth. Suppose that we are the subjects of a state
which fulfils this duty reasonably effectively in the case of its own
members, and does not actively violate the rights of outsiders. Then
it may be claimed that we may discharge our individual obligations
by supporting the state to which we belong. We have contracted into
a scheme of co-operation which can be justified in terms that the universalist accepts, and so we ought properly to acknowledge the special responsibilities that we incur under the scheme.

This approach still has to face the problem involved in viewing the
state as a voluntary association. States demand the allegiance of their
subjects: the long history of attempts to show that, appearances
notwithstanding, each of these subjects has actually *consented* to

membership of the state reveals the nature of the problem. It may be circumvented, however, by regarding political co-operation not as a voluntary matter in the strict sense but as *quasi-contractual* in nature. Here the emphasis is placed not on consent but on the mutual exchange of benefits. My obligations to the state and to my fellow-citizens derive from our common participation in a practice from which all may expect to benefit. The appeal here is to a principle of fair play which does not require that I should have made a voluntary decision to join the practice.[12] Now this principle has an important role to play in our understanding of the obligations of nationality, as I shall show in due course. But it cannot bear all the weight that it is being asked to bear here.

Observe that the quasi-contractual approach to limited obligations proceeds entirely by appeal to existing practices. Because, as a matter of fact, I am part of an on-going scheme of co-operation from which I derive benefits, I have an obligation to contribute to the scheme as its rules require. The fair play principle lays down some conditions on the kind of scheme that will generate obligations in this way—for instance, it cannot operate in such a way that one group of participants exploits another group by receiving a disproportionate share of the benefits—but it does not provide positive reasons for having such a scheme, or for preferring one such scheme to an alternative with a wider or a narrower membership. So, although it may show why individuals derive obligations from their participation in the state, it cannot show why *this* kind of practice is preferable to one that has a universal, or for that matter a much narrower, scope.

Putting this another way, the quasi-contractual approach only generates conditional obligations. It says that, *if* you are the beneficiary of a scheme of political co-operation, you should do your fair share to sustain the scheme. But it does nothing to show why such schemes should exist. It does not show that it is desirable for there to be such things as states; it only shows that, where they

---

[12] For formulations of the principle, see H. L. A. Hart, 'Are There any Natural Rights?' in A. Quinton (ed.), *Political Philosophy* (Oxford, Oxford University Press, 1967); J. Rawls, 'Legal Obligation and the Duty of Fair Play', in S. Hook (ed.), *Law and Philosophy* (New York, New York University Press, 1964). A full discussion can be found in G. Klosko, *The Principle of Fairness and Political Obligation* (Lanham, Rowman and Littlefield, 1992).

do exist, people may have special obligations as a result. And equally of course, it has nothing to say about the ethical significance o nationality. It attaches no weight to the fact that we feel a sense o common identity with this group of people rather than that. It i interested only in the fact of co-operation, regardless of whether thi is based on a shared national identity or upon the mere contingenc of being thrown together (metaphorically or actually) in a lifeboat.

However one tries to spell it out, the 'voluntary creation approach to special obligations is not going to endow nationalit with ethical significance (nor, indeed, will it even strongly justify th existence of states). What about the second strategy available to uni versalists, the 'useful convention' approach? This side-steps all th problems of consent and voluntariness, for there is no implicatio that useful conventions must be ones that have emerged by fre agreement. But it faces the same difficulty in explaining why an significance should attach to national boundaries as such.

Consider one example of this approach. Goodin writes: 'Specia responsibilities are, on my account, assigned merely as an adminis trative device for discharging our general duties more efficiently.'[1] To illustrate this account, he takes the case of a swimmer drownin off a beach that has an official lifeguard. To avoid chaos in the wate we need to be able to assign to someone the responsibility of rescu ing the swimmer, and since the lifeguard is the designated person, th duty falls in the first place on him. This is a convincing example o the way in which a duty borne by everyone—the duty to save life— can be assigned in a particular case to a specific person. But notic how the example works. First, there is a social convention—th appointing of an official lifeguard—which means that we can al recognize who bears the duty in this case. But the assignment is no purely arbitrary. The lifeguard will have been selected because he i a strong swimmer, and will have been trained in life-saving tech niques. So we all have good reason to think that the object of ou duty—saving the swimmer—will be served best by our getting ou of the lifeguard's way and letting him perform the rescue.

Now compare the case of obligations to compatriots as a way o discharging our general duties to humanity. Here again we find

[13] R. E. Goodin, 'What Is So Special about Our Fellow Countrymen?', *Ethics*, 9 (1987–8), 685.

convention whereby each state is held responsible for protecting the rights and serving the welfare of its own citizens. Although there is no act of assignment, as there has been in the case of the lifeguard, the convention in question seems to be universally recognized. But does this convention ensure that those who are assigned responsibility for each portion of humanity are the most competent to undertake that task? Why does it make sense to assign responsibility for the rights and welfare of Swedes to other Swedes and the rights and welfare of Somalians to other Somalians, if we are looking at the question from a global perspective? What is the equivalent here to the selection and training of the lifeguard?

Two bad answers to this question are physical proximity and administrative ease. Neither of these has any intrinsic connection with nationality. Physical proximity suggests taking responsibility for those in your locality regardless of their nationality. Administrative ease brings us back once again to states, as the institutions that are currently most effective in protecting rights and delivering welfare; but it provides no answer to such questions as 'Why should the boundaries of states be located here rather than there?' 'Why not have sub-national or supra-national units performing these tasks?' A better answer is that cultural similarities mean that co-nationals are better informed about one another than they are about outsiders, and therefore better placed to say, for example, when their fellows are in need, or are deprived of their rights. This, I think, is the strongest argument that can be given, from a universalist point of view, for acknowledging special obligations to compatriots. But it confronts an argument in the opposite direction which is at least as powerful. Nations are hugely unequal in their capacity to provide for their own members. In so far as the obligations we are considering include the obligation to provide for human needs up to a certain point, it would seem odd to put the well off in charge of the well off and the badly off in charge of the badly off. Simple co-ordination rules like 'Help the person standing next to you' make sense when, as far as we know, each is equally in need of help, and each equally able to provide it. But the international picture is very different from this. To put Swedes, with a per capita annual income of $24,000, in charge of their own needy, and Somalians, with a per capita annual income of $120, in charge of *their* needy would seem grossly irrational from a universal standpoint.[14] As Shue has argued, if we want to devise a reasonable institutional scheme to link together right-holders and duty-bearers, ability to pay would seem the natural way of assigning the duties.[15]

I conclude, therefore, that attempts to justify the principle of nationality from the perspective of ethical universalism are doomed to failure. The consistent universalist should regard nationality not as a justifiable source of ethical identity but as a limitation to be overcome. Nationality should be looked upon as a *sentiment* that may have certain uses in the short term—given the weakness of people's attachment to universal principles—but which, in the long term, should be transcended in the name of humanity. Thus, Sidgwick, representing the utilitarian brand of universalism, contrasted the national ideal with the cosmopolitan ideal. The latter was 'the ideal of the future', but to apply it now 'allows too little for the national and patriotic sentiments which have in any case to be reckoned with as an actually powerful political force, and which appear to be at present indispensable to social well-being. We cannot yet hope to substitute for these sentiments, in sufficient diffusion and intensity, the wider sentiment connected with the conception of our common humanity.'[16] Here is a consistent universalist, not trying *per impossibile* to demonstrate the moral worth of nationality, but arguing that practical ethics must, for the foreseeable future, bow to the force of national sentiments.

Nothing I have said so far is intended as a critique of universalism in itself. A universalist approach to ethics might still be the correct one. What I have been trying to dispel is the comforting thought that one can embrace universalism in ethics while continuing to give priority to one's compatriots in one's practical reasoning. The choice, as I see it, is either to adopt a more heroic version of universalism,

[14] Figures for 1990 are from *World Tables 1993* (Baltimore, Johns Hopkins University Press, 1993).

[15] H. Shue, 'Mediating Duties', *Ethics*, 98 (1987–8), 703.

[16] H. Sidgwick, *The Elements of Politics*, 2nd edn. (London, Macmillan, 1897), 308. Sidgwick's position has more recently been reaffirmed in C. Beitz, 'Cosmopolitan Ideals and National Sentiment', *Journal of Philosophy*, 80 (1983), 591–600. But compare the tougher-minded utilitarian universalism of Peter Singer: 'Sentiments like love, affection and community feeling are a large part of what makes life worthwhile. But sentiments are likely to lead us astray in moral reasoning, seducing us into accepting positions that are based, not on an impartial consideration of the interests of all involved, but rather on our own likes and dislikes' ('Reconsidering the Famine Relief Argument', 43).

which attaches no intrinsic significance to national boundaries, or else to embrace ethical particularism and see whether one can defend oneself against the charge that one is succumbing to irrational sentiment in giving weight to national allegiances.

III

The particularist defence of nationality begins with the assumption that memberships and attachments in general have ethical significance. Because I identify with my family, my college, or my local community, I properly acknowledge obligations to members of these groups that are distinct from the obligations I owe to people generally. Seeing myself as a member, I feel a loyalty to the group, and this expresses itself, among other things, in my giving special weight to the interests of fellow-members. So, if my time is restricted and two students each ask if they can consult me, I give priority to the one who belongs to my college.[17]

These loyalties, and the obligations that go with them, are seen as mutual. I expect other members to give special weight to my interests in the same way as I give special weight to theirs. This doesn't mean that the relationship is one of strict reciprocity. For various reasons it may not be possible for the person whose interests I promote to return the favour in kind: the student I advise is not likely to be in a position to reciprocate with advice of the same sort. But perhaps she has computing skills which I lack, in which case she may be in a position to offer help of a different sort, and then I expect her to weight my interests in the same way as I weight hers. If this mutuality fails—not in a particular case, but in general—the character of the group or community to which I think I belong is put in question. Perhaps I have the romantic belief that my college is an academic community, whereas in fact it is simply an agglomeration of self-interested individuals using the institution to advance their careers. It is important that the obligations I acknowledge may be either appropriate or inappropriate as the case may be, depending on the relationships that really obtain within the group in question.

---

[17] I am supposing that I have no formal responsibilities to either student; they just happen to be working on a subject where I am able to give them some guidance. I am not suggesting that obligations of membership should always take precedence over formally assigned or contractual obligations to outsiders.

The obligations that I should acknowledge in a case like this are likely to be coloured by the general ethos of the group or community. This will determine, to some degree at least, the interests that I can be called on to promote. The college example that I used above traded to some extent on the fact that a college is an academic institution, so that giving academic advice is a paradigm of the sort of act that I can be called on to perform. But if this point is pushed too far, we are in danger of reducing communities of all kinds to instrumental associations. My collegial obligations extend to general human interests, so that if there are two students who need to be driven urgently to hospital, and I can take only one, then again, I ought to give priority to the one who belongs to my college, taking the other only if his need is considerably more urgent. But the interests are interpreted in the light of the community's values. A good example is provided by the medieval Jewish communities described by Michael Walzer.[18] Members of these communities recognized an obligation to provide for one another's needs, but needs in turn were understood in relation to religious ideals; this meant, for instance, that education was seen as a need for boys but not for girls; that food was distributed to the poorest members of the communities on the eve of the religious festivals; and so forth.

Before going on to see whether this picture of the ethics of community can plausibly be extended to nations, it is worth dwelling for a moment on the motivational strengths of ethical ties of this kind. First, to the extent that I really do identify with the group or community in question, there need be no sharp conflict between fulfilling my obligations and pursuing my own goals and purposes. The group's interests are among the goals that I set myself to advance; they may of course conflict with other goals that are equally important to me, but we are far away from the position where an individual with essentially private aims and purposes has to balance these against the obligations of a universalist morality such as utilitarianism. In that position there would almost always be a simple trade-off: the more a person does what morality requires of him, the less scope he has to pursue his personal goals. If this were indeed a correct picture of ethical life, one might be forgiven for thinking that morality would have rather little motivational power.

[18] M. Walzer, *Spheres of Justice* (Oxford, Martin Robertson, 1983), 71–8.

But when I see my own welfare as bound up with the community to which I belong, contributing towards it is also a form of goal-ulfilment.

Second, because of the loose reciprocity that characterizes the ethics of community, a person who acts to aid some other member of his group can be sustained by the thought that in different circumstances he might expect to be the beneficiary of the relationship. I do not mean to suggest that such a person will act *in order* to receive some future benefit. From a self-interested point of view, it may be irrational to assume such an obligation, because it may be clear enough that the expected benefits are smaller than the expected costs. The point is a weaker one: the act of making a contribution is not a pure loss, from the point of view of the private interests of the person making it, because he is helping to sustain a set of relationships from which he stands to benefit to some degree. The point again is not that particularistic relationships serve to eradicate conflict between an individual's interests and the interests of others in the group or community, but that they soften the conflict so that ethical behaviour becomes easier for imperfectly altruistic agents.

Finally, we should observe that groups and communities form natural sites on which more formal systems of reciprocity can establish themselves. They mark out sets of people who are already well disposed to one another in certain respects, and this makes it easier to create formal practices for mutual benefit.[19] Thus, a group of neighbours may decide to form a shopping collective or share a school run. These practices are likely to be governed by tighter norms of reciprocity, in the sense that each person will have equal responsibilities and these will be more formally defined—it will be my job to visit the warehouse on the third Saturday of every month, say. When practices of this kind emerge, their effect will be

---

[19] I don't mean to suggest that communities are a necessary condition for mutual benefit practices to appear. If any set of individuals is so placed that there is mutual advantage to be gained by establishing a co-operative practice, there is some chance that the practice will emerge. But often there is a problem in deciding who should be included in the scope of the practice, and there may be set-up costs that no individual is willing to incur alone. (I have looked at this issue in some depth in D. Miller, 'Public Goods without the State', *Critical Review*, 7 (1993), 505–23.) In any case, the present point is not so much that communities facilitate mutual benefit practices as that, where they have this effect, the members' motivational ties to the group are reinforced.

to reinforce the less formal bonds that constituted the community in the first place, and to blur still further the contrast between a person's interests and her communal obligations.

How far, then, can these arguments be applied to nations? Does it make sense to regard nations as communities which generate rights and obligations in the same way as communities of a more immediate sort? Can the particularistic arguments I have been deploying serve to defend obligations to compatriots? In the last chapter I tried to bring out the various features that distinguish nations *qua* communities from communities of a more direct and immediate kind, and I want now to explore the ethical implications of this in somewhat greater depth.

Nationality is, as I have argued already, a powerful source of personal identity; but paradoxically, it is strangely amorphous when we come to ask about the rights and obligations that flow from it. It is capable of evoking fierce, and indeed often supreme, loyalty, manifested in people's willingness to give up their lives for their country; but if we were to ask those who share this loyalty what precisely their obligations consist in, we would I think receive answers that were very vague. People would no doubt say, first of all, that they had a duty to defend their nation and its ancestral territory, in other words to preserve the community's culture and its physical integrity. They would also say that they bore a special responsibility towards their fellow-nationals, that they were justified in giving them priority both when acting as individuals and when deciding upon public policy. But if asked to be more specific about the *content* of those special responsibilities, it would be hard to elicit any determinate general answer.

This reminds us of the abstract character of nationality, its quality of 'imagined community'. Whereas in face-to-face communities, especially perhaps those with defined objectives, there is a clear understanding of what each is expected to contribute towards the welfare of other members, in the case of nationality we are in no position to grasp the demands and expectation of other members directly, nor they ours. Into this vacuum there flows what I have called a public culture, a set of ideas about the character of the community which also helps to fix responsibilities. This public culture is to some extent a product of political debate, and depends for its dissemination upon mass media. (This will be particularly true, of course, where the nation in question has its own state, or equivalent system of political authority.) It will therefore have an ideological coloration. Some national cultures may attach value to individual self-sufficiency, for example, and will therefore construe their members' obligations to one another mainly in terms of providing the conditions under which individuals can fashion their own lives; others will lay greater stress on collective goods, and regard compatriots as having duties to involve themselves in various forms of national service, to enhance the literary and artistic heritage of the nation, and so forth. So, although at any time it may be possible to say roughly what the obligations of the members of nation A are, these obligations in their particular content are an artefact of the public culture of that nation.

Now this may at first sight appear a very unsatisfactory conclusion to reach. We set out to show that particular ethical obligations could legitimately be derived from membership in a national community. Normally we would expect such obligations to be independently derived, and to serve as reasons in the process of political decision-making. For instance, we might appeal to obligations to provide welfare in the course of advocating policies or institutions that would serve to meet the needs, for instance the medical needs, of fellow-nationals. But it turns out that the obligations themselves stem from a public culture that has been shaped by political debate in the past.

But although this shows that we cannot derive the obligations of nationality simply from reflection on what it means for a group of people to constitute a nation in the first place, we should not exaggerate the significance of this point. It certainly does not imply that my obligations *qua* member of nation A are merely whatever I take them to be. The culture in question *is* a public phenomenon: any one individual may interpret it rightly or wrongly, and draw correct or incorrect conclusions about his obligations to compatriots as a result. Moreover, although the public culture is shaped by political debate, this does not mean that it is easily manipulable by political actors in the short term. It is often quite resilient: a relevant example is the failure of the British Conservative Party under Mrs Thatcher to bring about any across-the-board changes in national culture, despite holding the reins of government for eleven years.[20] Because

[20] For evidence, see I. Crewe, 'Has the Electorate Become Thatcherite?' in R. Skidelsky (ed.), *Thatcherism* (Oxford, Blackwell, 1989).

of this relative stability, the idea that the public culture can serve as a source of ideas that may then be used to justify or criticize the policies of a particular government remains valid.

The fact that the public culture, and the obligations of nationality that derive from it, can be reshaped over time has a welcome consequence. I said that one main charge levelled against all forms of ethical particularism is that they amount to the sanctification of merely traditional ethical relations. To the extent that national identities, and the public cultures that help to compose them, are shaped by processes of rational reflection to which members of the community can contribute on an equal footing, this charge no longer applies. The obligations that we now acknowledge are not merely traditional, but will bear the imprint of the various reasons that have been offered over time in the course of these debates. Thus, if, in a democratic community, I have an obligation to support a national health service, that obligation is grounded in the reasons given for having the health service when it was first introduced, and reaffirmed from time to time when the health service is debated. (I may not know these reasons myself, and may simply take it for granted that supporting a national health service is part of what we believe in round here; none the less, the point remains that the obligations have a grounding in something more than mere tradition.) How far this ideal condition is met will depend on the political institutions we have, the quality of political debate both within the formal institutions and outside them, the general level of education, and so forth. These are matters that I shall return to in the next chapter, when I discuss the ideal of national self-determination.

I have so far claimed that the ethical implications of nationality differ from those of lesser communities in two main respects. The potency of nationality as a source of personal identity means that its obligations are strongly felt and may extend very far—people are willing to sacrifice themselves for their country in a way that they are not for other groups and associations. But at the same time, these obligations are somewhat indeterminate and likely to be the subject of political debate; in the best case, they will flow from a shared public culture which results from rational deliberation over time about what it means to belong to the nation in question. However, to grasp the full force of the obligations of nationality, we need to consider what happens when national boundaries coincide with state boundaries, so that a formal scheme of political co-operation is superimposed on the national community.

In this case people will have rights and obligations of citizenship as well as rights and obligations of nationality. Rights and obligations of the first kind stem simply from their participation in a practice from which they stand to benefit, via the principle of reciprocity. As citizens they enjoy rights of personal protection, welfare rights, and so forth, and in return they have an obligation to keep the law, to pay taxes, and generally to uphold the co-operative scheme.[21] To a very large extent, their obligations of nationality are discharged through the state, provided that the latter pursues the right kind of policies. And this has the immediate advantage that people can play their part in the scheme in the knowledge that most others will (if necessary) be compelled to play theirs. Whereas in small communities each member can see for himself whether others are carrying out their obligations or not, in a nation-state we have to rely on the presence of enforcement mechanisms to get that assurance.

It would, however, be a great mistake to suppose that, once a practice of political co-operation is in place, nationality drops out of the picture as an irrelevance—that we simply have the rights and obligations of citizens interacting with other citizens. The bonds of nationality give the practice a different shape from the one that it would have without them. Let us try to imagine how the rights and obligations of citizenship might look if the citizens were tied to one another by nothing beyond the practice of citizenship itself, and were motivated by the principle of fairness.[22] They would insist on strict reciprocity. In other words, each would expect to benefit from

---

[21] As will be apparent, I am here describing citizenship in a well functioning liberal democracy. For discussion of the circumstances under which the fair-play principle can generate obligations to the state, see Klosko, *Principle of Fairness*, especially chs. 2–4.

[22] Why not assume a higher degree of altruism? If we do this, we face the problem of explaining why altruistic concern should be directed towards one's fellow-citizens, rather than towards those who are neediest regardless of their citizenship. As I noted above, the only plausible argument here is one that appeals to our superior knowledge of the needs of our fellow citizens. So to show why citizens who were not linked by bonds of nationality should agree to compulsory redistribution among themselves, we would need to show (*a*) that they had sufficient general altruism, but also (*b*) that they had good reason to think that their altruism was best directed towards their fellow-citizens to whom, to repeat, they had no special ties beyond the institutions of common citizenship.

their association in proportion to his or her contribution, taking as a baseline the hypothetical state of affairs in which there was no political co-operation between them. So, for instance, redistributive taxation would be agreed to only in circumstances in which each person thought it was rational to insure him- or herself through the state against the possibility of falling below a certain level of resources.[23] Given the possibility of private insurance, we would expect states that lacked a communitarian background such as nationality provides to be little more than minimal states, providing only basic security to their members.[24] In particular, it is difficult to explain why states should provide opportunities and resources to people with permanent handicaps if one is simply following the logic of reciprocity. It is because we have prior obligations of nationality that include obligations to provide for needs that arise in this way that the practice of citizenship properly includes redistributive elements of the kind that we commonly find in contemporary states.

It may be asked how this analysis squares with the fact that citizenship is frequently extended to residents of the state who acknowledge a different nationality from the majority. Although it is possible to devise two categories of citizenship in these circumstances—e.g. by classifying non-nationals as 'guest workers'—there are strong reasons for extending a single common citizenship to everyone who is subject to the authority of the same state. When this happens, most citizens will find that their obligations of citizenship based on reciprocity are backed up by obligations stemming from common nationality; but some will not. Such a state of affairs may well be tolerated, particularly if the number of non-nationals is fairly small, but it is potentially unstable. The instability might be resolved either by slimming down the obligations of citizenship—turning the state into something closer to a minimal state—or by making state and nation coincide more closely. If the latter option is pursued, there are again two alternatives: to try to assimilate the non-

---

[23] This point emerges clearly in Brian Barry's analysis of the idea of reciprocity in 'Justice as Reciprocity' in his *Democracy, Power and Justice* (Oxford, Clarendon Press, 1989), although it is somewhat overlooked in his later paper in the same volume, 'The Continuing Relevance of Socialism'.

[24] A comparison between Canada and the USA might seem to rebut this claim: the USA has the stronger sense of national identity, yet redistributes less in favour of its worse-off members than does Canada with its welfare state. I discuss this issue in Ch. 4, S. I.

nationals so that they come to share in a common national identity, or to partition the state in such a way that the new political units are more exactly isomorphic with national divisions. The arguments for and against either alternative will be explored more fully in the chapters that follow. The point that I want to underline here is that there are strong ethical reasons for making the bounds of nationality and the bounds of the state coincide. Where this obtains, obligations of nationality are strengthened by being given expression in a formal scheme of political co-operation;[25] and the scheme of co-operation can be based on loose rather than strict reciprocity, meaning that redistributive elements can be built in which go beyond what the rational self-interest of each participant would dictate.

IV

The particularistic defence of nationality that I have been building up might seem convincing in its own terms; but the universalist will want to ask whether there are not also obligations to human beings as such, and if so how they can be reconciled with the picture so far presented. Does the ethics of nationality not entail moral indifference to outsiders? Here it is important to begin by recognizing that, when we talk about outsiders, we are not talking about isolated individuals, but about people who are themselves members of national communities. Of course there are exceptions to this—stateless persons, or refugees who for good reasons can no longer embrace their past national identity. But in general, in considering relationships to outsiders, we should not fall into the trap of thinking that our only relationship to them is of one human being to another. We are certainly related in that way; but, in considering my ethical relationship to, say, a Tanzanian, I should not forget that we are also related as Briton to Tanzanian. Each of us is linked internally to our own national community, and this creates a second dimension to our relationship alongside the first, which complicates the ethical picture.

[25] Strengthened in the sense that, besides the obligations that I have that stem directly from a shared national identity, I have largely overlapping obligations of citizenship based on reciprocity. If I ask myself: 'Why pay my taxes?' two answers can be given: I have a duty *qua* member of this nation to support common projects and to fulfil the needs of fellow members; and I have a duty *qua* citizen to sustain institutions from which I can expect in turn to benefit. Either of these reasons taken separately is vulnerable; together they make a powerful case for contribution.

If we consider just the first dimension, then the obligations that it imposes are probably best captured by a theory of basic rights. There are generic conditions for living a decent life which can be expressed in terms of rights to bodily integrity, personal freedom, a minimum level of resources, and so forth.[26] We have obligations to respect these rights in others that derive simply from our common humanity; mostly these are rights to forbearance of various kinds—rights to be left alone, not to be injured in various ways, etc.—but they may also include rights to provision, for example in cases where a natural shortage of resources means that people will starve or suffer bodily injury if others do not provide for them.

So much is relatively commonplace: nearly all ethical universalists would wish to endorse such a list of rights and their corresponding obligations, though many would argue that our responsibilities to other human beings go somewhat further than this. And I can see no reason why those who hold particularist views should not also endorse such a list of basic rights. The divergence occurs when we juxtapose relationships between persons abstractly conceived with relationships between persons as members of communities, including national communities.

For now the basic rights and the obligations that correspond to them are overlain by the special responsibilities that we have as members of these communities. Moreover, in each community there will be a specific understanding of the needs and interests of members which generate obligations on the part of other members. I argued above that a community will embody a common ethos which enters into the definition of the needs and interests that count for these purposes; in the case of nations, this common ethos takes the form of a public culture. Thus, in one national community (the Republic of Ireland, for example) religious education may be regarded as a shared need which should properly be funded by the community as a whole, whereas in another (the United States for example) it may be seen as a private matter which should be left to each person to consider, and to provide for their children as they saw fit. Given that there is a limit to the resources available in any given

[26] There are many accounts of basic rights. Among the best, not least because it resists the temptation to expand the list of basic rights to include things that are socially desirable but not really basic, is H. Shue, *Basic Rights: Subsistence, Affluence and American Foreign Policy* (Princeton, Princeton University Press, 1980).

community to meet these commonly recognized needs, conflicts may then arise in any of the following three ways.

First, there may be a simple conflict between providing for the needs people have as members of a national community and respecting the basic rights of outsiders, to the extent that the latter involves some form of positive provision. For example, given that there is no obvious limit to the quantity of resources that might be expended in providing for health needs, how should we weigh the demands of the domestic national health service against the costs of immunization programmes in other countries? Considerations of urgency point in one direction; the relative strength of our obligations to different groups of people points in the other. No simple doctrine of 'basic rights first' seems acceptable in such cases.

Second, it may turn out that our own understanding of basic rights, coloured as it will undoubtedly be by the ethos of our own community, conflicts in certain respects with the priorities attached to various needs in other communities. We might see formal education as a basic right; but there may be communities in which this is regarded as disruptive of cultural bonds and therefore as not, ultimately, in the best interests of the individuals concerned. In these circumstances, do we have obligations to promote basic rights as we see them, or should we rather give priority to community-based conceptions of need which we do not ourselves share?

Although these first two points seem to me quite powerful, they do not by themselves challenge a universal obligation to protect basic rights at a sufficiently fundamental level—say, to protect people from death by starvation. At this level we should expect conceptions of need to converge, and, provided the cost of protecting these rights is relatively small, it would be difficult to argue that the obligation must always yield to the demands of justice within the national community. But the third point cuts deeper still. *Who* has the obligation to protect these basic rights? Given what has been said so far about the role of shared identities in generating obligations, we must suppose that it falls in the first place on the national and smaller local communities to which the rights-bearer belongs. So why should we, as outsiders, have obligations to provide resources which ought to be provided in each case by fellow-nationals and/or local communities and other such groups?

The only answer that can be given here is that the rights will not be effectively protected unless there is provision across national boundaries. But again, we must ask why this should be the case. The most compelling argument for international provision is that it is simply impossible for the national community in question to protect the basic rights of its members—say, because of resource shortages caused by drought or flooding. In these circumstances we can say that there is a general obligation, falling equally on all those in a position to provide aid, to step in and safeguard the basic rights of those threatened by famine.[27] But if we take 'impossible' literally, this case is probably quite rare. Much more often, nations cannot protect the basic rights of their members because of other decisions they have taken: famines may result from misguided economic decisions made in the past, and they may be perpetuated by the institutional rules that continue to be applied.[28] Or again, the cause may simply be the unwillingness of better off people in the society in question to make the changes that would secure the rights of the worst off, for instance to introduce publicly funded welfare schemes.[29] What then follows for the obligations of outsiders?

Consider the general case in which B has a general right, primary responsibility for respecting which falls upon A (through some process of assignment), who fails to discharge his obligation. What responsibility does some third party, C, then have? We do not automatically conclude that C should herself provide what is needed to satisfy B's right. Her first obligation is surely to try to get A to acknowledge his responsibility, by persuasion if possible, but failing this by such force as is commensurate with the right in question. If these approaches fail, then at some point we will probably say that C should take care of B herself, though the obligation to do so would

---

[27] I am considering here the international obligations that would arise in the absence of any ongoing scheme of co-operation between the national communities in question. In the following chapter I discuss the obligations of reciprocity that occur when there exists a practice of mutual aid between states to cope with natural disasters of various kinds.

[28] The second alternative corresponds to Amartya Sen's thesis that starvation typically occurs because of failures of entitlement rather than unavailability of food in general; see A. Sen, *Poverty and Famines: An Essay on Entitlement and Deprivation* (Oxford, Clarendon Press, 1981).

[29] In saying this I do not mean to deny that the economic policies pursued by one nation-state may make it more difficult for another to protect the basic rights of its citizens. I return in the next chapter to consider the obligations towards other states that follow from the idea of national self-determination.

be weaker than A's original obligation. If we translate this pattern of reasoning to the international arena, then, if nation A fails to protect the rights of a set of its members B, the obligation of nation C is first of all to use all reasonable means to induce A to protect the rights of B. This might involve, for instance, trying by public condemnation to shame policy-makers in A to respect these rights, threatening to sever trade links or withdraw military co-operation unless the policy is changed, and in the last resort attempting directly to remove from power those responsible for the policies leading to the rights violations.

Measures such as this would be widely regarded as compromising the self-determination of the nation in question, and for that reason as unacceptable. This demonstrates the incongruity in holding together two principles which are indeed often held together by liberals: one attaches value to national self-determination and argues that nations have no right to interfere in one another's domestic affairs (except perhaps in very extreme cases); the other holds that we have a positive obligation to protect the basic rights of our fellow human beings. My point is that acceptance of the first principle places severe limits on the scope of the second. For if the obligation in question falls first of all on fellow-nationals, and if outsiders are prohibited by the first principle from intervening in a heavy-handed way when this obligation fails to be discharged, then it seems that they can at most have a weak obligation to provide the necessary resources themselves. If C is prohibited from compelling A to discharge his obligation to B when A defaults, C cannot then be placed under an equally strong obligation to fulfil B's rights.[30]

To put this point another way, I believe that ethical universalists who believe in a duty to protect basic rights of the kind I have been discussing—and, even more so, those who believe in a general utilitarian duty to promote the welfare of fellow human beings—ought to take seriously the case for benevolent imperialism. Given that many existing states signally fail to protect the basic rights of their

[30] I do not mean that C should not act to fulfil B's rights; this may still be the right thing to do. But it would be hard to blame C if she decided not to do this. This suggests that there could only be a humanitarian obligation to, for example, send relief to famine victims in circumstances where relief was being withheld by their own government (whereas if the government *cannot* send relief, then there is a good case for saying that outside agencies have a duty of justice to supply it).

members, and given also that on universalist grounds we can attach
no intrinsic value to the obligations of community or to national
self-determination, why not subject the members of these states to
benign outside rule? Of course in most cases this proposal would not
be practicable because of local resistance, but (again in universalist
terms) such resistance must be seen as misguided if we allow that the
imperialism is benevolent.[31] Why make a fetish of self-government if
your basic rights will be better protected by outsiders? That few of
those who now write as universalists are prepared to draw such conclusions shows, I think, that, while they are often ready to condemn
their own countrymen as blinkered for their attachment to the idea
of nationality, they are not prepared to pass the same judgement on
outsiders.[32]

There is an appealing compromise between ethical universalism
and ethical particularism which holds that it is justifiable to act on
special loyalties and recognize special obligations to compatriots
provided that this does not involve violating the basic rights of outsiders.[33] Basic rights come first; so long as they are respected, it is
ethically acceptable to give preference to the needs and interests of
fellow-countrymen (and to members of other such communities).
Unfortunately, this position turns out to be too simple. At the very
least, we need to draw a distinction between violating basic rights by

[31] Several readers have said that the objection to benevolent imperialism is simply that we have no reason to think that imperialism can be benevolent. I think this
is merely a way of avoiding a difficult question. Consider a proposal to put most of
sub-Saharan Africa under the administrative control of members of the EU, acting
perhaps on behalf of the United Nations. What reason is there to think that the
Dutch, the Austrians, or the Swedes—even perhaps the French or the British—
could not govern Tanzania, Angola, or Rwanda in a more efficient and humane way
than their present rulers? That proposals such as this are today ruled out on principle testifies to the force that the idea of national self-determination has for us.

[32] At one point Peter Singer makes the far weaker proposal that 'we might make
offers of aid to countries with rapidly increasing populations conditional on effective steps being taken to halt population growth'. But, he goes on, 'I imagine that
many people who have agreed with me up to this point will be reluctant to accept
this conclusion. It will be said that it would be an attempt to impose our own ideas
on other, independent, sovereign nations' ('Reconsidering the Famine Relief
Argument', p. 47). Singer goes on to defend his proposal, but he is fully aware of
how controversial it is to suggest even this.

[33] For examples of this position, see S. Gorovitz, 'Bigotry, Loyalty, and
Malnutrition', in P. G. Brown and H. Shue (eds.), *Food Policy* (New York, Free
Press, 1977); S. Nathanson, *Patriotism, Morality and Peace* (Lanham, Rowman and
Littlefield, 1993), especially chs. 4 and 13.

one's own actions, and allowing them to be violated by others. It is probably true that the ethical claims of nationality could not justify anyone in violating the rights of an outsider by, say, killing or injuring him.[34] But if we take nationality seriously, then we must also accept that positive obligations to protect basic rights (e.g. to relieve hunger) fall in the first place on co-nationals, so that outsiders would have strong obligations in this respect only where it was strictly impossible for the rights to be protected within the national community. If bad policies or vested interests in nation A mean that some of its citizens go needy, then, if nation C decides that its own welfare requirements mean that it cannot afford to give much (or anything) to the needy in A, it has not directly violated their rights; at most, it has permitted them to be violated, and in the circumstances this may be justifiable.

I shall have more to say about aspects of international distributive justice in the following chapter; and more to say, too, about the idea of national self-determination which has appeared already. So my account of the ethics of nationality is not yet fully executed. But since the argumentative strategy of this chapter has been a little oblique, let me conclude here by retracing its main steps. I began by distinguishing between ethical universalism and ethical particularism. I then argued that neither of the two approaches commonly used by universalists to justify special loyalties and duties—I call them the 'useful convention' and 'voluntary creation' approaches—stood much chance of accounting for commonly recognized obligations to fellow-nationals. The consistent ethical universalist ought to be a cosmopolitan. I then presented a justifying account of particularism, pointing out that, where obligations spring from communal relations, the opposition between self-interest and ethical obligation is diminished. I drew particular attention to the way in which communities can support formal practices of reciprocity in such a way that each reinforces the obligations deriving from the other. A nation-state in which a formal scheme of political co-operation is superimposed on a national community is a paradigmatic example of this. Finally, I asked whether ethical particularism of the kind defended here is compatible with the recognition of universal human rights. The answer is affirmative, but the obligations corresponding

[34] Unless this was necessary in order to protect the basic rights of a compatriot, as for instance in case of war.

to these rights turn out to fall primarily on co-nationals. One corollary of this is that we are not in most cases required by justice to intervene to safeguard the human rights of foreigners, though humanitarian considerations may lead us to do so.

This argument is something less than a frontal assault on ethical universalism, which would carry us far away from the main focus of my book. My aim has been the more modest one of showing that the ethics of nationality is plausible, resting as it does on well established facts about human identity and human motivation. The onus is on the universalist to show that, in widening the scope of ethical ties to encompass equally the whole of the human species, he does not also drain them of their binding force.

CHAPTER 4

National Self-Determination

I

The third and last proposition included in the idea of nationality that I am defending in this book holds that national communities have a good claim to be politically self-determining. As far as possible, each nation should have its own set of political institutions which allow it to decide collectively those matters that are the primary concern of its members. This is sometimes phrased in terms of a right to national self-determination, as it was, for example, in the UN Human Rights Covenants of 1966. But it devalues the currency of rights to announce rights which in their nature are sometimes incapable of fulfilment; and, for reasons that will emerge in the course of this chapter, this applies to the alleged right of national self-determination. I have therefore couched the proposition that I wish to defend in terms of a 'good claim' to political self-determination, recognizing that there will be cases where the claim cannot be met. Some nations—for instance those whose members are geographically intermingled with other groups—will have to settle for something less than full self-government.

I have also avoided saying bluntly that every nation has a good claim to a *state* of its own, even though that has historically been the chief vehicle for national self-determination. Later on I shall consider institutional devices for meeting the claim that fall short of independent statehood. But at the same time, I should not deny that an independent state is likely to provide the best means for a nation to fulfil its claim to self-determination, and in the earlier part of the chapter I shall take this as the paradigm case when asking what justifies the claim in question.

The plan of the chapter is as follows. First, I shall try to lay out the arguments *for* national self-determination, in other words the reasons why it is valuable for the boundaries of political units (paradigmatically, states) to coincide with national boundaries. Second, I shall ask about the rights and obligations of such states to one another, and in particular shall ask whether national self-determination demands a state that is sovereign in the traditional sense. Third, I shall look at some of the issues that arise when the boundaries of nation and political unit do not presently coincide, focusing especially on the question of when secession may be justified.

It is possible to look at the first issue from two different directions. We can begin with a nation as a source of personal identity, and as an obligation-generating community, and ask why it is valuable for such an entity to enjoy political self-determination. Alternatively, we can begin with a state as a political entity that wields certain powers and carries out certain functions, and ask why these tasks may be discharged better if the citizens of the state are also compatriots. I believe that both avenues must be pursued if we are fully to grasp the force of the claim for national self-determination. But notice one difference between them. The first set of considerations relies upon the arguments advanced in the last two chapters in defence of nationality. Unless national identities are defensible, and we are justified in acknowledging special obligations to compatriots, the arguments from nation to state will have no basis. On the other hand, the arguments from state to nation may appeal to those who doubt the cogency and appeal of nationality itself. That is to say, people who value the effective functioning of political communities may come to see the utility of national sentiments which they would otherwise dismiss as worthless. Of course this position is a somewhat uncomfortable one.[1] But I want to make it clear that some (but not all) of

---

[1] It is uncomfortable because the person who takes it may be in the position of having to recommend, on instrumental grounds, the fostering of attitudes and beliefs which he regards as intrinsically groundless. Should one try to encourage nationalism (because it helps to make the state function better) or to discourage it (because it is rationally unacceptable)? This is, for instance, the predicament of a utilitarian like Sidgwick, whose views I recorded in the last chapter, and it is interesting to compare Sidgwick's general ruminations on the question whether utilitarians ought to espouse their views openly, or keep them under wraps lest they should disturb 'the Morality of Common Sense'. (See H. Sidgwick, *The Methods of Ethics*, 7th edn., London, Macmillan, 1963, iv, ch. 5.)

the arguments of this chapter can be made independently of what has been said before; most importantly, some of them may be acceptable to ethical universalists.

Let us begin, then, with the reasons for thinking political self-determination valuable from a nationalist perspective. Now it might seem that the reason is very straightforward indeed, namely that those who think of themselves as forming a national community also think of themselves as self-determining, either actually or in aspiration, so that in granting self-determination one is simply giving people what they want. The assumption of nationhood and the quest for self-determination are merely two sides of the same coin. But granting the truth of this, the reason in this form could be only a weak one; after all, one group of people might want to subjugate another group, regarding them as naturally inferior on racial or some such grounds, and presumably we would attach little or no weight to such a desire. We must ask whether people *justifiably* conceive their nationality as carrying with it a claim to political self-determination.

The first, more substantial, reason for the claim concerns social justice, and restates a point made in the last chapter. Nations are communities of obligation, in the sense that their members recognize duties to meet the basic needs and protect the basic interests of other members. However, they are also large and impersonal communities, so in order for these duties to be effectively discharged, they must be assigned and enforced. Where a national state exists, it can develop and regulate a set of institutions—what Rawls has called 'the basic structure of society'—which together allocate rights and responsibilities to people in the way that their conception of social justice demands.[2] Of course, there is no guarantee that this will happen; it requires that the state should be responsive to people's views about what they can justly demand of one another, and also that it should be effective in regulating the basic structure. But where these conditions are met, as they are to some extent in existing liberal democracies, the obligations people have as members of national communities are given a definite content, and they can discharge them in reasonable confidence that others will play their part. Under these circumstances, as I argued in Chapter 3, obligations of

[2] See J. Rawls, *Political Liberalism* (New York, Columbia University Press, 1993), lecture VII.

citizenship based on reciprocity are superimposed on what would otherwise be somewhat loose and indeterminate obligations of nationality. In this way, social justice can become an effective force governing relationships within a national society.

To see the force of this argument, one needs to think about the alternatives: cases where political authority is either sub-national or super-national. I do not mean to suggest that a nation whose members were dispersed among a number of states—the case, say, of Germans or Italians prior to unification in the nineteenth century—could never achieve a regime of overall justice, but the obstacles are considerable. Unless the resource base of each state is approximately the same, a system of voluntary transfers from better endowed to worse endowed states would be needed, and it is likely to be hard to find an acceptable system: mistrust between the various units will make donor states reluctant to make the necessary transfers. (If the transfers are compelled, then what we have is an embryonic super-state capable of exercising authority over its constituent parts.) In the cases referred to, there were of course no such transfers; whatever solidarity Piedmontese and Tuscans, or Prussians and Bavarians, might have felt for one another was overwhelmed as far as policy-making was concerned by political rivalry and jealousy between the rulers of these states.

To turn now to the opposite case, where a single state embraces two or more nationalities, the problem will not be one of implementing a system of distributive justice, but one of legitimating it in the eyes of the populace. What reasons, for example, could have been given to the economically prosperous Slovenes to make them agree to subsidize investments in Serbia or Montenegro under the Yugoslavian federation?[3] Each community feels that it is entitled to the resources that its own members have created; it will agree to state transfers only if it has an assurance that it will not lose, overall, in relation to the other communities. In these circumstances the state

---

[3] At the end of the 1980s 'many Slovenes felt that their economically productive republic (in 1986 it provided 18 percent of total GNP and 23 percent of total exports) was contributing an unnecessarily high price for the operation of the federation. Particularly irksome to Slovenes was that each year their republic, with about 8 percent of Yugoslavia's population, contributed over 25 percent of the total federal budget and between 17 and 19 percent of the Federal Fund for Underdeveloped Regions' (L. J. Cohen, *Broken Bonds: The Disintegration of Yugoslavia*, Boulder, Colo., Westview Press, 1993, 59).

must choose between two alternatives: either it restricts the scope of its operations, providing only basic goods such as the protection of rights and national defence;[4] or it embraces a form of federalism, making each constituent nationality responsible for promoting social justice within its own area through, for instance, social insurance or poverty relief programmes. In the second case significant government functions are being devolved to national level, and a large measure of national self-determination has been effectively conceded. Provided, then, that we endorse ideals of social justice, and recognize that these take hold mainly within national communities, we have good reason for wanting the political systems that can realize these ideals to coincide with national boundaries.[5]

A second reason favouring national self-determination, one that is more likely to be directly in the minds of those demanding this when they do not already have it, is protection of the national culture.[6] We have seen already why we need to tread carefully in dealing with the idea of national culture. Nations tend to attribute to themselves a greater degree of cultural homogeneity than their members actually display. Nevertheless, if we think of national culture not as implying complete uniformity but as a set of overlapping cultural characteristics—beliefs, practices, sensibilities—which different members exhibit in different combinations and to different degrees, then, as I argued in Chapter 2, it is reasonably clear that distinct national cultures do exist. Moreover, it is valuable to the members in question that they should continue to do so. A common culture of this sort not only gives its bearers a sense of where they belong and provides

[4] Even here, there is room for disagreement about the level of provision and about how the burden of provision should be shared. To continue with the Slovenian case, 'Federal defense expenditures were also viewed as excessive by many Slovenes, particularly because Yugoslavia did not seem to be facing any imminent military threats and because citizens of their republic had traditionally played an extremely small role in the leadership of the armed forces' (ibid.).

[5] Equally, of course, those who oppose ideas of social justice will find in this a reason for advocating multinational states. This was Lord Acton's argument in his essay on 'Nationality' (in *The History of Freedom and Other Essays*, ed. J. N. Figgis, London, Macmillan, 1907), and it has since been reiterated by Hayek, whose advocacy of cross-national federations is explained by his view that socialism and nationalism are 'inseparable forces' (F. A. Hayek, *The Road to Serfdom*, London, Routledge, 1944, especially chs. 10 and 15; F. A. Hayek, *Law, Legislation and Liberty*, ii, *The Mirage of Social Justice*, London, Routledge, 1976, 134).

[6] This reason has been explored more fully in A. Margalit and J. Raz, 'National Self-Determination', *Journal of Philosophy*, 87 (1990), 439–61.

an historical identity, but also provides them with a background against which more individual choices about how to live can be made. Of course, any given person is likely to be a participant in more than one such culture—family, ethnic group, or class may each serve as a source of cultural values which exist alongside, and possibly in tension with, national culture. So a person's nationality is very far from being the only cultural resource available to him or her. But it is likely to be an important resource.

Does it follow, however, that people have an interest in the preservation of the particular national culture within which they have been raised? It is often suggested that, so long as people have access to *some* sufficiently rich culture, it does not matter which one that is. Indeed, it has sometimes been argued that it is positively beneficial to people to be inducted into a culture that is 'higher' than their original one. John Stuart Mill wrote:

Nobody can suppose that it is not more beneficial to a Breton, or a Basque of French Navarre, to be brought into the current of the ideas and feeling of highly civilized and cultivated people—to be a member of the French nationality, admitted on equal terms to all the privileges of French citizenship, sharing the advantages of French protection, and the dignity and prestige of French power—than to sulk on his own rocks, the half-savage relic of past times, revolving in his own little mental orbit, without participation or interest in the general movement of the world.[7]

It has to be said that this argument has yet to win the universal assent of the Bretons and the Basques. But in any case, the choice is not usually between remaining within your inherited national culture and assimilating to one that is equally good, or even perhaps better by some standard. To suppose this is to forget the part played by nationality in making someone the person that he or she is. Because national culture is in this sense constitutive, if it is destroyed those who had shared it either are left in a cultural vacuum or else have to undergo a difficult process of cultural adaptation, which is usually painful and disorienting while it is happening, and rarely wholly successful in its outcome. There will be large individual differences in this respect, but in general we can say that everyone has

---

[7] J. S. Mill, *Considerations on Representative Government*, in Mill, *Utilitarianism; On Liberty; Representative Government*, ed. H. B. Acton (London, Dent 1972), 363–4.

an interest in not having their inherited culture damaged or altered against their will.

There is still a significant step to be taken before we can conclude that national cultures need states to protect them. Plainly, many important cultures have survived without such protection; indeed, some have survived in the face of political persecution, such as the culture of Judaism. So why should national cultures give rise to political claims of a kind that other cultures do not—bracketing off, as we are, the fact that the wish to be politically self-determining is inherent in national identity (we are looking for reasons to justify that wish)?

It is important here that the elements that make up a national culture very often have an essentially public dimension; they concern features of a society whose existence is dependent upon political action. Consider some examples: the architecture of public buildings; the pattern of a landscape; the content of education; the character of television and film. If these are going to express and reproduce a common culture, they will have to be made subject to collective control (which doesn't of course mean that they must be politically regulated in every detail). The reason for regarding these cultural features as public goods is not that they cannot exist at all without state regulation. In principle, any of them might be entrusted to the care of private individuals—landowners might be given rights to do whatever they liked with their property; broadcasting might be thrown entirely on to the market; and so on. In this case it would still in theory be possible for people imbued with the culture to preserve it in their private dealings, but it would be very unwise to count on this happening. One reason is that many of the valued features are subject to collective action problems. We may all value a landscape in which small fields are divided by hedgerows rich in animal and bird life, but each of us has commercial reasons for rooting out the hedges and creating agricultural prairies. As owners of television stations we may sincerely want to make high-class drama and probing documentaries, but in a competitive market we may have to buy cheap imported soap operas in order to survive. So national cultures can decay without anybody intending that this should happen, and the only way to prevent this is to use the power of the state to protect aspects that are judged to be important. Very often this can be done by inducements rather than by coercion:

farmers can be given incentives to preserve their hedgerows; the domestic film industry can be subsidized out of cinema revenues important works of art can be purchased for national collections and so forth. The role of the state should not be to impose some preformed definition of national culture on people who may resist it, but to provide an environment in which the culture can develop spontaneously rather than being eroded by economically self-interested action on the part of particular individuals.

Why is a *national* state necessary to achieve this? Where a state exercises its authority over two or more nationalities, the dominant group has a strong incentive to use that authority to impose its own culture on the weaker groups. There are many historical instances of attempts to assimilate national minorities by force to the culture of the majority community, ranging from the enforced Magyarization of ethnic minorities in nineteenth-century Hungary to the consistent policy of the Turkish state to destroy the cultural identity of its Kurdish minority. So there are strong empirical reasons for thinking that national cultures will be protected most effectively when nurtured by states of their own. Now admittedly, there are some noteworthy exceptions to this rule: states with national minorities can go to some lengths to emphasize their commitment to the co-existence of different cultures within their borders, as for example states such as Canada and Belgium have done in recent years. But even if the commitment is made in good faith, the likely effect is that such states will offer weaker protection to each culture taken separately than would be expected in a culturally homogeneous state, since measures taken to protect one culture will be resisted by adherents of the other. (Canada has managed to hold an internal balance between French and English culture, but apparently at the cost of allowing a dominant American culture to pervade both.) Simply put, if you care about preserving your national culture, the surest way is to place the means of safeguarding it in the hands of those who share it—your fellow-nationals.

Finally, we must consider the case for national self-determination as an expression of collective autonomy. This argument is more speculative than the other two because it appeals to a contestable view of the person. It supposes that people have an interest in shaping the world in association with others with whom they identify. This interest can be pursued in various forms—for instance in enterprises in an economic setting—so it is not tied exclusively to national self-determination. But, given the many important ways in which states are able to impress their will on both their physical and social environments, being a participant in such a collective undertaking is likely to represent a significant form of collective autonomy.

This argument must immediately be qualified in several respects. People appear to vary a great deal in the value they attach to collective autonomy, just as they differ in the importance they attach to national identity. For some people it is enough to be in control of their personal lives. The idea of taking part in some collective enterprise which sets its stamp on the world has little appeal. So we are dealing here with a human interest that is widely shared but far from universal. Next, the quest for collective autonomy may take unacceptable forms, forms that are damaging to personal liberty. People may come to regard dictatorial leaders or authoritarian states as the embodiment of collective purposes, and sacrifice their own personal interests in the name of illusory 'self-determination'. This lies at the heart of the critique of 'positive liberty' delivered by Isaiah Berlin.[8] Collective autonomy may also be illusory for a different reason, namely that the state faces an external environment in which powerful economic and political forces effectively determine most of what it purports to control (for example, the chief parameters of the economy). Here, then, claims for national self-determination would be claims for a kind of autonomy that cannot, in fact, be achieved.

These qualifications show that appeals to the value of collective autonomy must be made with some care. In particular, autonomy of this kind requires more than that the state should coincide with the nation; it requires that what the state does should correspond to what we might call the popular will. The best guarantee of this is that the state should be democratic in form, with its decisions reflecting the judgements of its citizens as to what should be done. From this point of view, the historical association between ideas of democracy and ideas of national self-determination is hardly accidental: only a democratic state can ensure that the self-determination we are talking about is genuinely *national*, as opposed to the self-determination

[8] I. Berlin, 'Two Concepts of Liberty', in *Four Essays on Liberty* (Oxford, Oxford University Press, 1969) (abridged version in D. Miller (ed.), *Liberty*, Oxford, Oxford University Press, 1991).

of a class or a governing clique.[9] But it would be too strong to say that national self-determination strictly requires democracy. Provided there is indeed a genuine convergence in aims and interests between the population at large and those making decisions on their behalf, the interest in collective autonomy may be satisfied. We should see demands for self-determination in a colonial context in this light. It was not absurd for people to expect that they would have a greater sense of control over their destinies when ruled by local oligarchies than when ruled by imperial powers, even if in many cases these expectations have been frustrated.[10]

I have been looking so far at nationalist reasons for valuing national self-determination. As I noted earlier, the thesis that a nation should want its own state is at one level tautological, since the ambition to be politically self-determining is built in to the very idea of nationhood. What we have seen, however, is that this ambition flows naturally from other aspects of nationality. It is *conceivable* that someone should accept that national identities are valuable, and that nationality carries with it special obligations to compatriots, but find no value in nations being autonomous political units, but we can now see why this is such an unlikely position to hold.[11]

So let me now reverse the direction of the argument and ask why states, or more generally political authorities, are likely to function most effectively when they embrace just a single national community. The arguments here all appeal to the political consequences of solidarity and cultural homogeneity. They focus on the important role played by trust in a viable political community.[12] Much state activity involves the furthering of goals which cannot be achieved

[9]   I shall explore the connection in the reverse direction shortly.

[10]   See the careful discussion of this question in J. P. Plamenatz, *On Alien Rule and Self-Government* (London, Longmans, 1960).

[11]   One could, for example, cite the case of the German anarchist Gustav Landauer, who argued for a complete dissociation between nation and state. Landauer, drawing upon the ideas of Herder, saw nations as cultural communities whose unique qualities were mutually enriching, and between which, therefore, there was no natural antagonism. Self-government should be based in sub-national communes which might federate in various ways. See E. Lunn, *Prophet of Community: The Romantic Socialism of Gustav Landauer* (Berkeley, University of California Press, 1973), ch. 5.

[12]   This is also stressed in B. Barry, 'Self-Government Revisited', in D. Miller and L. Siedentop (eds.), *The Nature of Political Theory* (Oxford, Clarendon Press, 1983); reprinted in B. Barry, *Democracy, Power and Justice* (Oxford, Clarendon Press, 1989).

without the voluntary co-operation of citizens. For this activity to be successful, the citizens must trust the state, and they must trust one another to comply with what the state demands of them. Let me give a couple of examples. One concerns the provision of public goods such as a clean and healthy environment. The state can do certain things directly—it can fine polluters, for instance—but to achieve real results it must also very often rely on education and exhortation. Since adhering to the rules the state proposes will usually have costs, each person must be confident that the others will generally comply—and this involves mutual trust.[13] For another example, consider state grants or concessions to particular groups within the population, say financial support to an industry hard hit by changes in the terms of trade, or special funding for local authorities with inner-city problems. These dispensations are made on the understanding that other sections of the community would qualify for similar favourable treatment in the event that they too faced new and unforeseen difficulties. Such a practice cannot evolve if each sectional group jealously guards its own interests and insists that each dispensation should be strictly egalitarian. Again, what is needed is mutual confidence which allows you to sanction aid to group G on this occasion with the assurance that group G will give you its reciprocal support when it is your turn to ask for help.

Now a state might attempt to diminish its reliance on mutual trust by restricting its role to that of a night-watchman, merely presiding over a market economy in which outcomes depend on separate individuals pursuing their own interests. Yet, quite apart from the question whether this is a viable possibility for a state in the late twentieth century, certain kinds of trust are still required to support the ground rules of a market: individuals must have confidence in one another to deal fairly, to keep contracts, and to refrain from using their industrial or financial muscle to oblige the state to intervene in the market on their behalf.[14]

[13] I mean this to be a necessary condition for co-operation with the policy, not a sufficient condition; after all, each individual, or each enterprise, will usually have self-interested reasons for defection. My point is that agents will often be prepared to co-operate with policies, in situations where doing so has costs that may put them at a competitive disadvantage unless others co-operate too, *provided* they can expect reciprocal co-operation.

[14] It may be true, however, that a lesser degree of trust is required to support a

I take it as virtually self-evident that ties of community are an important source of such trust between individuals who are not personally known to one another and who are in no position directly to monitor one another's behaviour. A shared identity carries with it a shared loyalty, and this increases confidence that others will reciprocate one's own co-operative behaviour. So far this does not discriminate between the various communities that a person may belong to. The importance of national communities here is simply that they are encompassing communities which aspire to draw in everyone who inhabits a particular territory. This aspiration is not always achievable, giving rise to problems that we shall consider later in this chapter. But in contrast to, say, religious communities, which tend to define themselves exclusively, requiring adherence to a particular creed, nationality becomes a self-defeating idea if it is not accommodating. Suppose that we are members of a national community forming the dominant group in the territory we aspire to control, but that we share it with a minority group who have much in common with us, but who differ in one respect—religion, say. Unless our religion is crucial to our identity—and I suggested earlier that with most nations no single feature is likely to be crucial—we have good reason to de-emphasize this feature, and to stress instead, as a basis of unity, those cultural traits that we already share with the minority. To the extent that we succeed in doing so, we can form a territorial community in whose self-determination all can share. From this springs mutual trust. Again, to say this is not to say that an adequate degree of trust will in fact materialize—this is a perennial problem in modern states—but at least the basis is there. In states lacking a common national identity—states such as Nigeria, for instance, which are little more than umbrella organizations holding together two or three national or ethnic groups—politics at best takes the form of group bargaining and compromise and at worst degenerates into a struggle

night-watchman state. I have argued elsewhere that redistributive policies of the kind favoured by socialists are likely to demand a considerable degree of social solidarity if they are to win popular consent, and for that reason socialists should be more strongly committed than classical liberals to the nation-state as an institution that can make such solidarity politically effective. See D. Miller, 'In What Sense must Socialism be Communitarian?' *Social Philosophy and Policy*, 6 (1988–9) 51–73.

for domination. Trust may exist within the groups, but not across them.[15]

Trust assumes particular importance if we ask about the conditions under which individuals will give their support to schemes of social justice, particularly schemes involving redistribution to those not able to provide for their needs through market transactions.[16] States which in this sense aim to be welfare states and at the same time to win democratic legitimation must be rooted in communities whose members recognize such obligations of justice to one another. As we saw earlier, national communities are indeed of this kind. Thus, political philosophers such as Rawls, who argue in defence of principles of justice that require redistribution in favour of the worst-off members of society, tacitly presuppose that these principles are to operate in the context of a community whose members acknowledge ties of solidarity. Although Rawls does not devote any attention to the national character of the political community he is describing, it is noteworthy that he sees the problem of justice as arising in a society whose membership is taken to be fixed and given. The task of the parties in the original position, he says, 'is to agree on principles for the basic structure of the society in which it is assumed they will lead their life. . . . The attachments formed to persons and places, to associations and communities, as well as cultural ties, are normally too strong to be given up, and this fact is not to be deplored.'[17] These assumptions are hard to justify unless we suppose that the parties in question share a common nationality.[18]

[15] I have emphasized the role of nationality in creating trust among the members of large, anonymous societies, but one might also refer to Gellner's argument that industrial societies, if they are to function effectively, require their members to share a high culture transmitted by a common education system, and must therefore organize themselves politically along nationalist lines. See E. Gellner, *Nations and Nationalism* (Oxford, Blackwell, 1983). These two arguments strike me as complementary rather than competitive. Both stress the role played by nationality under specifically modern social conditions.

[16] I shall make the argument only briefly here, since I have expounded it at greater length in Miller, 'In What Sense must Socialism be Communitarian?' and in *Market, State and Community* (Oxford, Clarendon Press, 1989), ch. 9.

[17] Rawls, 'Basic Structure', *Political Liberalism*, 277.

[18] When analysing schemes of justice in his earlier book, Rawls says: 'I assume that the boundaries of these schemes are given by the notion of a self-contained national community' (J. Rawls, *A Theory of Justice*, Cambridge, Mass., Harvard University Press, 1971, 457). It is clear from his general discussion, however, that 'national community' means no more than 'state whose citizens together subscribe

It might be said in reply that there is no hard evidence connecting states that rest on common national identities with redistributive schemes of social justice. On the one hand, states such as Belgium, Canada, and Switzerland are to some degree multinational, yet sustain effective systems of public welfare. On the other hand, American national identity is strong, but the United States has been singularly reluctant to implement redistributive schemes of social justice. So it seems as though a shared national identity is neither necessary nor sufficient for a practice of social justice along Rawlsian or similar lines. The thesis I am advancing cannot, however, be refuted by these examples, for two reasons at least. First, it is not only the *strength* of national identity (supposing that can be measured) but also the *character* of national identity that matters from the point of view of social justice. I pointed out in Chapter 2 that national identities embodied a shared public culture. The quality of that culture—in particular, the extent to which the nation conceives itself along solidaristic or individualistic lines—is clearly going to be of vital importance in determining which practices of justice are seen as legitimate. So we have two variables rather than just one to consider when explaining welfare policy and so forth, and this may sufficiently account for the case of the United States, whose public culture is by common consent unusually individualistic.

Second, in the case of those states that appear to support redistributive social policies despite their communal divisions, two points must be made. The first is that they cannot be described simply as multinational states. Rather, they are states whose members have both national and communal identities and allegiances. Take the cases of Switzerland and Canada. In Switzerland a national identity was quite deliberately fostered in the course of the nineteenth century, a process bearing all the usual hallmarks of nation-building—myths of origin, the resurrection of national heroes like William Tell and so forth—with the result that the Swiss today share a common national identity *as Swiss* over and above their separate linguistic

to principles of justice'. He says, for instance, that 'the citizen body as a whole is not generally bound together by ties of fellow-feeling between individuals, but by the acceptance of public principles of justice' (p. 474). Rawls's failure to investigate the sense of community that his principles of justice presuppose forms the basis for Michael Sandel's critique in *Liberalism and the Limits of Justice* (Cambridge: Cambridge University Press, 1982). See also J. W. Nickel, 'Rawls on Political Community and Principles of Justice', *Law and Philosophy*, 9 (1990), 205–16.

religious, and cantonal identities.[19] The Canadian case is more complex, because there seems to have been a shift in identity among the French-speaking community in Quebec over the last decades.[20] Originally this community thought of itself as belonging to *la nation canadienne-française*; that is to say, they identified themselves as Canadian, but more specifically with the French-speaking population scattered throughout Canada. More recently the Québécois have tended to think of themselves as belonging to a separate Quebec nationality whose place in the Canadian state must be understood entirely in instrumental terms.[21] If this trend continues, Canada will indeed become a multinational state, though with the peculiarity that one constituent unit sees itself as distinct while the other does not (the English-speaking population continuing to think of the Québécois as French-Canadians).[22] At the same time, the future of Canada as a single state will increasingly be called into question. The point I want to make about Canada is that its institutions and policies stem from a period in which, although French- and English-speakers thought of themselves as different kinds of Canadians, they held in common a Canadian identity that was more than merely the fact of membership in a single state. So once again, we find that democratic states that have successfully pursued policies aiming at social justice have a unifying identity, even if the unity is not as complete as in the case, say, of Norway.

The second point is that where communal divisions are sharp, as in the cases under discussion, policy has to be made in such a way that each community feels that it is getting a fair deal, and is not going to be a winner or loser in the long term. Power has to be less centralized in such states, and a high premium is placed on agreement between the constituent parts—the Swiss in particular being legendary for the consensual nature of their decision-making. This might pose problems if fairness required radical redistribution

[19] For an account of the building of Swiss national identity, see H. Kohn, *Nationalism and Liberty: The Swiss example* (London, Allen and Unwin, 1956).

[20] I draw here upon C. Taylor, 'Shared and Divergent Values', in G. Laforest (ed.), *Reconciling the Solitudes* (Montreal, McGill-Queen's University Press, 1993).

[21] For a recent account, see M. Ignatieff, *Blood and Belonging: Journeys into the New Nationalism* (London, Vintage, 1994), ch. 4.

[22] See here B. Rodal, 'The Canadian Conundrum: Two Concepts of Nationhood', in U. Ra'anan, M. Mesner, K. Armes, and K. Martin (eds.), *State and Nation in Multi-Ethnic Societies* (Manchester, Manchester University Press, 1991).

across the communities (rather than between better endowed and worse endowed individuals within them). Social justice will always be easier to achieve in states with strong national identities and without internal communal divisions. Belgium, Canada, and Switzerland work as they do partly because they are *not* simply multinational, but have cultivated common national identities alongside communal ones, and partly because they have developed institutions (federalism, decentralization) to ensure that each community has its interests protected against incursions by the rest.[23]

Finally, states require citizens to trust one another if they are to function effectively as democracies; in particular if they are guided by the ideal of *deliberative* democracy.[24] This is the ideal of a political community in which decisions are reached through an open and uncoerced discussion of the issue at stake where the aim of all participants is to arrive at an agreed judgement. If a democracy is to function with this as its regulative ideal, at least two conditions are necessary. One is that the reasons given in political debate should be sincerely held, and not merely adopted as an expedient way of promoting sectional interests. Connected with this is a requirement of consistency, namely that if you advance an argument in one case

---

[23] There is also a danger here of saving the thesis by trivializing it: where a state works effectively and promotes social justice, it must by the same token be a national state. I do not wish to trivialize the thesis in this way, though I should be the first to admit that the causal relationships are complex. In the Canadian case, for instance, Canadians will often point to their national health service as a source of national pride and as something that marks Canada off from its American neighbour. So here the existence of the institution becomes a component of national identity. I should want to argue, however, that this works only on the condition that the institution is taken to heart and regarded as expressing the underlying values of Canadians. The fact that in reality institutions shape values as well as expressing them—that Canadians may not have believed very strongly in a public health system prior to its introduction—takes us back to the questions about the origins of national identity canvassed in Ch. 2.

[24] This ideal has recently been advocated and discussed by a number of political theorists. The most incisive presentation is probably J. Cohen, 'Deliberation and Democratic Legitimacy', in A. Hamlin and P. Pettit (eds.), *The Good Polity* (Oxford, Blackwell, 1989). See also B. Manin, 'On Legitimacy and Political Deliberation', *Political Theory*, 15 (1987), 338–68; J. Dryzek, *Discursive Democracy* (Cambridge, Cambridge University Press, 1990); and my own earlier discussions in Miller, *Market, State, and Community*, ch. 10, and in 'Deliberative Democracy and Social Choice', *Political Studies*, Special Issue, 40 (1992), 54–67 (reprinted in D. Held (ed.), *Prospects for Democracy*, Cambridge, Polity Press, 1993).

where it works in favour of an interest or cause of yours, you should be willing to concede that the same argument applies to other cases that are similar except that now it counts against your personal interests. Insincerity quickly devalues the currency of political argument. Once arguments are no longer to be taken at their face value, but simply regarded as indicators of the interests that different groups want to pursue, there is no longer any point in searching for grounds of agreement. Democracy can still exist in some form—interests can be aggregated by procedures that give each person's preferences approximately equal weight—but the deliberative ideal has been abandoned.

The second condition is that citizens should be willing to moderate their claims in the hope that they can find common ground on which policy decisions can be based. Given that spontaneous agreement is unlikely to occur even if all the arguments are sincerely made, those who hold extreme views on the issue under discussion have to be prepared to shift to a more moderate position in the search for a consensus. Thus, in a debate on the subject of nuclear weapons, those who on pacifist grounds believe that all weapons of destruction should be abolished cannot simply rely on this premiss; they must be willing to present and consider other arguments against nuclear weapons—arguments that they presumably endorse —such as the argument that nuclear devices are likely to inflict indiscriminate damage on civilian populations. Again, this requires trust among those doing the deliberating. If I am now willing to abandon some position that I feel strongly about in an effort to reach a compromise that commands widespread support, I must expect others to reciprocate either now or in the future. Otherwise every concession will be regarded as a sign of weakness, and there will be no incentive to move towards agreement.

No democracy that we can envisage will ever perfectly match the deliberative ideal. Unless a democracy includes some deliberative elements, however, its legitimacy will be put in question, and it is likely to make bad policy. If sectional groups look upon policy-making as a zero-sum game in which they fight for financial concessions and legal privileges in competition with other groups, then what emerges will reflect nothing more than the balance of forces on each occasion. Moreover, as J. S. Mill saw, such groups have no common interest in containing the power of government itself:

Their mutual antipathies are generally much stronger than jealousy of the government. That any one of them feels aggrieved by the policy of the common ruler is sufficient to determine another to support that policy. Even if all are aggrieved, none feel that they can rely on the others for fidelity in a joint resistance; the strength of none is sufficient to resist alone, and each may reasonably think that it consults its own advantage most by bidding for the favour of the government against the rest.[25]

Mill's conclusion was that 'free institutions are next to impossible in a country made up of different nationalities'.[26] If Mill had meant that free institutions require complete national homogeneity, cases such as those of Canada, Belgium, and Switzerland might be brought forward to prove him wrong. But Mill was well aware that a common sentiment of nationality could co-exist with linguistic and other cultural differences, and indeed used the Swiss and the Belgians as examples to make the point. His thesis remains sound: to the extent that we aspire to a form of democracy in which all citizens are at some level involved in discussion of public issues, we must look to the conditions under which citizens can respect one another's good faith in searching for grounds of agreement. Among large aggregates of people, only a common nationality can provide the sense of solidarity that makes this possible. Sharing a national identity does not, of course, mean holding similar political views; but it does mean being committed to finding terms under which fellow-nationals can agree to live together.

We have now explored the main arguments favouring national self-determination. Where a nation is politically autonomous, it is able to implement a scheme of social justice; it can protect and foster its common culture; and its members are to a greater or lesser extent able collectively to determine its common destiny. Where the citizens of a state are also compatriots, the mutual trust that this engenders makes it more likely that they will be able to solve collective action problems, to support redistributive principles of justice, and to practise deliberative forms of democracy. Together, these make a powerful case for holding that the boundaries of nations and states should as far as possible coincide. Some of the practical difficulties

[25] Mill, *Representative Government*, 361.
[26] For a recent restatement of this case, see C. Taylor, 'Cross-Purposes: The Liberal–Communitarian Debate', in N. Rosenblum (ed.), *Liberalism and the Moral Life* (Cambridge, Mass., Harvard University Press, 1989).

that this gives rise to will be considered later. But our next task is to look more closely at what national self-determination entails for the question of sovereignty and the obligations of one state to another.

II

This is not the place to embark on a full analysis of the idea of sovereignty, one of the more confusing concepts in the repertoire of political thought. A sovereign body, I shall assume, is the body that has the final authority to decide, and especially to legislate, on a set of issues. Thus, we might say that the International Rugby Football Board is sovereign in matters of international rugby, meaning that it has the authority to establish the rules and other conditions under which international matches are played. In the case of states, sovereignty is usually taken to have two aspects: states are said to be sovereign internally in so far as they are recognized as the final authority on all matters that arise within their boundaries; and they are sovereign externally in so far as their decisions cannot be overridden by any other body, whether another state or an international institution.[27] Putting the point this way shows that the scope of sovereignty may vary. A state might be sovereign with respect to one subject-matter but not with respect to another. Conventionally, states are assumed to exercise sovereignty with unrestricted scope, but the question I want to address is whether the idea of national self-determination necessarily requires this.

Clearly, there are forms of nationalism that do point towards unlimited sovereignty as a political ideal. If you believe that nations are justified in doing whatever best promotes their interests, including trampling on the interests of their neighbours, then you will also see states as having no limits to their authority. But the principle of nationality that I am defending here is not of this kind. It gives grounds for favouring national self-determination, but these grounds apply equally to all peoples who meet the criteria for nationality. Thus, reiteration is built into the principle itself. In justifying the special obligations that I owe to my fellow-Britons, I am

[27] See the discussion in C. Beitz, 'Sovereignty and Morality in International Affairs', in D. Held (ed.), *Political Theory Today* (Cambridge, Polity Press, 1991). For an historical account of the evolution of the idea of sovereignty, see F. H. Hinsley, *Sovereignty*, 2nd edn. (Cambridge, Cambridge University Press, 1986).

also justifying Americans in acknowledging and acting on special obligations to fellow-Americans, Frenchmen to Frenchmen, and so forth. Likewise, in justifying my own country's claim to be an independent political unit, I am also justifying the corresponding claims of others. This does not yet tell us how we should act when these claims come into conflict; but perhaps, if the principle is specified correctly, such conflicts will be relatively rare. The question, then, is to see how far national states must exercise sovereign powers if national self-determination is valued on the grounds set out in the previous section.

The guiding ideal here is that of a people reproducing their national identity and settling matters that are collectively important to them through democratic deliberation. To achieve that, they need a political unit with authority of the relevant scope, but what that scope must be will depend on the particular identity of the group in question, and on the aims and goals that they are attempting to pursue. Thus, one nation may include religious affiliation as part of its self-definition, in which case it is very likely to want the political authority it exercises to extend to religious questions, whereas another nation may define itself in ways that make no reference to religion. It is therefore going to be difficult to set a priori limits to the proper scope of sovereignty from this perspective. Moreover, we cannot tell in advance which particular features of a society's way of life will come to assume importance as markers of national identity. To take one example, there has recently been some debate in Britain (paralleled elsewhere in Europe) about the conditions under which it would be acceptable for a European currency to replace British currency. Some of those involved would wish to argue that the British people have a right not to have the European currency imposed on them without their consent. (The implication would be that a referendum would be needed to legitimize the replacement of the pound by the ecu.) Now we might think this was an absurd argument; no one could claim a constitutive attachment to a particular currency. But I do not believe that one can rule out a priori the possibility that having one's own currency could come to symbolize national self-determination. In this area, a collective belief that something is essential to national identity comes very close to making it so. Once you combine the principle of national self-determination with the proposition that what counts for the purposes of national identity is what the nation in question takes to be essential to that identity, it follows that nothing in principle lies beyond the scope of sovereignty.

It does *not* follow, on the other hand, that nation-states must rigidly demand complete sovereignty over their internal affairs; there may be good reasons for transferring powers of decision upwards to confederal bodies, for instance. But such transfers must in the last resort be regarded as provisional, in the sense that nations have a residual claim to re-appropriate rights of decision where they believe that vital national interests are at stake. So there is a presumption here in favour of national sovereignty together with a recognition that in practice many decisions may sensibly be delegated upwards.

Perhaps this perspective can be better understood by seeing what it would mean in a few key policy areas. Take national defence first. In a post-imperial world, there seems no reason why defence should not be managed at a supra-national level, say in a European context by a collective European defence force. Each nation has an interest in its security, plainly, but no particular interest in that security being provided by its own armed forces as opposed to a collective European force. This is in line with the traditional idea of a confederation, which was that of an alliance for mutual defence and security but with the domestic policy of each member state being left in its own hands.[28] The essential element of state sovereignty here is simply that each state has the right to ensure that it is adequately defended; but this is consistent with entering into a binding pact with others to provide that defence.

At the other end of the spectrum lies social policy. Social policy is both the vehicle whereby common ideals can be expressed and the means whereby a society consciously reproduces its own identity. The latter aspect is particularly clear if one takes the example of public education. What is taught in schools and how it is taught reflects the priorities of a particular culture and tends to instil those priorities in the rising generation. (This should not be understood in a narrowly political sense: consider the case of Japanese children spending long hours learning precisely how to paint the characters

[28] See the historical analysis in M. Forsyth, *Unions of States: The Theory and Practice of Confederation* (Leicester, Leicester University Press, 1981), especially chs. 2–3.

of the Japanese alphabet.) As to the former aspect, consider how social policy is bound to reflect common definitions of need which none the less may vary substantially across cultures. For these reasons, there is a clear case for national governments retaining direct control over the making of social policy.

Somewhere between these extremes lies economic policy. Or perhaps one should rather say that if we look at economic policy-making there are strong arguments pulling in both directions. In favour of transmitting decision-making powers upward to a supra-national authority is the fact that decisions on economic policy taken at state level often appear to place the participants in a Prisoner's Dilemma. For instance, assuming the standard arguments for free trade as the means of bringing about an efficient global division of labour, each country taken separately may have an incentive to implement policies to protect its own industry; but if all do, economic performance falls to a level below that achievable under free trade. This would suggest removing the power to protect from the nation-state, either through some binding pact or through the creation of an international authority. Against this, however, is the fact that economic policy and social policy are intertwined. Consider unemployment levels, which are not only parts of an economic equation but have a profound impact on the general character of a society. Or consider agricultural policy, often now regarded as merely a tug-of-war between the vested interests of farmers and the interests of consumers inside and outside the country in question, but also of course a major determinant of the physical shape of the landscape in that country—something in which its members have a very different sort of interest. Most radically, think of a state which for reasons of social justice makes a significant departure from standard capitalist patterns of industry—implementing, say, a scheme of workers' ownership; it is plausible to assume that such an initiative would need sheltering to some degree from international competition, at least in the sense that capital investment could not be left to the free play of market forces.[29] All of these examples suggest that the members of a nation-state have a legitimate interest in keeping

---

[29] For the reasons why this is so, see my 'Market Neutrality and the Failure of Co-operatives', *British Journal of Political Science*, 11 (1981), 309–29, and *Market, State, and Community*, ch. 3.

control of economic policy-making and tell against any transfer of rights in this area in an upwards direction.

I do not know how to escape from this quandary, which indeed seems to me one of the major dilemmas facing the human species at present. The case for a stable international order is strong, not least from the point of view of the poorer nations, who need above all open access to world markets and commodity prices that are reasonably predictable in the long term. But who could gainsay the right of a nation to set off along its own path and to set in place the protective institutions that would be needed to make that path feasible—say, a nation that decided to adopt a radical environmental policy? The dilemma can perhaps be resolved formally by saying that states should be prepared to make conditional transfers of decision-making rights in this area, while always retaining the ultimate right to opt out of whatever collective arrangements are made. But this does not give much practical guidance.[30]

It is clear, at any rate, that from the perspective I am developing there is no reason to make a fetish out of national sovereignty. The questions to ask will always be: how much does it matter, from the point of view of preserving our national identity and exercising self-determination on questions that concern us, that we should retain such-and-such rights of decision? On the other hand, are there real gains to be made by vesting them in a higher authority? Let us turn then to the second issue to be addressed in this section, namely the limits placed by *others'* claims to national self-determination on *our* exercise of rights of sovereignty.

Suppose we have to deal with states embodying claims to national self-determination that are prima facie as good as our own, and sup-

---

[30] What a nation does in practice will no doubt depend on how closely its policies are seen to be aligned with those of the international authority in question. To take a local example, the parties in Britain have performed a small pirouette on the question of Britain's relations with the European Community. For most of the post-war period, the Labour Party, and especially its left wing, has been deeply suspicious of the Community as a capitalist club, membership of which would seriously inhibit the implementation of socialist policies in Britain. Over the last decade, however, the position has been reversed: Labour has come to see the EC/EU as a haven of social democracy, whereas the Thatcherite Right believes that economic union would prevent the carrying out in Britain of genuine free market policies. At one moment it is the Left that is 'nationalist', at another moment the Right. I am sure that many other examples of this phenomenon could easily be found.

pose that these states are not engaged in acts of aggression or other unjust acts against their neighbours: what obligations ought we to acknowledge towards them? In answering this question, we are to be guided by the idea that each nation has a good claim to develop a scheme of social justice, to protect its distinctive culture, and to make autonomous decisions about its future. This idea appears to entail four obligations that are already quite widely recognized, together with a fifth that is somewhat more problematic. These obligations are as follows.

1. The duty to abstain from materially harming another state, either by acts of military aggression or by physical damage in the form, say, of pollution that is exported across national boundaries. States, that is, have a right to territorial integrity which holds against any sort of physical encroachment by other states.

2. The duty not to exploit states that are one-sidedly vulnerable to your actions. This would include the case where a powerful state threatens the use of military force against a weaker state in order to force the latter to change its policies in some respect; but also the more difficult case of economic dependency, whereby state A can devastate the economy of state B by, for instance, suddenly demanding the repayment of a loan or altering the terms of trade in some commodity that plays a vital role in B's economy. (The relationship between the United States and the countries of Central America such as Guatemala and Honduras might be taken as an example.) Here there is an obligation to refrain from using the power that the international situation provides you with, however the power imbalance has arisen.[31]

3. The duty to comply with whatever international agreements have been made, including of course treaties to establish confederal institutions. We need to distinguish what it is right or advisable to undertake by way of international co-operation, and the obligations a state has once it has entered into co-operative arrangements, whether wisely or not. Here I am pointing to the latter; I shall shortly consider what we should say in cases where obligations arising from agreements clash with basic rights of national self-determination.

[31] The best analysis of the general principle at stake here is R. Goodin, *Protecting the Vulnerable* (Chicago, University of Chicago Press, 1985).

4. Obligations of reciprocity, arising from practices of mutual aid whereby states come to one another's assistance in moments of need. These obligations arise whether or not there is a formal agreement to provide aid. (If there is a formal agreement, then duties in the present category plainly overlap with duties in the previous one.) An example of what I have in mind is the emerging convention whereby countries struck by earthquake, flood, or certain kinds of famine can count on assistance from other countries in the form of emergency relief. What we have here is essentially an informal scheme of mutual insurance whereby the costs of unforeseeable natural disasters are shared among countries roughly on the basis of each country's ability to contribute to the scheme. Given such a scheme, each country has an obligation to contribute as the occasion arises.[32]

5. More problematically, obligations to ensure the fair distribution of natural resources. Nations cannot provide for the basic needs of their members and cannot exercise any sort of collective autonomy unless they have a sufficient resource base to be economically viable. Moreover nation-states are interdependent in so far as the value of the resources available within the territorial boundaries of any one state depends on global institutions such as the international commodity market. Since states are enriched and impoverished in seemingly arbitrary ways by such institutions, this triggers an obligation on the part of resource-rich states to aid those that are resource-poor.

It is less easy to settle on the principles that should govern such redistribution. One fairly radical proposal is the principle that each inhabitant of the world has an equal basic entitlement to natural resources, so that states should be entitled to resources in proportion to the number of their citizens.[33] But such a principle faces some

[32] We may expect to see such schemes extended in the future, particularly in response to the impact of large-scale environmental change, where it is likely to be difficult to see in advance how particular countries will be affected. Uncertainty about the future allows such schemes to embrace a certain amount of redistribution between countries in practice, although it is not in their underlying logic that they should be redistributive.

[33] For this argument see B. Barry, 'Humanity and Justice in Global Perspective' in Barry, *Democracy, Power and Justice*. Barry, however, pulls back from the extremely radical implications of attempting to implement this principle directly in favour of taxes on GDP and on mineral extraction.

serious difficulties of implementation. One is the absence of a common metric by which resources of different kinds can be valued. In the case of exchangeable commodities, the global market provides a metric of sorts, but this overlooks the specific use-value that a resource may have for the community that possesses it. Can the value of the city of Jerusalem to the Israeli nation be estimated by the revenue that that piece of real estate is capable of producing? Second, resources are not simply there for the taking: they need to be discovered, extracted, and made serviceable for human use, all at some cost.[34] So the question how many resources does any particular society possess has no straightforward answer. (Do you have coal if it is prohibitively expensive to mine, or if you do not have the technology to extract it?) The resource base of each society will depend on its cultural features and on political decisions already taken, such as decisions about which productive skills to cultivate through the education system. The apparent simplicity of 'global equality of resources' dissolves in the face of these problems.[35] What can be coherently argued for is the much weaker claim that resource transfers should be made so as to allow each national community to reach a threshold of viability, giving it an economic base from which national self-determination can meaningfully be exercised.[36]

Obligation 3 also requires a brief comment. My general line has been that nation-states have an underlying right to decide for themselves which rights of sovereignty they should continue to exercise

[34] The extreme view here is that of Israel Kirzner, who argues that, in the morally relevant sense, the person who discovers a resource also creates it. 'What no one thought worthy of taking, was something valueless; economically—and morally—speaking, it did not exist. My discovery of the natural resource, my realizing its potential value, has meant that I have brought it into existence' (I. Kirzner, *Discovery, Capitalism, and Distributive Justice*, Oxford, Blackwell, 1989, 155). I do not wish to endorse this view, but to steer a mid-course between it and the manna-from-heaven view which sees natural resources as simply lying available for use in production.

[35] Equality of resources is in any case an ideal fraught with difficulties, as I have argued in 'Equality' in G. M. K. Hunt (ed.), *Philosophy and Politics* (Cambridge, Cambridge University Press, 1990). Trying to apply it on a global as opposed to a societal basis merely adds to these.

[36] Although his starting point is somewhat more voluntarist than mine, Thomas Baldwin reaches a similar conclusion on the related question of what *territory* a political community is entitled to claim in 'The Territorial State', in H. Gross and R. Harrison (eds.), *Jurisprudence: Cambridge Essays* (Oxford, Clarendon Press, 1992).

and which rights they can sensibly transfer to some confederal or global agency. What, then, if a state undertakes a binding commitment to transfer a right which it later finds that it wants to re-appropriate (assuming that the confederation is unwilling to restore this element of sovereignty to the state in question)? If the right is vital to continuing national self-determination, then it may be taken back at the expense of the pact. One reason for such an about-turn might be that in international society circumstances may change to the point where the reasons for entering the pact no longer obtain. Suppose for instance that at one moment an alliance is formed to provide security against a common aggressor, but at a later time this threat has receded while one member state alone faces some new external threat; in these circumstances that state seems justified in withdrawing its forces from the alliance if this is necessary to deter the new threat.[37] I do not think this argument is destructive of the very idea of confederation. Confederations are sustained by a sense of mutual advantage and by the sanctions, economic or political, that members can impose on those that default for no good reason. To allow states the residual right to recover their rights of sovereignty in the event that they judge it vital to do so does not imply that the pact has no binding force.

The picture of international justice that I have sketched portrays a world in which nation-states are self-determining, but respect the self-determination of others through obligations of non-interference and in some cases of aid. This is very different from the picture presented by, for example, Charles Beitz, who argues that we are justified in regarding the world as a single scheme of co-operation, and who therefore conceives international justice in Rawlsian terms. In particular, he argues for applying the Rawlsian difference princi-

---

[37] International lawyers have addressed the general question of when states are justified in renouncing treaties because of radically changed circumstances. The doctrine of *clausula rebus sic stantibus* has been read as holding that a treaty ceases to be binding when a 'vital change of circumstances' has occurred subsequently to its enactment: see J. L. Brierly, *The Law of Nations*, 6th edn. (Oxford, Clarendon Press, 1963), ch. 7. Brierly himself argues that the doctrine should be taken to mean that 'the obligation of a treaty comes to an end if an event happens which the parties *intended*, or which we are justified in presuming they would have intended, should put an end to it' (p. 338). This narrower interpretation would apply to the example given in the text, but not to cases where a state reclaims a right of sovereignty because it has since come to believe that the right is vital to national self-determination.

ple internationally.[38] It follows from the Beitz position that states would have an obligation to accept outside economic management in the event that this proved to be the most effective way of raising the living standards of the worst-off members of the poorer states. In the present picture there is no general obligation to help poorer states. (Equally, of course, there is no *prohibition* on a state deciding to do this on humanitarian or other grounds.) This fits with the account of international ethics presented in Chapter 3, where I argued that international obligations should be seen as humanitarian except in cases where people's basic rights were put at risk and it was not feasible for their own national state to protect them. Such a view may appear heartless, but we now see that it is entailed by respect for the self-determination of other national communities. To respect the autonomy of other nations also involves treating them as responsible for decisions they may make about resource use, economic growth, environmental protection, and so forth. As a result of these decisions, living standards in different countries may vary substantially, and one cannot then justify redistribution by appeal to egalitarian principles of justice such as the Rawlsian difference principle.

III

Up to now I have been looking at cases in which the boundaries of nation and state presently coincide, and asking what the principle of national self-determination implies for the issues of sovereignty and confederation. In this final part of the chapter I look at the more difficult problems that arise when the above condition fails to hold, and in particular at the question when a national community presently incorporated in a multinational state is justified in demanding secession. An objection that is frequently raised to the principle of self-determination itself is that it cannot possibly be applied to the real world: there is no feasible way of drawing state boundaries that would simultaneously meet all demands for national self-determination. Thus, serious attempts to apply the principle would inevitably lead to political chaos.[39]

[38] C. Beitz, *Political Theory and International Relations* (Princeton, Princeton University Press, 1979), pt. III.

[39] This charge runs throughout E. Kedourie, *Nationalism* (London, Hutchinson, 1966). It is succinctly stated by Gellner, *Nations and Nationalism*, 2 (though the

We can better appreciate the guidance which the principle of national self-determination offers on this question by contrasting it with liberal answers to the same question. It is interesting to observe that liberalism can generate two radically opposed doctrines on the issue of state boundaries.[40] One view subordinates the issue entirely to considerations of individual rights and justice. The state has certain obligations to its citizens, and, provided it discharges these obligations in a satisfactory manner, no group can be justified in claiming a right to secede; conversely, if the existing state is falling down in this respect, exploiting or oppressing the members of one particular group, and it seems likely that the group can protect its rights more effectively by setting up its own state, then it would be justified in so doing.[41] In classical liberal theory, the rights in question were conceived in roughly Lockean terms as life, liberty, and property, and this view underlay Lord Acton's defence of the multinational state, recently echoed by Kedourie.[42] Modern liberals take a more expansive view of the state's responsibilities, but they may approach the questions of boundaries and secession in the same way: a group's wish to secede has little or no force unless it can establish that it is receiving unfair treatment from existing political institutions. Birch, for example, lays down four conditions under which a regional group might justifiably claim to secede from a larger state: the prior forcible inclusion of the region within the state; serious failure to protect the rights and security of the inhabitants; failure to safeguard the legitimate political and economic interests of the region; and reneging on an explicit or implicit bargain designed to safeguard the essential interests of the region (e.g. by constitutional change).[43] With the possible exception of the first, these conditions

remainder of Gellner's book is a powerful attempt to show why the drive to national self-determination is endemic to industrial societies, and why for that reason the political problems it brings with it are inescapable).

[40] See also here Barry, 'Self-Government Revisited', 126–30.

[41] The dominant view among politicians in the international community appears to be an even more restrictive version of this one: secession is justifiable only when the fundamental rights of the seceding group are threatened by the state they wish to secede from—in particular when genocidal or similar policies put the group's very existence at stake.

[42] Acton, 'Nationality'; Kedourie, *Nationalism*.

[43] See A. H. Birch, 'Another Liberal Theory of Secession', *Political Studies*, 32 (1984), 596–602; A. H. Birch, *Nationalism and National Integration* (London, Unwin Hyman, 1989), ch. 6.

reflect an underlying view that each citizen has a range of basic interests which she may expect the state to promote, and it is only in the event that she finds herself in a group that is systematically getting a raw deal that she has a prima facie case for opting out. Demands that spring from a wish to preserve cultural identity are quite specifically excluded.[44]

The most sophisticated version of this liberal view can allow culture to stand as one of the things in which individuals may have an interest, along with their liberties and material possessions.[45] This might converge in practice with the nationalist view in circumstances where the policies of the state threaten a minority with cultural destruction. Even here, however, there is a difference: the liberal view may acknowledge a person's interest in having *some* culture, but it finds no particular value in a group's wish to preserve and develop the particular culture into which it was born.[46] In a revealing metaphor, Buchanan portrays minority groups as clinging to a 'sinking ship' (and demanding timbers and pumps to keep it afloat) when they have the chance to 'board another, more seaworthy cultural vessel'.[47] Why insist on clinging to your old, competitively unsuccessful, culture when nearby there is an alternative to which you can assimilate? To which the nationalist will reply, first, that cultures, unlike ships, are not vessels to be boarded and abandoned at will, but conditions for a person's having an identity and being able to make choices in the first place; second, that the culture in question may not be defective in itself, but merely unable to flourish without the protection that political self-determination can provide.

The first liberal view says, in effect, that the wishes of a minority community should not count unless it can show that it is not getting a fair deal out of the existing state. The second view makes the wishes

[44] See the concluding page of Birch, 'Another Liberal Theory'; in *Nationalism* he describes those who argue for self-determination simply on cultural grounds as 'romantics'.

[45] See e.g. A. Buchanan, *Secession* (Boulder, Colo., Westview Press, 1991), which sets out what is essentially a liberal view with considerable sophistication. Buchanan makes it clear, however, that he regards arguments for secession based on cultural claims as far weaker than those alleging 'discriminatory redistribution' of material resources by the existing state.

[46] On this point see C. Taylor, 'Can Liberalism be Communitarian?' *Critical Review*, 8 (1994), 257–62.

[47] Buchanan, *Secession*, 54–5; there are clear echoes here of John Stuart Mill's view cited on p. 86 above.

hemselves paramount. This view also has a Lockean pedigree, for it 1olds that the boundaries of states should as far as possible depend)n individual consent. The practical implication is that any sub-:ommunity in any state has the right to vote to secede from that state, provided that it is in turn willing to allow any sub-sub-:ommunity the equivalent right, and so on indefinitely. (Beran calls his the 'recursive' version of the majority principle.[48]) The princi->le for fixing the borders of states is simply the will of the majority n any territorial area.

This might seem to be nothing more than a recipe for anarchy. 3eran attempts to ward off such a charge by laying down a number)f conditions that a would-be state should meet if it is to make good ts claim to secession: for instance, it must not create an enclave within the existing state, it must not occupy an area that is culturally, :conomically, or militarily essential, etc. But the effect of this is to substitute a charge of arbitrariness for a charge of anarchy. Consider, ·or instance, a case like that of Nagorny Karabakh, within which the dominant group is Armenian. Since it would constitute an enclave, t cannot, on the principles we are considering, vote to secede from Azerbaijan.[49] But by including a suitably defined corridor strip con-1ecting Nagorny Karabakh to Armenia, it would be relatively easy .o demarcate a territory in which there was still a majority for acced-ng to Armenia. Are the inhabitants of the corridor strip then per-nitted to take a subsequent vote to rejoin Azerbaijan?[50] According .o the principle of recursion, they must be; but the effect of a 'Yes' /ote in this second referendum would be to make Nagorny Karabakh into an enclave once again, in violation of the no-enclaves ·ule. The consent principle together with the prohibition of enclaves 3ives no determinate answer to the borders question in these cir-:umstances. If the inhabitants of Nagorny Karabakh are not allowed ·o hold a referendum in a territory of their choosing, this violates the

---

[48] This position is spelled out clearly in H. Beran, 'A Liberal Theory of 3ecession', *Political Studies*, 32 (1984), 21–31; see also H. Beran, 'More Theory of 3ecession: A Response to Birch', *Political Studies*, 36 (1988), 316–23.

[49] Beran allows that an enclave might be viable as an independent state if the sur-ounding state shows it 'goodwill', but this would clearly not be so in the case under discussion.

[50] This is a conjectural question. The strip between Armenia and Nagorny Karabakh is in fact inhabited mainly by Kurds, who would probably prefer Armenian to Azeri rule if they were given the choice.

basic principle of consent. If the inhabitants of the corridor strip are not permitted to hold a subsequent referendum in a territory of their choosing, this violates the principle of recursion. And if both referendums are permitted, leading to the designation of Nagorny Karabakh as an enclave affiliated to Armenia, this violates the no-enclaves rule.

Quite apart from the difficulties created by Beran's additional conditions, the original principle that majority will should determine borders has little intuitive appeal. Consider a state whose population is presently made up of 60 per cent cultural group A and 40 per cent cultural group B. It includes a small region within which 60 per cent of the population belongs to B and 40 per cent to A (but these populations are closely mingled so no further division is possible). Suppose the majority in the region vote to secede: we would then have a small state with 60 per cent Bs and 40 per cent As, and a large state with, let's say, 65 per cent As and 35 per cent Bs. Even from the point of view of consent, is this a real gain? The 60 per cent in Small are presumably happy with the outcome, and the 40 per cent are presumably unhappy. On the other hand, the 35 per cent of Bs left in Big may be less happy with the new arrangement than the old (perhaps with the secession of Small important cultural centres are taken away from them, etc.). My point is that it is an illusion to think that by (repeatedly) applying the majority principle everyone can end up in the state they would ideally like to be in. Instead, from any redrawing of boundaries there are almost certain to be both gainers and losers, and to assess a proposed redrawing we need to estimate the gains and losses, not merely to count heads.

In contrast to these liberal views, the principle of nationality focuses attention neither on material interests nor on individual preferences for boundaries, but on the political conditions for securing national identities. The principle tells us to further the cause of national self-determination wherever possible. So to begin with, existing boundaries are put in question only where a *nationality* is currently denied self-determination. This is to be distinguished from the situation of an ethnic group which feels it is currently denied rights of cultural expression, or treated unfairly in some other way, and for which the remedy is reform of existing arrangements and policies within the state. Now as we saw in Chapter 2, the distinction between nationality and ethnicity is not a hard and fast one: historially, national identities have very often developed out of prior ethnic identities, and where a cohesive ethnic group finds that its legitimate claims are ignored by the state, a natural response is for the group to begin to think of itself as an alternative nationality. But, equally, such a development is not pre-ordained. It is quite possible for a state to include several groups with separate ethnic identities but a common national identity: Switzerland and the United States are both in their different ways good examples of this. How this is to be achieved is a question that will occupy us in the following chapter, where I consider what policies towards ethnic minorities are consistent with the principle of nationality I am defending.

Once we are clear about the distinction between ethnicity and nationality, we can avoid the error of thinking that the principle of national self-determination requires every cultural group to have its own state. The problem of secession arises only in cases where an established state houses two or more groups with distinct and irreconcilable national identities—irreconcilable because, for instance, each takes a different religion to be constitutive of its identity, or because each includes as part of its historical self-understanding its separation from, and antagonism towards, the other; a case such as that of the Jews and the Palestinians in Israel. Let us take it, then, that group G is a group in this position, having national claims that cannot be accommodated by the state in which it is presently incorporated (S). Its representatives demand that G should secede from S and establish its own state. In order to recognize this as a valid demand, we need to be persuaded that what is contemplated is indeed the formation of a nation-state. One condition has already been met: we have established that group G has a national identity that is distinct from that of the remaining members of S, and that cannot be adequately protected and expressed by granting G a limited measure of political autonomy within S. But there is also a second condition: we would need to be convinced that the territory demanded by G did not contain minorities whose own identities were radically incompatible with that of G, so that, rather than creating a viable nation-state, the secession of G would simply reproduce a multinational arrangement on a smaller scale. Again, this is not simply a matter of the strength of feeling expressed by those minorities. They might resist simply because in the G-state they would lose certain privileges they are able to enjoy in the S-state. But

if they could show, for instance, that their ethnic identity was reasonably secure under S but would be seriously threatened under G,
then this would be a good reason for blocking G's demand.[51]

Finally, some consideration must be given to those minority
groups that would be left in S when G secedes, particularly members
of G who do not live in the seceding territory. The effect of secession
may be to destroy a *modus vivendi* and leave these groups in a very
weak position. With most of G gone, the majority group in S may no
longer feel the need to conciliate G politically, or to attempt to define
a common identity in which G might be included. It is, for instance,
a strong argument against the secession of Quebec from the
Canadian federation that it would effectively destroy the double-
sided identity that Canada has laboured to achieve, and leave
French-speaking communities in other provinces isolated and politically helpless.[52] If national self-determination is our governing principle, we need to ask whether the realization of that principle
through the creation of the G-state is not matched by its weakening
in the rump of S.

The principle also suggests a number of further practical conditions that need to be fulfilled before a sub-community could
justifiably claim to form its own state.[53] The new state would need

---

[51] If G can make out a good case for leaving S in terms of its own identity, but
the minorities within G's territory also have a good case against the creation of a G-
state, then the nationality criterion is plainly indeterminate in application. This is
the current situation in Ireland, which represents the case where the G-state has
been formed. The Protestant majority in Northern Ireland had and still has a good
case for separation from a Catholic-dominated Irish Republic, whereas the Catholic
minority in the North can reasonably claim that their identity has not been
respected in the Protestant state. Until there is movement on one side or the other
(and the election of a liberal president in Eire is an unexpected and hopeful sign),
neither solution—separation or union—can be preferred on grounds of nationality
alone.

[52] For this argument, see e.g. P. Trudeau, 'Quebec and the Constitutional
Problem', in *Federalism and the French Canadians* (Toronto, Macmillan, 1968).

[53] Some of these correspond to the conditions that Beran proposes in his liberal
theory of secession; however, I believe that they make better sense from a nationalist perspective than from the perspective of individual consent. Why, for instance,
should one insist from the latter perspective that the seceding group should be 'sufficiently large to assume the basic responsibilities of an independent state' (Beran,
'A Liberal Theory', 30)? If a group agrees to set up a political unit that then turns
out not to be viable because, for instance, it cannot defend itself adequately, why
should that matter if individual consent is our watchword? To prohibit secession on
those grounds would be like prohibiting people from marrying when we knew they

o be viable in the sense that it could secure itself territorially; at the same time, it should not radically weaken the parent state by, for instance, making it extremely difficult to defend militarily. Another condition sometimes suggested, for instance by Sidgwick, is that the seceding territory should not contain the state's entire supply of some important natural resource.[54] Here I think the following point needs to be made. If a sub-community wishes to secede simply on the grounds that it could do better for itself by hogging all of the resource in question, then by the criterion I am proposing its claim must fail; on the other hand, if its claim to national independence is essentially a good one, then it should not be blocked by the fact that the resource would go with it, not even if the current demand for independence is to some degree driven by that perception.[55] As noted in Section II, all that it seems realistic to impose in relation to natural resources is a rather general obligation on resource-rich countries to help out countries whose economic viability is put in question by lack of resources. It was morally arbitrary that state S originally had the resource in question; so members of S have no real complaint against the seceding G that they are taking the resource with them, unless this would leave S itself in the category of bread-line states.

If we put the various conditions for justifiable secession together, we can see that the principle of national self-determination is very far from licensing a separatist free-for-all. We can also see that there are cases in which no redrawing of boundaries between states could implement the principle fully, and here we must look for solutions that fall short of traditional statehood. There are various devices by which groups can achieve partial autonomy inside an existing territorial state. I do not intend to examine these in detail, since the best

were unsuited to one another, or prohibiting people from setting up business enterprises which we thought were too small to compete effectively in the market. On the other hand, if our criterion is the furthering of national self-determination, then it is relevant to ask whether a secessionist group has any prospect of being genuinely self-determining, or whether it is inevitably going to be the puppet of some large neighbouring state.

[54] H. Sidgwick, *The Elements of Politics*, 2nd edn. (London, Macmillan, 1897), 228.

[55] I am thinking, for instance, of Scottish nationalism, where it has frequently been remarked that there is a correlation between the strength of nationalist feeling and the prospect of extracting substantial quantities of oil from what would become Scottish territorial waters.

solution in a particular case will depend on the character of the group involved and its relationship to the majority community,[56] but essentially, what is required is a constitutional settlement which creates a representative institution for the people in question and assigns to it legislative and policy-making powers over matters that are essential to their identity and material welfare.[57] A current example would be the governmental institutions established in Catalonia and the Basque country, which under the Spanish constitution are given responsibility for many issues in those regions, including environmental policy, social welfare, and cultural matters. For smaller groups, such as the Lapp or Saami people in the Nordic countries, an elected council or parliament, which can negotiate with the relevant government over the use of resources in traditional Saami territory and exercise some control over education and cultural issues, is a more effective solution.[58] There seem to be broadly three types of case in which such schemes of partial self-determination make better sense than outright secession.

The first is where the nationality in question and/or the territory it aspires to control is very small, and so could not realistically function as an independent state. It might fall short of economic viability, or be unable to secure its borders. Here continued affiliation to a larger national state, with appropriate constitutional guarantees, provides the best means of realizing the principle of national self-determination. The native peoples of North America fall into this category, and in recent years a few have succeeded in negotiating forms of self-government that give them control over land use,

---

[56] For a sustained argument to the effect that we should not be looking for a universal solution to the national minorities problem, see M. Walzer, 'Notes on the New Tribalism', in C. Brown (ed.), *Political Restructuring in Europe: Ethical Perspectives* (London, Routledge, 1994). 'Secession, border revision, federation, regional or functional autonomy, cultural pluralism: there are many possibilities and no reason to think that the choice of any one of these in this or that case makes a similar choice necessary in all the other cases' (p. 199).

[57] A wide range of examples is described and discussed in H. Hannum, *Autonomy, Sovereignty and Self-Determination: The Accommodation of Conflicting Rights* (Philadelphia, University of Pennsylvania Press, 1990). I have drawn on Hannum's work in the following paragraphs.

[58] Such councils were first elected in Norway in 1989 and in Sweden in 1993. See H. Runblom and H. I. Roth, *The Multicultural Baltic Region*, i (Uppsala, Baltic University Secretariat, 1993).

ealth and social services, etc.[59] Other examples can be found among he inhabitants of small islands, such as the Cook Islanders who emain in 'free association' with New Zealand.

The second case occurs where the territory of the national group ve are considering contains a very substantial minority whose iational affiliation is with the larger state. Thus, if we suppose for he moment that the French-speaking inhabitants of Quebec can e treated as a distinct nation having a prima facie case for self-letermination, it becomes relevant that the province includes a sub-tantial English-speaking minority whose aspiration to national self-letermination would be denied if Quebec became an independent tate.[60] As we saw above, the principle of nationality is not equiva-ent to the principle that territorial boundaries should be settled by najority preference. Assume that a constitutional settlement can inally be reached in Canada which (as the present Constitution loes) gives considerable self-determination to the people of Quebec »ver matters such as language policy that are regarded as vital by that ommunity, while at the same time the continued overarching uthority of the Canadian government gives expression to the iden-ities of those inhabitants who think of themselves as Canadians ather than as Québécois. Such a settlement may represent the best ulfilment of the principle of nationality, whereas outright secession /ould realize it for one group but deny it to the other.

The third, and in some ways most interesting, case arises where nany inhabitants of the relevant territory have national identities hat are somewhat ambivalent. (This case often coexists with the sec-ond.) They see themselves as the bearers of both a wider and a nar-ower identity. Thus, to take one example, in an opinion survey aken in Catalonia in 1982, '26% of the population considered itself Catalan; 40% felt dual Catalan–Spanish identity; and 30% felt pri-narily Spanish'.[61] A rather similar picture emerges when Scots are sked about their Scottish or British identities.[62] Assuming that

[59] See A. Fleras and J. L. Elliott, *The 'Nations Within': Aboriginal–State Relations in Canada, the United States, and New Zealand* (Toronto, Oxford University Press, 1992).

[60] See the figures cited in B. Rodal, 'The Canadian Conundrum: Two Concepts of Nationhood', in U. Ra'anan, M. Mesner, K. Armes, and K. Martin, *State and Nation in Multi-Ethnic Societies* (Manchester, Manchester University Press, 1991).

[61] Hannum, *Autonomy*, 268.

[62] I discuss the Scottish case more fully in Ch. 6 below.

these identities are genuinely national as opposed to ethnic, the prin
ciple of nationality here points rather directly towards a constitu
tional arrangement which allows both identities appropriate
recognition and expression. Complete independence for Catalonia
or Scotland would violate that part of the identity of both of these
peoples which seeks to participate in the self-determination of the
larger nation. Regional autonomy of the kind currently enjoyed in
Catalonia and aspired to by many in Scotland realizes the principle
more effectively.

In discussing these cases, I have been assuming that there is an
identifiable territory within which the smaller nationality forms a
majority, and over which, therefore, some form of partial autonomy
can be exercised. Under these circumstances it may still be possible
for co-nationals not currently resident in the territory to participate
in the process of self-determination, as happens for instance in the
case of elections to Saami councils in Sweden. However, the position
changes when two different nationalities are commingled more or
less evenly throughout a geographical area—the position, for
instance, in Bosnia before the civil war. Here partial autonomy over
territory cannot be the answer, and the only feasible solution that
preserves the integrity of the state appears to be a form of power-
sharing between the groups to guarantee each at least some measure
of self-determination. But before we reach this conclusion, we need
to examine much more widely the issues that cultural minorities
pose for the principle of nationality, and to this I turn in the chapter
that follows.

CHAPTER 5

Nationality and Cultural Pluralism

I

For the greater part of this century, nationalism has stood accused above all of engendering fearsome conflicts between states over territory and spheres of influence. Even while conceding the internal advantages of national unity, many liberals have thought that this was bought at an intolerable price in the slaughter and oppression of outsiders. But recently this assessment has changed. The experience of liberal states in the period following the Second World War suggests that, among these states at least, international disputes can be resolved non-violently without sacrificing national autonomy. The focus of attention has switched instead to the internal effects of nationality. Are national allegiances not secured at the cost of suppressing the more specific identities of individuals and groups within the boundaries of the nation-state? Does nationality not involve the imposition of a fixed identity deriving from the dominant group in a society on other groups whose own cultural values are thereby disparaged and undermined? The new charge is that nationalism is necessarily an illiberal force, where liberalism involves showing equal respect for the many different personal and group identities that would otherwise flourish in a modern plural society.

Responding to this charge involves asking what the principle of nationality implies for the internal politics of the state. If we value national allegiances and want them to continue to serve as the basis for political association, what stance should we adopt towards subnational group identities, especially perhaps ethnic identities whose substance may be at odds with the national identity itself? The position I want to map out stands in contrast to two others which I shall sketch briefly to set the scene and explore in greater detail shortly. These are conservative nationalism and radical multiculturalism.

Conservative nationalism resolves the question decisively in favour of nationality. Our national identities are given to us by the past; they are (or at least ought to be) the collective identities that matter most to us; and it is essential to the stability of the state that these identities should be protected against subversion and transmitted to new generations of citizens. So although the state may have liberal features (if that is what our particular sense of national identity prescribes), individual liberty should cede to the demands of nationality in cases of conflict. Therefore, in considering issues such as the education of children or immigration, we should be guided not by the supposed basic rights of individuals but by the need to preserve a common national identity.

Radical multiculturalism, by contrast, regards the state as an arena in which many kinds of individual and group identity should be allowed to co-exist and flourish. The state should not merely tolerate but give equal recognition to each of these identities. No special weight should be given to national identities; indeed, such identities are somewhat suspect, in so far as they are likely to be the product of political manipulation, whereas identities stemming from gender, ethnicity, religious belief, and so forth are to be celebrated as authentic expressions of individual difference.

Neither of these positions is in my view adequate, but to see why we need to look in greater detail at the way in which cultural pluralism poses a problem for the principle of nationality. If we consider possible sources of personal identity apart from nationality, we should be struck by their number and variety. People may identify themselves by their occupation, their class, their locality, their gender, their sexual orientation, their hobbies, their membership of associations, their religion, their party allegiance, their ethnicity, and in other ways besides. Any one of these may become a primary source of identity. One person may think of herself as above all a woman, another as a bird-watcher, a third as a Muslim. In plural societies most are likely to have composite identities in which different affiliations come to the fore on different occasions. Some of these identities are chosen, some unchosen, but it will be to a considerable degree a matter of choice which aspects any particular person makes central to their conception of themselves.[1]

Why should there be conflicts between identities such as these and the idea of nationality? Unless one takes the view that nationality is the *only* legitimate source of collective identity—and even the conservative nationalist would recoil from saying this—there seems no reason why one should not acknowledge French or American identity alongside one's identity as a woman, a trade unionist, a Christian, and so forth. Discord will arise only where the national identity includes elements that are incompatible with these other allegiances. This will depend on what nationhood means in a particular case. If I belong to a nation whose self-definition includes Catholicism—being Catholic is what separates this people from its neighbours, say—and I decide to join a Protestant church, then inevitably there will be a clash between my religious and national identities. But at the other extreme, national identity might have no religious component, and the state might remain studiously neutral as between the various religious confessions of its citizens. As we shall see, it is harder to achieve such an outcome in practice than it might seem in theory. But let us at least begin by reminding ourselves that national identities are not all-embracing, but can co-exist peacefully with other commitments and loyalties in a person's conception of himself.

The hardest cases are likely to be ethnic identities, and I shall focus on these in the discussion that follows. Why is this? Although I have argued (in Chapter 2) against the assimilation of ethnic and national identities, it is important to acknowledge what they have in common. Like nations, ethnic groups tend to think of themselves as extended families; indeed, the belief in common descent plays an even stronger role here than it does in most national identities. They share cultural and sometimes physical features which make assimilation to and from other groups difficult. There is also often a sense of a family home, a territory with which the group has a special relationship. Ethnicity is a pervasive phenomenon, in the sense that it is something that a person carries with her wherever she goes: you may be a fanatical bird-watcher at weekends, but this has no particular implications for the way in which you are treated in the weekday

[1] Though not in all circumstances, a point that I illustrated in Ch. 2 n. 52 with the example of Hannah Arendt's Jewishness.

world, whereas if you are ethnically black in a white-dominated society, or ethnically Tamil in a society dominated by Sinhalese, this is likely to condition your experience in all spheres of life: in work, in leisure, in politics, and so forth. As a result, ethnic identities very often give rise to demands for political recognition. Unless the group you belong to has its identity confirmed in symbolic and other ways by the relevant state, you are likely to feel vulnerable and demeaned. So although ethnicity is not an essentially political phenomenon in the way that nationality is, it is likely in practice to foster demands on the state, demands which may not be easily reconciled with the demands of nationality. To take a rather obvious example, in a society in which language divisions are markers of ethnicity, giving equal recognition to the languages spoken by different ethnic groups in the public sphere may conflict with the idea of a common public language as the expression of a common national identity. Language recognition, however, is often of great importance to ethnic groups for both instrumental and symbolic reasons.[3] Fierce disputes, such as that currently raging in the United States over whether, in view of the substantial numbers of Spanish-speaking immigrants in some states, English should be entrenched as the primary language in education, workplaces and government, are to be expected when ethnicity and nationality collide in this way.

One response to this predicament might be to say that ethnicity *should* be treated as a private cultural phenomenon, on a par with other forms of personal identity such as those I listed above. Even if ethnic groups in practice are always liable to trespass across the boundary with nationality, they have no justification for doing so, and politically we should take no notice of their demands, attempting all the while to educate the members of ethnic groups into regarding their shared identity as a private matter. But this response overlooks the fact that national identities invariably contain some ethnic ingredients. Very often a nation has been formed from the ethnic group that is dominant in a particular territory, and bears the hallmarks of that group: language, religion, cultural identity. This

---

[2] See the exploration of this point in C. Taylor, *Multiculturalism and 'The Politics of Recognition'*, ed. A. Gutmann (Princeton, Princeton University Press, 1992).

[3] See D. Horowitz, *Ethnic Groups in Conflict* (Berkeley, University of California Press, 1985), 219–24.

1as typically been the case with the nations of Europe. Other 1ations, created out of political necessity from a *melange* of ethnic groups, have felt the need to give themselves an ethnic coloration, as 5mith explains:

Even where a nation-to-be could boast no ethnic antecedents of impor-.ance and where any ethnic ties were shadowy or fabricated, the need to forge out of whatever cultural components were available a coherent nythology and symbolism of a community of history and culture became everywhere paramount as a condition of national survival and unity. Without some ethnic lineage the nation-to-be could fall apart.[4]

It is this ethnic ingredient in national identity that makes the rela-:ionship between ethnicity and nationality inherently problematic. Groups outside the ethnic core cannot be expected straightfor-wardly to embrace the national identity that is on offer, since this poth creates internal strains and puts them at a practical disadvan-·age (if they speak the 'wrong' language or practise the 'wrong' reli-:ion). So, even if their ethnic identity is itself devoid of political elements, they are bound to seek to alter the national identity so as :o make it more hospitable to their cultural traits. Thus, to bear a Muslim identity in Britain today is not inherently political, but it pecomes so if British national identity and the practices that express t are seen as containing an Anglo-Saxon bias which discriminates against Muslims (and other ethnic minorities).[5]

So we cannot sidestep the problems of cultural pluralism by sup-posing that we can legitimately require all identities other than 1ational ones to be 'privatized'. Or at least, in order to reach that conclusion, we need to have some argument to show why the polit-ical demands of ethnic groups should be dismissed in this way. An argument to this effect can be found in the writings of those I call conservative nationalists. This is a doctrine with a long pedigree, but I shall principally consider recent restatements by British conserva-ives, made in a context in which the reality of cultural pluralism can 1ardly be overlooked.

---

[4] A. D. Smith, *National Identity* (Harmondsworth, Penguin, 1991), 42.
[5] Whether this perception is valid is another matter; see my discussion of British 1ational identity in the following chapter.

II

At the core of conservative nationalism stands the idea that national identity integrally involves allegiance to authority. To think of one-self as British is *ipso facto* to acknowledge the authority of institutions such as the monarchy which form the substance of national life. This view does not involve a crude identification of nation and state; indeed, the conservative nationalist's main charge against the liberal is that the latter overlooks the need for a pre-political source of unity to underpin the state. But the nation is conceived not merely in terms of horizontal ties to fellow-members, past and present, who share whatever features are taken to constitute the common identity, but in terms of vertical ties to established institutions, which are regarded as authoritative. In an illuminating analogy, the nation is compared to the family, a human community which has built into it the unequal relation of authority between parent and child. The family requires of its junior members not merely loyalty but *piety*, and it is this that, on the conservative view, forms the proper disposition of the patriot. As Scruton puts it:

Impiety is the refusal to recognize as legitimate a demand that does not arise from consent or choice. And we see that the behaviour of children towards their parents cannot be understood unless we admit this ability to recognize a bond that is 'transcendent', that exists, as it were 'objectively', outside the sphere of individual choice. It is this ability that is transferred by the citizen from hearth and home to place, people and country. The bond of society— as the conservative sees it—is just such a 'transcendent' bond, and it is inevitable that the citizen will be disposed to recognize its legitimacy, will be disposed, in other words, to bestow authority upon the existing order.[6]

Without this disposition of piety, conservative nationalists claim, a person cannot properly understand herself as forming part of an historic national community, and with this *deracinement* goes a loss of moral direction. As Casey expresses this thought,

A man who lacks piety does not know, in the widest sense, how to behave and feel. To compile a random list of his failings: he would not know how to speak of the dead; he would not fully understand what constitutes insult; he would lack a sense of place; he would not see old age as 'venerable'. On

---

[6] R. Scruton, *The Meaning of Conservatism* (Harmondsworth, Penguin, 1980), 32–3.

a larger scale he might be unable to understand love of country. He would tend to lack all attachment to traditions, customs, forms and manners. This suggests that he would lack attachment to all those ways in which men imprint their character and national identity upon economic arrangements.[7]

This view of nationality has a number of corollaries which bear directly on the problem of cultural pluralism. Since the state draws its own authority in part from the authority of the nation, it needs to give formal recognition to the institutions through which the latter is expressed. Scruton refers to this as *establishment*. The institutions in question need not be formally constituted as parts of the state, but they must be given a legal status. Thus, the national church should be an established church with special rights and duties. This immediately militates against the idea that the state should be neutral towards, or give equal recognition to, the many different cultural practices that may arise in a plural society. It should not, for instance, confer the same status on the religious institutions of minority ethnic groups as it does on the national church, because to do so would be to weaken the authority of the national institutions.

Second, it is implicit in the conservative understanding of nationality that the beliefs and practices that compose it may need to be protected against the corrosive acids of criticism. For these are to have authority, but the authority in question is that of tradition, and tradition is notoriously vulnerable to rational criticism. Scruton refers to the importance of myths that 'constitute the great artifact whereby institutions enter the life of the state and absorb the life of the citizen'.[8] It is therefore a legitimate task of the state to ensure that national myths are preserved and, to the extent to which this conflicts with liberal commitments such as those to freedom of thought and expression, liberalism must be transcended. As Scruton says of 'communitarian' liberals, 'none of them is prepared to accept the real price of community: which is sanctity, intolerance, exclusion, and a sense that life's meaning depends upon obedience, and also on vigilance against the enemy'.[9] This remark seems to me to

[7] J. Casey, 'Tradition and Authority', in M. Cowling (ed.), *Conservative Essays* (London, Cassell, 1978).

[8] Scruton, *Meaning of Conservatism*, 169.

[9] R. Scruton, 'In Defence of the Nation', in *The Philosopher on Dover Beach* (Manchester, Carcanet, 1990), 310.

illuminate well the kind of community that conservative nationalists take the nation to be, and the political implications that follow.

Mention of exclusion leads to the third corollary: the conservative conception of nationality is bound to entail a discouraging if not prohibitive attitude towards would-be immigrants who do not already share the national culture. Conservative opposition to immigration is sometimes put down simply to racism, but a deeper ground is that, if you regard a common national identity as essential to political stability, and also think that national identity involves an allegiance to customary institutions and practices, you cannot help but regard an influx of people not imbued with a suitable reverence for these institutions and practices as destabilizing. Casey, for example, argues that both the West Indian and the Indian community in Britain embody values that are antipathetic to the British sense of nationality, and proposes the voluntary repatriation of substantial sections of these communities as the only feasible way of preserving nationhood.[10] To say that the national identity, and its institutional expressions, should change and adapt to welcome the newcomers is, in conservative eyes to abandon the very feature of nationality that makes it so valuable namely its authority over the present generation.

What is wrong with this view? Notice to begin with that the modern conservative does not really regard national identity as authoritative in the way that he pretends to do. He is fully alive to the fact that national identities are in constant flux, and that the traditions he wishes to uphold may be of recent invention. So in counselling deference and piety towards these traditions, he cannot help being disingenuous: he is recommending to his readers that they should adopt attitudes that he does not himself share (for instance, to take a British example, that they should be entranced by royal ceremonies which the conservative intellectual himself may recognize as Victorian or Edwardian contrivances). The modern conservative is not in the position of, say, Burke, who seems really to have believed in the antiquity of the constitutional arrangements he wished to defend, and who could therefore appeal wholeheartedly to the

[10] J. Casey, 'One Nation: the Politics of Race', *Salisbury Review*, 1 (1982), 23–8. West Indians are said to manifest 'an extraordinary resentment towards authority' to have 'a family structure which is markedly unlike our own', etc. Indians are conceded to be industrious and peaceable, but because of 'their *profound* difference of culture, they are most unlikely to wish to identify themselves with the traditions and loyalties of the host nation'.

authority of tradition to combat the rationalism of liberal reformers. His modern counterpart has to recommend an attitude of deference to 'traditions' which, by his own admission, cannot claim the authority that that label implies.

National identities are not cast in stone: as we saw in Chapter 2, they are above all 'imagined' identities, where the content of the imagining changes with time. So although at any moment there will be something substantial that we call our national identity, and we will acknowledge customs and institutions that correspond to this, there is no good reason to regard this as authoritative in the sense that excludes critical assessment. The alternative to piety is not 'the lonely heights of abstract choice [where] nothing comforts and nothing consoles', in Scruton's evocative phrase,[11] but common membership in a nation where the meaning of membership changes with time. Ideally, the process of change should consist in a collective conversation in which many voices can join. No voice has a privileged status: those who seek to defend traditional interpretations enter the conversation on an equal footing with those who want to propose changes. The conversation will usually be about specific issues: which language or languages should be given official status; which version of national history should be taught in schools; what changes, if any, should be made to the constitutional arrangements; and so forth. But behind these lie the wider questions: what kind of people are we? What do we believe? How do we want to conduct ourselves in future? In this perspective established institutions have no sanctity; they serve as a point of reference, but have authority only in the sense in which a cookery book has authority for an aspiring chef, namely that it lays out the existing principles of cuisine and provides a base from which experimentation and innovation are possible.

From this perspective—which, I have argued, the modern conservative cannot help but acknowledge, much as he may hanker after the certainties of the past[12]—liberal freedoms play a vital role in

---

[11] Scruton, 'In Defence of the Nation', 326.

[12] Indeed, this acknowledgement may be quite explicit, as in the following passage by Casey:

The best account of tradition in the twentieth century—that given by T. S. Eliot—sees it as something that is both impersonal and at the same time open to personal appropriation; as both something existing in its own right and yet as needing recreation in every age. This recreation, which is also the acquiring of an 'historical sense', involves the finding of a language that is the language of the

providing the conditions under which the conversation can continue. Without freedom of conscience and expression, one cannot explore different interpretations of national identity, something that takes place not only in political forums, but in the various associations that make up civil society. (Think of a street association deciding how to commemorate some national event such as a military victory or a coronation.) These discussions must proceed on the basis that no one should be penalized or excluded for expressing views that challenge the traditional understanding of national symbols and historic events. So, although I have yet to examine how far the principle of nationality lends support to or conflicts with liberalism in general, on this issue of basic freedoms there will certainly be convergence.

From the same perspective, the conservative nationalist's hostility to immigration can be dissipated. Why should immigrants pose a threat to national identity once it is recognized that that identity is always in flux, and is moulded by the various sub-cultures that exist within the national society? Immigration might pose a problem only in two circumstances. One occurs where the rate of immigration is so high that there is no time for a process of mutual adjustment to occur; consider recent Mexican immigration to California, where a large number of immigrants have arrived in a relatively short space of time. In such cases the education system and other such mechanisms of integration may be stretched beyond their capacity. The receiving community, recognizing the social problems that the immigration causes, may turn a cultural difference into a perceived cultural incompatibility and seek to deter further immigration (as some Californians have tried to do with Proposition 187, which would prevent illegal immigrants from receiving education, medical aid, and other forms of social security). One community feels threatened, the other feels demeaned, and there is no chance in the short term for cultural accommodation to take place.[13] In the longer term,

present, and which at the same time re-establishes real relations with the past. Such a picture of tradition . . . assumes that the individual must in some sense subordinate himself to what is historical and impersonal, and yet must re-create his sense of the past in the light of creative possibilities in his own time . . . (Casey, 'Tradition and Authority', 98)

[13] Although I am addressing the issue in the light of the principle of nationality, the same point recurs in discussions of immigration from a liberal perspective. See e.g. the essays in B. Barry and R. E. Goodin (eds.), *Free Movement: Ethical Issues in the Transnational Migration of People and Money* (Hemel Hempstead, Harvester Wheatsheaf, 1992).

immigrant identity and national identity can adjust to one another, as they have with so many other ethnic groups in America, but in the meantime the political system has to resolve group conflicts without being able to rely on a shared sense of nationhood to create mutual trust. All of this points, however, not towards preventing immigration, but to limiting its rate according to the absorptive capacities of the society in question.

The other circumstance is where the immigrant group is strong and cohesive enough to constitute itself as an independent nation. This is not likely to arise unless the group in question has been expelled *en masse* from some other place. If the situation does occur, however, the receiving nation may have good reason to guard itself against being turned into a bi-national society, particularly where it foresees deep conflicts between the two peoples. Thus, the Palestinian Arabs had good grounds for resisting large-scale Jewish immigration into their territory in the 1930s and 1940s, given their own nationalist aspirations and the small likelihood that a viable bi-national state could be established in Palestine.[14] Once again, however, this suggests setting upper bounds to immigration, not a policy of preserving existing national identities by refusing to admit those who do not already share them.

The conservative nationalist moves from a valid premiss—that a well functioning state rests upon a pre-political sense of common nationality—to a false conclusion—that this sense of common nationality can be preserved only by protecting the present sense of national identity and the authority of the institutions that now express it. In contrast to this view, I have argued that nationality need not be (and as a matter of fact is not) authoritative in the way that the conservative supposes. That the national identities of, say, France and the United States have altered considerably over the last century does not imply that these countries now stand on the brink of dissolution. Because nationality does not require deference to established institutions or the myths that sustain them, it need not outlaw dissent or select as new members only those who already share the existing national identity. All it needs to ask of immigrants

---

[14] In saying this, I do not mean to deny that the Jewish settlers also had strong claims, given the reluctance of the Western states to offer them sanctuary from the persecution they were suffering in Germany and elsewhere. Their human rights have to be set against the legitimate national claims of the Palestinian Arabs.

is a willingness to accept current political structures and to engage in dialogue with the host community so that a new common identity can be forged.[15]

So far, then, the principle of nationality is consistent with liberal political ideals. But can it travel all the way down the road to multiculturalism?

III

The terms 'multicultural' and 'multiculturalism' have no clear or fixed meaning.[16] They may be used simply to record the fact that all contemporary societies—or at least all contemporary liberal democracies—contain a plurality of distinct cultural groups, and that this cultural pluralism is going to persist for as far ahead as we can reasonably foresee. In this sense multiculturalism is something to be taken for granted which it makes little sense to oppose (or recommend) on grounds of principle. More commonly, however, multiculturalism implies some views about the *nature* of cultural differences and about how we should respond to them individually and politically. This means that there can be different versions of multiculturalism (and of

---

[15] Cf. H. Van Gunsteren:

> The prospective citizen must be capable and willing to be a member of this particular historical community, its past and future, its forms of life and institutions within which its members think and act. In a community that values autonomy and judgement, this is obviously not a requirement of pure comformity. But it is a requirement of knowledge of the language and the culture and of acknowledgement of those institutions that foster the reproduction of citizens who are capable of autonomous and responsible judgement. ('Admission to Citizenship', *Ethics*, 98 (1987–8), 736)

[16] Cf. J. Horton, 'Liberalism, Multiculturalism and Toleration', in J. Horton (ed.), *Liberalism, Multiculturalism and Toleration* (London, Macmillan, 1993). Horton notes that some commentators prefer 'pluralism' to 'multiculturalism' on the grounds that the latter suggests that each culture is homogeneous and separate from the rest. Parekh, however, makes precisely the opposite move, arguing that 'the term multicultural does not adequately express, and even seems to obscure, the kinds of differences that obtain between different communities in modern Britain', because it suggests that ethnic communities are merely groups of people who happen to have chosen to adopt the same culture; he believes that 'plural society' better signals the tenacious nature of communal divisions in societies like Britain (see B. Parekh, 'Britain and the Social Logic of Pluralism', in G. Andrews (ed.), *Citizenship* (London, Lawrence and Wishart, 1991)). Both Horton and Parekh note the tendency to slide from descriptive to normative uses of 'multiculturalism'.

the corresponding policies such as multicultural education), and the question is not whether one wants to be a multiculturalist at all but the kind of multiculturalist one wants to be.[17]

The version of multiculturalism that poses the most direct challenge to the principle of nationality is radical multiculturalism. Its core principle is the idea of respect for difference, where this means something more than toleration. A multicultural society must allow each of its members to define her identity for herself, by finding the group or groups to which she has the closest affinity, and must also allow each group to formulate its own authentic set of claims and demands, reflecting its particular circumstances. The state must respect and acknowledge these demands on an equal basis. It cannot hold up one model of the good life at the expense of others, nor may it base its policies on principles of justice that some groups but not others regard as legitimate. Thus, to illustrate radical multiculturalism through one of its expressions,

Today most gay and lesbian advocates seek not merely civil rights, but the affirmation of gay men and lesbians as social groups with specific experiences and perspectives. Refusing to accept the dominant culture's definition of healthy sexuality and respectable family life and social practices, gay and lesbian movements have proudly created and displayed a distinctive self-definition and culture. For gay men and lesbians the analogue to racial integration is the typical liberal approach to sexuality, which tolerates any behavior as long as it is kept private. Gay pride asserts that sexual identity is a matter of culture and politics, and not merely 'behavior' to be tolerated or forbidden.[18]

More generally:

Implicit in emancipatory movements asserting a positive sense of group difference is a different ideal of liberation, which might be called democratic cultural pluralism. . . . In this vision the good society does not eliminate or transcend group difference. Rather, there is equality among socially and

[17] I can, for instance, find very little to quarrel with in the 'liberal multiculturalism' defended by Joseph Raz. This 'affirms that in the circumstances of contemporary industrial or postindustrial societies, a political attitude of fostering and encouraging the prosperity, cultural and material, of cultural groups within a society, and respecting their identity is justified by considerations of freedom and human dignity' (J. Raz, 'Multiculturalism: A Liberal Perspective', *Dissent*, 41 (1994), 78).

[18] I. M. Young, *Justice and the Politics of Difference* (Princeton, Princeton University Press, 1990), 161.

culturally differentiated groups, who mutually respect one another and affirm one another in their differences.[19]

This requires an interpretation of politics which has variously been described as a 'politics of identity', a 'politics of difference', or a 'politics of recognition'.[20] Group identity, whether sexual, cultural, or ethnic, should not merely be expressed in private settings, but should be carried into the arenas of politics—that is, one should participate politically *as* a gay, a religious fundamentalist, or a black—and political institutions should operate in such a way as to respect these group differences. On the one hand, they must validate group identities by ensuring that the various groups are represented in politics *as* groups; on the other hand, they must ensure that the policies that emerge show equal respect for the values and cultural demands of each group—there should, if necessary, be subsidies for the activities that each group regards as central to its identity; educational materials must avoid discriminatory judgements which imply that one cultural norm might be superior to another; and so forth. Radical multiculturalism reaches far beyond mutual tolerance and the belief that each person should have equal political opportunities regardless of sex, class, race, etc., to the view that the very purpose of politics is to affirm group difference.

It is not hard to see how someone taking up this perspective would be led to reject the principle of nationality. National identities will appear to impose an artificial homogeneity on a culturally plural society, and moreover they will be seen as serving to legitimate the norms of some cultural groups at the expense of others—the long-established at the expense of the newly arrived, the dominant ethnic groups at the expense of the minorities, the sexually 'normal' at the expense of the sexually 'deviant'. Thus Young, citing George Mosse, argues that nineteenth-century nationalism represented 'white male bourgeois unity and universality'.[21] Although this has been somewhat diluted in more recent understandings of nationhood, the idea of a homogeneous public identity standing over and above group

---

[19] I. M. Young, *Justice and the Politics of Difference* (Princeton, Princeton University Press, 1990), 163.

[20] For these descriptions see, respectively, W. E. Connolly, *Identity/Difference* (Ithaca, NY, Cornell University Press, 1991); Young, *Justice*; Taylor, *Multiculturalism*.

[21] Young, *Justice*, 138.

differences serves to benefit dominant groups at the expense of those they dominate. As Young puts it, 'this norm of the homogeneous public is oppressive. Not only does it put unassimilated persons and groups at a severe disadvantage in the competition for scarce positions and resources, but it requires that persons transform their sense of identity in order to assimilate. Self-annihilation is an unreasonable and unjust requirement of citizenship.'[22]

Conversely, 'a just polity must embrace the ideal of a heterogeneous public. Group differences of gender, age and sexuality should not be ignored, but publicly acknowledged and accepted. Even more so should group differences of nation and ethnicity be accepted. In the twentieth century the ideal state is composed of a plurality of nations or cultural groups . . .'[23] And although Young favours participatory politics, this should not presuppose that there are shared principles of justice or of common good on which policies might be based. Rather,

the repoliticization of political life does not require the creation of a unified public realm in which citizens leave behind their particular group affiliations, histories and needs to discuss a mythical 'common good'. In a society differentiated by social groups, occupations, political positions, differences of privilege and oppression, regions, and so on, the perception of anything like a common good can only be the outcome of public interaction that expresses rather than submerges particularities.[24]

I have quoted fairly extensively from Young's work lest readers should think that radical multiculturalism is merely a straw construction of my own. What is wrong with the multiculturalist critique of nationality?

To begin with, it relies upon a false contrast between the allegedly authentic group identities that a multicultural politics is supposed to express, and an artificially imposed common national identity. The group identities themselves are socially constructed, and may be foisted on individuals who are quite unwilling to accept them. Take the example I cited at the beginning, gay pride, or the belief that gay sexuality should be affirmed in public and political ways. This is an identity shared by many gay activists, but not by many other homosexuals and lesbians, who prefer to see their sexuality as a private matter, and not as an overriding public identity. Nor are there any

[22] Ibid. 179.   [23] Ibid. 179–80.   [24] Ibid. 119.

grounds for saying that gay pride is an 'authentic' identity while private homosexuality is an identity imposed by the dominant culture; that is nothing more than an arbitrary assertion. Both are social constructions: both come about through some mixture of voluntary choice on the part of those who have them, outside pressures, power struggles, and so forth—the story will always be a messy one. Nor again can one say that one version of this sexual identity serves the interests of homosexuals better than another, because this too will depend upon a partisan account of interests which will be in dispute among both homosexuals and heterosexuals.[25]

The case is somewhat similar with ethnic and other group identities. As I indicated above, ethnic identities in particular tend to be pervasive, and usually a person has little choice about which ethnic group he belongs to—even if the identity is not one that he willingly embraces, others will treat him in ways that make it clear that they regard him as an Asian or a Catholic, etc. But such identities are by no means fixed, and groups adapt their self-conceptions to their surroundings. Very often the identity of one group is worked out in relation to other groups, and develops along with changes in the group's relative standing.[26] We can often see this process at work when political boundaries are redrawn: Horowitz cites the carving out of a separate Telugu-speaking state from the Indian state of Madras, divided mainly between Telugus and Tamils: 'When many other people in the territory were Tamils, it was vitally important whether one was a Tamil or a Telugu. But when virtually everyone is a Telugu, being Telugu is less important than being, say, Kamma or Reddi, Telangana or Coastal, Muslim or Hindu.'[27] In the smaller state, these subgroups came to define political identities. A similar process of ethnic redefinition is likely to occur when one section of an existing group advances economically while the other stagnates. Each subgroup may wish for different reasons to distinguish itself from the other, and small cultural differences may be amplified to create a new sense of ethnic identity for each. In thinking

[25] It will depend, for example, on highly controversial claims about the nature of sexuality and the place it should occupy in human lives generally.

[26] See the general account in D. Horowitz, 'Ethnic Identity', in N. Glazer and D. P. Moynihan (eds.), *Ethnicity: Theory and Experience* (Cambridge, Mass., Harvard University Press, 1975).

[27] Horowitz, *Ethnic Groups in Conflict*, 66.

about ethnicity, we need to steer a mid-course between hyper-voluntarism—the notion that ethnic identities are simply chosen to suit each momentary encounter with another person—and hyper-determinism—the idea that ethnic groups are the bearers of unchangeable identities from which no member or sub-group can escape.

What we must avoid, once again, is thinking of the ethnic identities that we wish to support as 'genuine' or 'authentic' in contrast to other identities which are 'manufactured' or 'imposed'. These contrasts cannot survive a cool empirical look at the way in which collective identities of all kinds emerge and change over time. What we find, in all cases, is a complicated picture in which the ambitions and interests of particular subgroups jostle with cultural beliefs and values to create identities that are always impure when measured against the hypothetical standard of a group of people sitting down together to think out what it means to them to be Jewish or black. In this respect, national identities themselves are in no worse shape than ethnic and other sub-national identities. Indeed, they may be in better shape, in favourable cases, because they are shaped more deliberately by political discussion in the course of which, in democratic states, each smaller group can make its voice heard. Consider, for example, the evolution of Australian national identity over the last quarter-century: no one, I think, could seriously deny that the mosaic of cultural groups that now inhabit Australia have played their part in the quite self-conscious reformation of national identity that has taken place, a reformation that seems very likely to conclude with the severing of the remaining constitutional ties with the United Kingdom, which are taken to symbolize the old 'White Australian' identity. In cases like this, national identities are transformed in a way that is more open and democratic than is the case with the identities of the ethnic groups that contribute to them.

Radical multiculturalism, I am suggesting, wrongly celebrates sexual, ethnic, and other such identities at the expense of national identities: there is no obvious sense in which identities in the first group are 'better' or more 'genuine' than those in the second. It also fails to recognize the importance of secure national identities to minority groups themselves. This point emerges most vividly in the case of ethnically distinct immigrant groups. Such groups are not yet fully socially integrated with the established majority communities.

Their personal, and to some extent their political, values may be quite sharply at odds with the values of the receiving society. Yet they want to be included on an equal footing, and to have their membership recognized by the majority, and one way to do this is to embrace their new national identity wholeheartedly. Harles, for example, has shown how immigrant groups in the United States typically espouse a form of American patriotism that is somewhat exaggerated and uncritical, provoked partly by the contrast between the freedoms and benefits of American society and the conditions they left behind, but also by a desire to affirm their commitment to their new country and to win acceptance from other Americans. Those escaping from authoritarian regimes do not find it easy to embrace the whole panoply of liberal and democratic values at once; what they can more easily do is to identify themselves *as Americans*, aided in this by the fact that this is as much a symbolic and emotional identification as a commitment to certain principles. As Harles puts it:

The possession of an unqualified patriotism gives time for the American creed to percolate into immigrant attitudes and behavior, gradually orienting them to the core beliefs defining American identity. And immigrants are usually willing communicants, eager to assume the full trappings of loyal Americans. Yet for them, patriotism precedes assimilation of the dominant political culture; the American political community is embraced before the valuational consensus that defines the community is internalized.[28]

In the American case, this process is aided by the fact that American national identity has ceased to have any marked ethnic content: ethnic groups naturally think of themselves as having hyphenated identities (Irish-American, Asian-American, etc.) which is possible only where the second term carries a meaning that transcends ethnic differences.[29] In European states, where national

[28] J. Harles, *Politics in the Lifeboat: Immigrants and the American Democratic Order* (Boulder, Colo., Westview Press, 1993), 100.

[29] The hospitable character of American identity has often been remarked upon. As Walzer puts it, 'American symbols and ceremonies are culturally anonymous, invented rather than inherited, voluntaristic in style, narrowly political in content: the flag, the Pledge, the Fourth, the Constitution' (M. Walzer, 'What Does it Mean to Be an "American"?' *Social Research*, 57 (1990), 602). This allows us to see 'American nationality as an addition to rather than a replacement for ethnic consciousness' (p. 611). See also P. Gleason, 'American Identity and Americanization', in S. Thernstrom (ed.), *The Harvard Encyclopaedia of American Ethnic Groups* (Cambridge, Mass., Harvard University Press, 1980).

identities typically reflect to a much higher degree the culture of the dominant ethnic groups, it may be more difficult for incoming minorities to find a suitable focus for their loyalties even though the need and desire for such a focus remains. As Modood notes in the case of Britain:

As a matter of fact the greatest psychological and political need for clarity about a common framework and national symbols comes from the minorities. For clarity about what makes us willingly bound into a single country relieves the pressure on minorities, especially new minorities whose presence within the country is not fully accepted, to have to conform in all areas of social life, or in arbitrarily chosen areas, in order to rebut the charge of disloyalty. It is the absence of comprehensively respected national symbols in Britain, comparable to the constitution and the flag in America, that allows politicians unsympathetic to minorities to demand that they demonstrate loyalty by doing x or y or z, like supporting the national cricket team in Norman Tebbit's famous example.[30]

This, however, is not an argument against national identities, but an argument for national identities that have a clear focus and are as far as possible independent of group-specific cultural values. It is not feasible to aim for complete cultural neutrality: a national language, for instance, is invariably to some extent the bearer of the culture of the people whose language it originally was. But in other areas national symbols and institutions can be detached from group-specific norms: in a society divided along religious lines, for example, they can be multi-faith or else purely secular in form.[31]

It might be claimed here that the value attached by minority ethnic groups to the chance to share in their country's national identity merely reflects the prejudice shown to their members by the majority. Because they feel that they are discriminated against and

---

[30] T. Modood, 'Establishment, Multiculturalism and British Citizenship', *Political Quarterly*, 65 (1994), 64–5.

[31] Neither of these options is quite as straightforward as it may at first seem. To take the multi-faith option first, if national events such as state openings of parliament or commemorations of war dead are to have a religious content, the framework of some particular religion must be used, even though within that framework it may be possible to include, say, the reading of sacred texts from other religions. The secular option may be challenged on the ground that it does, in practice, privilege a secular world view, and for that reason alienate groups for whom the public recognition of religious beliefs is seen as essential. The second argument is developed in Modood, 'Establishment'.

undervalued, they desperately try to assimilate to the norms of the dominant group even at the cost of weakening or abandoning their own cultural traditions. Remove the prejudice and ensure that each group is shown equal respect, and the wish to share in a common identity will evaporate.

This claim is wrong, I believe, both in respect of the minority groups and in respect of the majority; it fails to grasp the psychological needs that are met by a common sense of nationality. The minority groups want to feel at home in the society to which they or their forebears have moved. They want to feel attached to the place and part of its history, even if they also feel some attachment to their place of ethnic origin. So they need a story that they share with the majority, though a story that can be told in different ways and with different emphases by different groups. To see themselves only as bearers of a specific ethnic identity, let's say, would be to lose the chance to join a larger community whose traditions and practices have inevitably left their mark on the environment they inhabit. Their need is for a national identity which can be embraced, to use Walzer's phrase, 'as an addition to rather than a replacement for ethnic consciousness'.

It is not hard to find this argument endorsed explicitly by members of minority groups. Jonathan Sacks, now chief rabbi of Anglo-Jewry, has put it well:

we each have to be bilingual. There is a first and public language of citizenship which we have to learn if we are to live together. And there is a variety of second languages which connect us to our local framework of relationships: to family and group and the traditions that underlie them. If we are to achieve integration without assimilation, it is important to give each of these languages its due. . . . The more plural a society we become, the more we need to reflect on what holds us together. If we have only our second language, the language of the group, we have no resource for understanding why none of our several aspirations can be met in full and why we must restrain ourselves to leave space for other groups.[32]

Sacks also emphasizes that the first language cannot simply be a language of abstract rights: it must be the language of the national culture, even if that language has mainly been shaped by the ethos of

[32] J. Sacks, *The Persistence of Faith* (London, Weidenfeld and Nicolson, 1991), 66–7.

the dominant groups, for instance by Christianity in the British case.[33]

If radical multiculturalism overlooks the need and desire on the part of ethnic minorities to belong as full members to the national community, it also makes unrealistic demands upon members of the majority group. In the absence of a shared identity, they are being asked to extend equal respect and treatment to groups with whom they have nothing in common beyond the fact of cohabitation in the same political society. But why should these groups rather than others further afield be singled out for favourable treatment? Why should an immigrant Turk in Holland be provided with benefits that are not provided for Turks in Turkey? A common sense of nationality is needed to underpin the claim for equal respect: I respect the other person *as* a fellow-American or fellow-Briton, and this means someone who shares an identity and belongs to the same community. (I don't mean to deny that there are forms of respect that we owe to all human beings as such, but this is not the kind of recognition that advocates of radical multiculturalism have in mind when they demand equal recognition for all cultural groups *within* a political society.) The radical multiculturalist is relying on an appeal to the majority which makes sense only if a common identity is assumed, while at the same time arguing that minority groups should throw off an identity that is seen as 'oppressive' from the standpoint of group difference.

The dilemma becomes clearer still if we think about the politics of multiculturalism. Radical multiculturalists portray a society that is fragmented in many cross-cutting ways, but they aspire to a politics that redresses the injustices done to hitherto-oppressed groups. Since, however, the injustices will be group-specific, how will it be possible to build a majority coalition to remedy each of them? Given finite resources, why should gays support favourable treatment for Muslims, or Jews for blacks? Behind multiculturalist rhetoric, there seems to lie the assumption that to expose an injustice is already to have created a constituency willing to abolish it. Young writes: 'In a humanist emancipatory politics, if a group is subject to injustice, then all those interested in a just society should unite to combat the powers that perpetuate the injustice. If many groups are subject to

[33] For this reason, Sacks supports the continued establishment of the Church of England.

injustice, moreover, then they should unite to work for a just society.'[34] As exhortation this may sound fine, but who with any experience of politics could suppose either that there will be spontaneous agreement about what are injustices and what are not, or that groups will of their own accord fight to redress the injustices done to other groups? As I argued in the last chapter, if we believe in social justice and are concerned about winning democratic support for socially just policies, then we must pay attention to the conditions under which different groups will trust one another, so that I can support your just demand on this occasion knowing that you will support my just demand at some future moment. Trust requires solidarity not merely within groups but across them, and this in turn depends upon a common identification of the kind that nationality alone can provide.[35]

Radical multiculturalists want to affirm group difference at the expense of commonality, and they want to encourage deprived groups to develop their own organizations to express their demands in political arenas, but they do not think hard enough about how a politics of group difference is supposed to work. Much more rests on the majority's sense of fairness than multiculturalists appreciate, and that sense of fairness is liable to be contracted if groups issuing demands reject the identity by virtue of which they belong in the same community as the majority. Minority groups must in the end rely on appeals and arguments; in the nature of the case, they are rarely in a position to back up their assertions with serious threats.[36] So the instinct of the immigrant groups noted above, to want to be better Americans than the native-born Americans themselves, is essentially a sound one, and the multiculturalists are *faux amis* to the groups whose interests they seek to promote.

[34] Young, *Justice*, 167.

[35] For discussion of the decline of trust between ethnic groups as an effect of radical multiculturalism in contemporary America, see A. M. Schlesinger, Jr., *The Disuniting of America* (New York, W. W. Norton, 1992).

[36] Radical spokesmen for ethnic minorities do sometimes threaten violence or other forms of disruption if their demands are ignored, but at least in the case of small and dispersed minorities these demands have little force. The case is rather different with geographically concentrated secessionist movements, who may well be able to support a terrorist wing. The Black Power movement in the USA may be a good case study in how far a dispersed ethnic group can use the threat of violence to advance its political goals.

IV

We saw in the American case that the national identity that immigrant ethnic groups were keen to acquire had the fortunate feature that it was expressed in values and symbols that were accessible to all ethnic groups, so that in embracing an American identity no one is required to give up his or her pre-existing cultural identity.[37] It has been suggested that multiculturalism and nationality might in general be reconciled by thinning national identities to the point where they cease to have any content that could compete with ethnic or other such cultural identities. Nationality would be defined in strictly political terms, as allegiance to a set of institutions and their underlying principles. Even in the American case, however, the relationship between ethnicity and nationality has been worked out over a long period of time in which the present inclusive meaning of American identity had to compete with narrower, ethnically loaded meanings—for instance with Anglo-Saxon conceptions for much of the nineteenth century.[38] In the process, America gathered a history and a culture which distinguished it from all other nations. The idea, then, that to be an American is *simply* to subscribe to a set of underlying values—liberty, rights, equal opportunities—is a misconception. As Gleason puts it,

the abstract quality of the American ideology does not mean that American identity is without what might be called the grandfather effect. In the eight generations since independence, many series of grandfathers have revered the symbols of national loyalty, fought to uphold them, and thought of themselves as full-fledged Americans. Even for descendants of more recent immigrants, what Abraham Lincoln called the mystic chords of memory are intertwined with homes, and graveyards, in the new land, as well as with traditions from beyond the seas.[39]

The American example is a helpful one because it suggests how a common identity can evolve that is accessible to all cultural groups, an identity that is expressed partly through allegiance to a body of principles embedded in the Constitution, but also includes the more concrete ideas of common membership and shared history that are

[37] As noted in Ch. 2, n. 5, this claim cannot be extended without qualification to blacks and American Indians.
[38] See Gleason, 'American Identity and Americanization'.   [39] Ibid. 56.

essential to nationality. Clearly, it cannot be taken literally as a model for other places: where a political community contains sub-communities with distinct identities that nest somewhat precariously within the national identity (the Canadian case, for instance), or where such a community embraces a single old nation with more recently arrived cultural minorities (the case in many West European states), the making or remaking of common nationality must proceed differently. What must happen in general is that existing national identities must be stripped of elements that are repugnant to the self-understanding of one or more component groups, while members of these groups must themselves be willing to embrace an inclusive nationality, and in the process to shed elements of *their* values which are at odds with its principles.

In pursuit of the latter aim, states may legitimately take steps to ensure that the members of different ethnic groups are inducted into national traditions and ways of thinking. This applies particularly in the sphere of education. Whereas the radical multiculturalist is likely to regard education as a means whereby specific cultural identities can be handed down intact from one generation to the next, and therefore to favour educational separatism, or at least pluralism within schools, the principle of nationality implies that schools should be seen, *inter alia*, as places where a common national identity is reproduced and children prepared for democratic citizenship. In the case of recently arrived ethnic minorities whose sense of their national identity may be insecure, schools can act as a counterweight to the cultural environment of the family. It follows that schools should be public in character, places where members of different ethnic groups are thrown together and taught in common.[40] It follows too that there should be something like a national curriculum, a core body of material that all children should be expected to assimilate (though this can leave scope for teachers to emphasize different ele-

---

[40] This is not meant to prescribe how schools should be organized and funded, but to make the point that, however they are constituted—whether as state schools in the traditional sense or in some other way—they should be culturally inclusive rather than sectarian in nature. Nor shall I try to establish how far ethnic and cultural mixing must be taken: see the discussion in M. Walzer, *Spheres of Justice* (Oxford, Martin Robertson, 1983), ch. 8. Walzer concludes: 'It is not necessary that all schools be identical in social composition; it is necessary that different sorts of children encounter one another within them' (p. 223).

ments according to the cultural backgrounds of their charges, which
is how national curricula seem to work in practice).

Here the French example may be instructive. Since the Revolution
at least, French ideas of nationality and citizenship have been open
and inclusive: anyone might become a French national who resided
on French soil and displayed attachment to French values. But along
with this in the nineteenth century went a deliberate policy of 'making Frenchmen' out of the various communities living on French
soil.[41] The two main instruments were compulsory education in
public schools and military service. The former was secular in character and patriotic in intent.

The nation . . . was at the heart of the intellectual and moral curriculum of
the schools. History and geography, which had pride of place in the
Republican school curriculum, made the nation a central cognitive and
moral category, using new textbooks to render concrete, palpable, and
emotionally resonant the previously distant and abstract notion of France,
and to surround patriotic duty with a penumbra of dignity and grandeur.[42]

We might now think that this attempt was over-strenuous, but the
basic logic is sound: if you want to extend full rights of citizenship
to everyone who resides on French soil regardless of cultural background, and at the same time to have generous immigration laws,
then you must take steps to ensure that the incoming groups are
properly incorporated into French nationality.

What of cultural groups who claim that exposure to a common
education system would destroy their own identity—that, rather
than adding a national identity to an ethnic identity, say, the latter
identity would be disrupted and their children culturally disabled? I
think we are entitled to treat such claims with some scepticism when

[41] The classic study is E. Weber, *Peasants into Frenchmen* (London, Chatto and
Windus, 1979). An integral part of the process was the substitution of French for
the various regional dialects and languages that were still in common use in large
areas of rural France. In schools, unwilling pupils were forced to speak French (see
Weber, *Peasants*, ch. 18). This may offend present-day multiculturalist sensibilities,
but it is important to understand that France could not have been economically and
politically integrated if the many local patois had not been superseded. These
dialects were very often useless to their speakers beyond their own localities.
Breton, for example, was not a unified language, but a collection of dialects whose
speakers could barely if at all comprehend one another.

[42] R. Brubaker, *Citizenship and Nationhood in France and Germany*
(Cambridge, Mass., Harvard University Press, 1992), 107–8.

they are made on behalf of cultural groups rather than by their young members themselves. The latter are often eager to embrace the national system of education, not least because it provides them with the linguistic and cultural skills to get ahead economically. Thus, recent backtracking in the French education system from the nationalist ideal has not been particularly successful. Immigrants' children may now be taught in primary school in their 'language and culture of origin', but the children themselves may not welcome this: 'in Marseille, children of Maghrebin origin desert classes in classical Arabic, practice their Marseillaise slang and prefer Latin or German, in order to get into a good *lycée*'.[43] It might be argued that such children mistake their own interests, putting economic opportunity ahead of cultural solidarity, but it seems more likely that they feel no damaging conflict between an Arabic ethnic identity and a French national identity, and are seeking to hold on to the best elements of both.

The most difficult problems are likely to be posed by fundamentalist religious groups who claim that their cultural values can be transmitted only through a closed educational system, so that if their children are obliged to attend public schools they will invariably be alienated from their parents' religion. This was the claim made by Amish parents in the United States which resulted in the exemption of their children from mandatory high school attendance in the case of Wisconsin *v.* Yoder.[44] But why should public education oriented towards a common national identity have this effect? In the case of religious education, the options are presumably that state education should be purely secular—the traditional solution both in France and America—or that it should be multi-faith in character—the solution currently favoured in Britain. Thus, there is no question of fundamentalist children being inducted into some opposing faith. The argument is rather that either option is likely to have the effect of inducing religious scepticism: in the multi-faith option, children brought up in the home to believe in the absolute truth of certain religious tenets will be confronted with the fact that different people

[43] R. Brubaker, *Citizenship and Nationhood in France and Germany* (Cambridge, Mass., Harvard University Press, 1992), 149.

[44] The case has been widely discussed. For a brief description, see S. M. Davis and M. D. Schwartz, *Children's Rights and the Law* (Lexington, Mass., D. C. Heath, 1987), ch. 4.

reasonably adhere to different faiths; in the secular option, the argument is that, by keeping religion out of schools, by treating it as a private rather than public matter, one is effectively marginalizing it, discouraging children from taking it seriously. If you take the view that religious belief should permeate life in all its aspects, you are bound to reject the kind of segmentation that a system of national education in a multi-faith society necessarily implies.

I shall not consider here the issues this raises about individual rights and autonomy, but look at the problem from the perspective of nationality. Assume that the fundamentalists' claim is correct, that obligatory participation in public education will indeed have a corrosive effect on their community. How should we respond? We may feel that a community that can preserve itself only by isolating its members from the intellectually disturbing influences of the outside world is not worth safeguarding. Alternatively, we may feel that we should be tolerant, and that the principle of nationality is not seriously compromised by allowing to live within the borders of the state small pockets of people who do not share in the national identity, and are not in the full sense citizens. Consider, for example, the position of those orthodox Jews who live in Israel but do not recognize the legitimacy of the Israeli state. This is anomalous, certainly, but, in so far as such groups are self-contained and make as few demands as possible on the state, we may think that they should be left alone. It will depend on their size and number, and also on the likely effects of trying to integrate them into nationhood and citizenship.

What is clear is that religious fundamentalists and other such groups cannot have it both ways. They may choose to withdraw from citizenship and live, so to speak, as internal exiles within the state. Alternatively, they may assert their rights of citizenship along with their cultural identity, and make demands on the state on behalf of their group. But in the second case they must also recognize the obligations of membership, including the obligation to hand on a national identity to their children so that the latter can grow up to be loyal citizens. In this case fundamentalists can legitimately argue about the content of public education—they can complain if their children are taught in ways that unnecessarily bias them against their parents' faith—but they cannot claim the right to withdraw from it altogether.

V

So far I have been looking at the demands that nationality may make on the members of cultural minorities. But, as I emphasized earlier, we should also consider ways of making national identities more hospitable to the minorities. One way of doing this might be to recognize cultural groups by granting them special rights within the nation-state, or to institute what is sometimes called multicultural citizenship. How far can such policies be justified?

Let me begin here by drawing a couple of distinctions. We need first of all to separate the claims of ethnic and other cultural groups in general from the more specific demands made by national minorities, groups within the existing state with a distinct sense of their national identity. It may well turn out that these two kinds of group require a quite different response on the part of the state.[45] At the end of the last chapter, I argued that the principle of nationality itself pointed towards special rights for national minorities, the precise form that these rights should take depending upon the case in hand. Here I am considering cultural groups that do not conceive of themselves in national terms, for instance territorially dispersed ethnic groups, always bearing in mind that the distinction is not watertight, and that groups may over time move from one category into the other.

Second, I want to distinguish between groups being given substantive rights to certain advantages—special freedoms, special forms of protection, additional resources, and so forth—and groups being given political rights, in the form, say, of a right to be consulted over certain issues, or a right to be represented in a parliament or other such decision-making body. Let me begin with the case for substantive rights.

Defenders of group rights often claim that the very same arguments I have deployed in defence of national self-determination count equally in defence of the rights of ethnic and other cultural groups. In particular, the nationalist case for protecting a common culture as a source of identity and a condition for personal choice can be extended to sub-national cultures, which may be equally essential to a person's sense of her own identity, and equally important in

[45] See the general argument to this effect in W. Kymlicka, *Multicultural Citizenship* (Oxford, Clarendon Press, 1995).

providing a rich array of options to choose between. In so far as group rights are needed to protect such cultures, there appears to be a solid case for granting them.[46]

But why should members of these groups need special rights over and above those general rights which, in a liberal society, allow them to pursue their cultural activities singly or in association? Why are freedom of expression, association, occupation, and the like not sufficient to allow minority cultures to flourish? One argument, running parallel to the case made on behalf of nationality in the last chapter, might be that cultures are to some extent public goods: individuals may be tempted to free-ride, enjoying the benefits of cultural membership without paying the costs involved in sustaining the institutions through which the culture is transmitted. If one tries to think of examples to bear out this argument, they tend to involve territorially based communities, and this may be significant. But suppose we could find a convincing case where the culture of a dispersed group was a public good in the sense sketched above: what would follow? Most people have a number of interests which give rise to public goods questions, and there is a difficult general issue about how to determine what justice requires in the provision of public goods where these interests diverge. One person wants access to areas of wilderness; another is interested in forms of art that require collective provision; a third belongs to a minority group whose culture is under threat. Clearly, some means must be found to weigh up these interests and decide what resources the state should allocate to each of these projects. Minorities should not be discriminated against merely because their cultural aspirations may be seen as eccentric by the majority, but is there any reason to give them more than equal consideration?

---

[46] This argument is made in W. Kymlicka, *Liberalism, Community and Culture* Oxford, Clarendon Press, 1989), chs. 8–11, and in V. Van Dyke, 'The Individual, the State and Ethnic Communities in Political Theory', *World Politics*, 29 (1976–7), 343–69. The premiss has been criticized by J. Waldron in 'Minority Cultures and the Cosmopolitan Alternative', *University of Michigan Journal of Law Reform*, 25 1991–2), 751–93, who argues that a cosmopolitan cultural kaleidoscope may provide a perfectly good setting for individuals to choose their life-plans; and the entailment to group rights by C. Kukathas in 'Are There any Cultural Rights?' *Political Theory*, 20 (1992), 105–39, who appeals to the shifting character of ethnic identities and conflicts of interest within cultural groups to claim that group rights would merely entrench the existing power-holders within each group.

Defenders of group rights argue that minorities do have a special case. Kymlicka, for instance, argues that, because a person's cultural identity is given to them (by birth and upbringing), 'members of minority cultures can face inequalities which are the product of their circumstances or endowment, not their choices or ambitions'.[47] As I pointed out above, it is possible to exaggerate the extent to which ethnic and other such identities are fixed or 'primordial', but suppose for the sake of argument that we are dealing with an identity the core of which is not adaptable to changing circumstances: how far can its bearers justly claim compensation in the form of special rights? To claim that compensation is due whenever a person is worse off by virtue of having the identity that he or she has would lead to bizarre consequences. It is well known, for instance, that different group cultures tend to produce differential rates of success in business or working life, but it would be odd, to say the least, to claim extra remuneration because I was born a Catholic rather than a Protestant, or a Sinhalese rather than a Tamil, and therefore was not inducted as forcefully as I might have been into an ethic of work or 'getting ahead'; similarly if my ethnicity biases me against entering certain occupations or discourages me from marrying an eligible partner from outside my community. What members of minority groups can justly demand, it seems, is that their opportunities should not be restricted in ways that merely reflect the conventions or the convenience of the majority group: hence the justified claims by religious minorities that the law on working and shopping hours should be flexible enough to accommodate their Sabbaths and their festivals.

So far, then, we have found that respect for minority cultures requires nothing beyond equal treatment, though clearly 'equality' (always a slippery notion) must be interpreted in a way that is sensitive to cultural factors. (You do not treat Christians and Jews equally by prohibiting everyone from trading on a Sunday.) There is, however, one further argument that might back up the claim for group rights. This is the claim that cultures and their bearers cannot flourish in the absence of recognition, that is public acknowledgement of the value of the culture in question. From this perspective, the value of group rights is symbolic rather than substantial, but none the less important for that. They are a way of assuring a minority group that

---

[47] Kymlicka, *Liberalism*, 190.

their culture and way of life is seen as no less valuable than the culture of the mainstream.

As a general thesis about cultural survival, this argument is almost certainly false. Minority cultures have survived for centuries under conditions in which they were merely tolerated by the majority, or even actively discriminated against; some cultures, it could reasonably be claimed, have actually been strengthened by their members' sense of being an embattled minority in a hostile society: think of Jewish minorities in Eastern Europe, or the French-speaking community in Canada. So the claim about recognition could hold good only in certain circumstances. What circumstances are these? Like Taylor, I think that the demand for the public recognition of cultural values is a distinctively modern phenomenon.[48] More specifically, it has two preconditions. First, the cultural group in question must already see itself as part of a larger community, so that it matters that your culture is recognized in public. (Otherwise the only people whose recognition would count for you would be those who already belong to your group.) Second, public recognition must be currently being given to some cultures but not to others. (If the state grants recognition to no cultural values, then it cannot be said that any one culture is being devalued.) Paradoxically, then, the search for recognition by minority communities testifies to the fact that they share a common national identity with the minority. Once again, the demand for group rights turns on closer inspection into a demand for equal treatment. (And, once again, equality will prove to be a slippery notion to apply; very often members of the majority are unaware that current public practices may be seen as endorsing some cultural values at the expense of others.)

I turn now to the question whether cultural minorities should be given special political rights: whether, for instance, a certain proportion of seats in a legislature should be reserved for members of each minority, or whether parties should be required to produce lists of candidates that are balanced according to ethnic or other relevant

---

[48] As Taylor puts it, 'what has come with the modern age is not the need for recognition but the conditions in which the attempt to be recognized can fail. That is why the need is now acknowledged for the first time. In premodern times, people didn't speak of "identity" and "recognition"—not because people didn't have [what we call] identities, or because these didn't depend on recognition, but rather because these were then too unproblematic to be thematized as such' (*Multiculturalism*, 35).

criteria. (Proposals like these assume that in the absence of such measures minority groups would not be adequately represented despite having formally equal opportunities to stand for office.) This question cannot be answered until we know what political rights are *for*: how we should understand the nature and purpose of political authority. Here I want to contrast the conception of politics implicit in the principle of nationality with the conception favoured by multiculturalists, which as I noted above has been variously described as the 'politics of identity', the 'politics of difference', or the 'politics of recognition'.

The principle of nationality points us towards a republican conception of citizenship and towards deliberative democracy as the best means of making political decisions. If a nation is to be self-determining, its members should aim as far as possible to achieve consensus about the policies they wish to pursue, and the only way to achieve this is through an open dialogue in which all points of view are represented. The institutions of politics should be structured in such a way as to maximize the chances for such an open dialogue. It would take us too far afield to consider the whole set of arrangements needed to support deliberative democracy, but let us consider the specific issue of minority representation.

Here two powerful considerations pull us in opposite directions. On the one hand, if political deliberation is to issue in genuine agreement that all sections of the community can recognize, then it is vitally important that the views of each group should be represented in the deliberating body. Not knowing what issues may arise for resolution, or how opinion is likely to divide on them, we cannot assume that one cultural group can adequately be represented by members of another. On the view I am defending, the public culture that constitutes a shared national identity is not set in aspic, but changes over time under the impact of ethnic and other group cultures. As concrete issues are decided, people's sense of what it means to belong to this political community gradually shifts. For this to happen in a democratic way, each cultural group must be in a position to make its voice heard, and that requires representation in legislatures and other such bodies. Lobbying behind closed doors is inadequate precisely because what is at stake is the gradual remaking of a *public* culture.

On the other hand, deliberative democracy aims at reaching *agree-*

ment wherever possible, and that requires that each group should be willing to listen to others and moderate its demands where this is necessary to obtain a compromise. If a representative speaks for a group, his or her role is not simply to table a list of non-negotiable demands, but to use the resources of the common culture to find principles that place the claims of the group in a wider context—for instance, principles of equal treatment in the supply of public goods. To use Sacks's metaphor cited earlier, representatives must speak the first and public language of citizenship as well as the language of their group.[49] Now here it is important that they should not only be advocates for their group, but citizens who take part in deciding a wide range of issues, including some to which the group's particular interests are irrelevant. It is potentially dangerous, therefore, for representatives to be chosen simply to represent a particular ethnic group, for this immediately casts them in a narrow role, and discourages them from taking up the wider role of citizen; it may also put them under undue pressure from the constituency they have been elected to represent. The danger is of a narrow sectarianism. Sunstein puts this point well:

From the republican point of view . . . the most significant problems with proportional representation are that it threatens to ratify, perpetuate, and encourage an understanding of the political process as a self-interested struggle among 'interests' for scarce social resources, that it may discourage political actors from assuming and understanding the perspectives of others, and that it downplays the deliberative and transformative features of politics.[50]

Because of these conflicting considerations, I share Sunstein's view that formal minority group representation may be justifiable as a second-best solution, but it is not the ideal.[51] If there is a danger

---

[49] In D. Miller, 'Citizenship and Pluralism', *Political Studies*, 43 (1995), 432–50, I have argued at greater length that the republican conception of citizenship is better able to accommodate the claims of minority groups than either the liberal or the libertarian conceptions that are currently its main rivals. In particular, I attempt to rebut I. M. Young's charge that republican citizenship involves the imposition of oppressive norms of impartiality on such groups.

[50] C. R. Sunstein, 'Beyond the Republican Revival', *Yale Law Journal*, 97 (1988), 1587.

[51] For a stronger republican position that is hostile to group representation, see C. Ward, 'The Limits of "Liberal Republicanism": Why Group-Based Remedies and Republican Citizenship Don't Mix', *Columbia Law Review*, 91 (1991),

that the voices of ethnic or religious minorities might go unheard in the legislature, then some device to guarantee representation must be sought; but it would be far better if this outcome were achieved spontaneously through open selection procedures, so that each person knew that he or she had been elected to serve as a representative *citizen* over and above speaking for a geographical constituency and the claims of the cultural minorities to which he or she may belong.

This view of political representation stands in sharp contrast to the politics of identity favoured by radical multiculturalists, and I should like to end by recording my sharp disagreement with the latter view. The politics of identity sees politics as an arena in which group identities are publicly expressed and validated in the eyes of other groups. The main requirement of group representatives is *authenticity*: they should speak with the authentic voice of their group and not be co-opted into a homogenizing public discourse.

If authentic cultural expression is your aim, however, the political arena is a poor place to look. To begin with, the politics of identity raises in its most acute form the old question, 'How can one person represent another politically?' Cultural groups subdivide into subgroups—Jewish identity fractures into Orthodox, Liberal, and secular versions and so forth—and there is no reason to think that the process will stop before we get down to individuals: the only person who can really express my cultural identity is me. Schemes for group representation are much cruder than this—they single out some relatively objective factor such as skin colour or sex, which may not matter much if the point is to have a wide range of voices represented in political dialogue, but does matter a good deal if politics is supposed to express authentic group identities. The likely outcome of the politics of identity with minority representation schemes is that spokesmen are chosen whose version of group identity is not shared by many of those they claim to represent.

The second problem is that politics is a process geared towards the making of decisions, and therefore necessarily a matter of com-

581–607. Ward amplifies the charge that proportional representation of minorities would lead to a rigid form of interest-group politics that is destructive of deliberative community, but she does not address the problem of how republicans can ensure that all sections of society are included in the deliberation.

promise between competing demands—competing principles as well as competing interests. If a group enters the political arena making demands which it claims authentically express its cultural identity, then when it is rebuffed, as it inevitably will be sooner or later, it will feel that its identity has been publicly demeaned. The stakes have been raised too high, and so when the group loses it feels that it has not merely lost a political argument, but has been judged all the way through, as it were. Thus, in the recent British debate about lowering the age of consent for male homosexuals below 21, many gay activists claimed that only a change to 16 (the age of consent for heterosexual sex) would show them equal respect—anything less would label them as second-class citizens. After strong arguments on both sides, the House of Commons voted to set the age of consent at 18—a fairly predictable compromise. Inevitably, this was experienced as deeply wounding by those who had committed themselves to the activists' claim. Whatever substantive position one takes on the issue, it is surely misguided to hinge the whole of one's identity in this way on a political decision. The politics of identity, rather than including hitherto-excluded groups in the political community, tends to create political alienation among those who fail to get what they see as their essential demands accepted.

In general, then, the principle of nationality supports equal citizenship rather than a form of politics that is fragmented along group lines. I have attacked the idea of nationality as a collective identity that must be authoritatively imposed on dissenting minorities; but equally, I have attacked the suggestion that national identities should be allowed to evaporate, so that people are the bearers only of specific group identities. My claim is that in multicultural societies group and national identities should co-exist, the challenge being to develop forms of each that are consonant with one another. This idea of nationality is liberal in the sense that the freedoms and rights defended by liberals are valued here as the means whereby individuals can develop and express their ethnic and other group identities, while at the same time taking part in an ongoing collective debate about what it means to be a member of this nation. It is also democratic in so far as it insists that everyone should take part in this debate on an equal footing, and sees the formal arenas of politics as the main (though not the only) place where the debate occurs. But the principle of nationality is resistant to special rights for groups, over and above what equal treatment requires, because of the fear that this will ossify group differences, and destroy the sense of common nationality on which democratic politics depends.

CHAPTER 6

Nationality in Decline?

It is often said, for the purpose of undercutting arguments in defence of nationality such as those made in this book, that the era of nations and nation-states is drawing to its close: perhaps not everywhere, but at least so far as the populations of Western liberal societies are concerned. Various factors—I shall touch on some in a moment—have contributed to the decline of national identities, with the result that political systems based on such identities must either collapse or find some other source of legitimacy. So the arguments I have been making so far, whatever their general validity, are fast becoming anachronistic in the liberal democracies. This has the unhappy consequence that in those places where nationality might support democracy and social justice it is becoming an irrelevance, while in places where nationalism remains strong it is likely to be used to prop up authoritarian and repressive regimes.

Why is nationality thought to be declining in this way? The catalogue of reasons is a familiar one. The first is the ever-growing impact of the world market on individual consumption and style of life, taking the market here to include the market in cultural commodities like television, film, and the printed word. As the volume of international trade expands, consumption patterns everywhere become more alike, not only the food people eat and the clothes they wear, but also the books they read and the programmes they watch. Moreover, these cultural uniformities are to a large degree conscious ones: the same media that tell us what we should be eating, wearing, or reading also tell us how people in other places are doing these things. And so it becomes harder for people to think that they are living in a way that distinguishes them from others, or indeed that it matters very much where they choose to live.

Increasing geographical mobility has a similar effect. People travel and experience at first hand the not-so-very-different ways of life of foreigners, with the result that the foreigners seem less foreign. Orwell thought that encountering a different culture was the best way of understanding what was distinctive about your own, but that thought was expressed at a time when crossing the English Channel meant experiencing quite unfamiliar kinds of food, drink, dress, and so forth.[1] Crossing the Channel now (or tunnelling underneath it) serves only to disabuse the traveller of most of the notions he might have about the peculiarities of the British, for instance that they are excessively fond of supermarkets. In so far as our belief that we share a distinct national identity depends upon a certain degree of igno-rance about how people are actually leading their lives in other places, it is eroded by direct contact with those cultures.

Third, people increasingly define themselves in terms of groups and communities that many be either sub-national or supra-national. Their religious beliefs may bind them to a local sect, or on the other hand to a global faith like Islam. Scientists and professionals find themselves interacting and identifying with fellow-practitioners regardless of national borders. Political activists may find their fulfilment either in local campaigns or in international groupings like Amnesty or Greenpeace rather than in national parties. Now although (as I argued at some length in the previous chapter) there need be no incompatibil-ity between acknowledging a national identity and acknowledging cul-tural identities of other kinds—religious, ethnic, professional, or political—it may still be the case that the *strength* of national identities, the extent to which they *matter* to people, has diminished as these other loyalties and allegiances have strengthened.

Finally, the nation-state as a locus of political decision-making has to some extent been superseded by regional and supra-national organs of government, the EU being the most prominent example of the latter. It may not be so clear why this should affect people's sense of nationality. But recall here that, as I argued in Chapter 2, it is an integral part of national identities that nations should be conceived

---

[1] At least, this was so for all social ranks below the upper class; consumption pat-terns among the aristocracy had shown cross-European influences for several cen-turies.

of as actors, as collectivities that are able to influence events around them and determine their own futures. Now it is one thing for this aspiration to self-determination to be blocked by an external force such as a colonial power: this may simply strengthen people's sense of their national identity. But it is quite another matter if people see that it makes sense to have different decisions made in different places, national governments being on the one hand not sufficiently sensitive to local needs, and on the other hand not powerful enough by themselves to combat external forces such as the unwanted side-effects of the world market. If on these grounds there is popular acquiescence in membership of bodies like the EU, then people will stop thinking of themselves for political purposes as exclusively Spanish or German, and will begin thinking of themselves as at least in part European, or moving in the other direction as Catalan or Bavarian.

These seem to me to be the main trends underlying the decline of nationality in Western liberal societies, and I want in this chapter to ask how we should respond to this process: whether we should welcome or deplore it, whether national identities should be abandoned or reshaped in such a way as to take account of the changing cultural and political configurations that surround us. I shall consider the case of British national identity in some detail, partly in order to illustrate in more concrete terms some of the claims about nationality that I have made in previous chapters, partly because it seems to provide a particularly telling example of the problems facing the national idea in the contemporary world. Most commentators have taken Britain to be the first historical instance of a successful nation-state,[2] and until quite recently it would still have been held up as a prime example of Western or liberal nationalism. So if there is indeed now a crisis in British national identity, this might tell us something more general about the fate of nationality in our time.

Before delving into the British case, however, let us look a bit more critically at the reasons for thinking that national identities should matter less to people than they once did, and also at such evidence as is available on this question.

I shall start with the cultural homogenization issue, and here I want to observe that convergence in patterns of consumption by no

[2] See e.g. L. Greenfeld, *Nationalism: Five Roads to Modernity* (Cambridge, Mass., Harvard University Press, 1992).

means necessarily indicates convergence in political identity. To suppose so would be to ignore a distinction I have already insisted upon, the distinction between private and public culture, where a public culture is a set of understandings about the nature of a political community, its principles and institutions, its social norms, and so forth, and a private culture is all those beliefs, ideas, tastes, and preferences that may be unique to an individual, or more likely shared within a family, a social stratum, an ethnic group, or what has been called a 'lifestyle enclave'.[3] Just as a common public culture can coexist with a multiplicity of private cultures, so there can be convergence in private culture without there being any tendency for public cultures and national identities to assimilate to one another. Indeed, the opposite may occur: Taylor points out that in Canada the Québécois have in recent decades become more like the English Canadians in general attitudes and style of life, while at the same time their political identity, their understanding of Quebec as a political community, has become more sharply distinct.[4] Or, for a somewhat different case, think of the Croatian and Serbian communities who in many parts of former Yugoslavia lived side-by-side and in very much the same way before the war, but who none the less retained separate national identities which could be mobilized once questions were raised about where and on what terms political boundaries should be drawn.[5] If (private) cultural convergence were enough to erase national differences, there would be no Quebec problem and no Bosnian problem.

I want to turn next to the issue of cultural fragmentation, the claim that people increasingly have multiple identities, sub-national and supra-national, and that the effect of this is to diminish the impor-

[3] I borrow this term from D. Bell, *Communitarianism and its Critics* (Oxford, Clarendon Press, 1993), 170, who borrows it in turn from R. Bellah *et al.*, *Habits of the Heart* (Berkeley, University of California Press, 1985).

[4] C. Taylor, 'Shared and Divergent Values', in G. Laforest (ed.), *Reconciling the Solitudes* (Montreal, McGill-Queen's University Press, 1993).

[5] See the illuminating description in M. Ignatieff, *Blood and Belonging: Journeys into the New Nationalism* (London, Vintage, 1994), ch. 1. Ignatieff tends to blame the political élites for fomenting nationalism, but this overlooks the fact that, if the identities of the various communities had not already been national as well as ethnic, it would not have been possible to put the issue of political boundaries so quickly and centrally on the agenda. What the various leaderships *can* justifiably be blamed for is promoting an exclusive and antagonistic understanding of national identities in a situation where this was bound to lead to bloodshed.

tance of surviving national identities. Without dismissing this claim outright, it is important to take note of a countervailing trend. This is the decline of social cleavages which in the past have stood as obstacles to a shared national identity: I am thinking particularly of class and religious divisions. In societies divided sharply by social class or religious confession, there is an obvious tension between the solidarity that a common nationality requires and the antagonism provoked by these divisions. How can I think of myself as sharing a common identity with the boss who is trying to screw my wages down to subsistence level, or the Protestants who would suppress me if they could, and in any case will discriminate against me on every possible occasion? These questions are somewhat rhetorical: national identities have triumphed over such divisions, as the historical record shows. Yet national solidarity will plainly be easier to achieve to the extent that social cleavages are less sharp, and the factors producing cultural fragmentation have also helped to blur these cleavages. (The effects of ethnic differences on class divisions are well known, for instance, and in the case of religious divisions I should claim that the *proliferation* of religious (and non-religious) identities in contemporary liberal societies has had the effect of weakening traditional binary divisions such as that between Protestants and Catholics.) The picture that emerges is of societies that are culturally fragmented in many different directions, but in which none of the fracture lines is sufficiently deep to prevent people from sharing a *national* identity which underpins their political institutions.

But now we must respond to the final challenge, the claim that national institutions have themselves become something of an anachronism, and that the citizens of nation-states are perfectly willing to see decision-making powers transferred to different levels of government. The question here is whether this represents the passing of national identities or rather their remaking. Perhaps what we are witnessing is the slow emergence of new nationalities, such as a European nationality, so that national identities will co-exist at different levels—people will think of themselves as French or German at one level, European at another. We have seen that established nations often contain territorial minorities whose national identity appears to be split in this way; perhaps we can look forward to more complex nested identities whose stability will depend on the larger unit giving proper recognition to the political and cultural demands of the smaller. This would mean the passing of nationality as a simple, all-embracing source of political identity, but not of nationality as a differentiating factor which binds together a given set of people and makes them a community to the exclusion of outsiders.

Although the development I have just sketched is certainly a possible one, we should be wary of assuming that it has already taken place. Consider Europe as the most promising site in the contemporary world for the emergence of a new higher-level identification beyond the nation-state. Despite attempts by Euro-ideologists to create a European national identity, drawing upon the common cultural background of the European states, very few Europeans actually acknowledge this in preference to their traditional national identities. They support membership of the EU on practical grounds, but their emotional loyalty (feelings of national pride, etc.) continues to be directed towards their country of origin. As Wilterdink puts it, they exhibit

a mainly utilitarian acceptance of the integration process, that is not (or hardly) accompanied by a European consciousness, by sentiments of 'we-Europeans' comparable to the feelings of national pride. The majority expects European integration to bring advantages such as free travel, freedom of residence, being able to study where one chooses, being able to choose from a wide assortment of consumer goods—but the Euro-nationalistic symbolism proposed in the context of the 'Citizens of Europe' program (flag, anthem, etc.) has no appeal. The European Community is associated, and not without cause, primarily with industrial–economic interests. The integration process in the Community context is accepted as useful and perhaps necessary (in line with historical developments) but only as long as and insofar as national autonomy is not fundamentally threatened.[6]

Thus, when asked about some practical question that requires them to choose between displaying national loyalty and displaying a European loyalty, large majorities of people across Europe will choose their nation (the exceptions mainly being those who are connected in some way to European institutions). Another indication can be found in the findings of the Eurobarometer poll, where peo-

---

[6] N. Wilterdink, 'An Examination of European and National Identity', *Archives Européennes de Sociologie*, 34 (1993), 119–36. Wilterdink gives several cogent reasons why this state of affairs is likely to persist.

ple were asked about their willingness to give support to another member-state of the EC (as it then was). Most gave affirmative replies when asked the rather general (and costless) question, 'If one of the countries of the European Community finds itself in major economic difficulties, do you feel that the other countries (including your own) should help it or not?' But in contrast, most gave negative replies to the more specific and pointed question, 'Are you, personally, prepared or not to make some personal sacrifice, for example paying a little more taxes [*sic*], to help another country in the European Community experiencing economic difficulties?'[7] This pattern of response corresponds to a view of Europe as an association of states for mutual support rather than as a genuine community each of whose members acknowledges a responsibility for the welfare of the rest.

It is also noteworthy that, despite the political integration of Europe, and the hugely increased flows of people and goods across Europe that have come with it, there is no observable tendency for beliefs and values in the component nations to converge. A European Values survey, carried out in 1981 and again in 1990, and covering a wide range of topics from political principles to sexual morality to religious beliefs, showed that over that decade value diversity between the nations increased over as many issues as it decreased.[8] On the specific topic of national identity, two questions were asked: 'How proud are you to be [British, German, etc.]?' and 'Would you fight for your country?' Once again there were fairly large national differences in response to these questions, differences that sometimes point in opposite directions. (Thus, the Italians scored above the mean on the national-pride question, but came decisively bottom on the willingness-to-fight question.) More significantly, if we can take answers to these questions to give some indication of the strength of national identities, there was barely any erosion over the decade in question: a very small drop in the national-pride figure, no drop across Europe as a whole in the

[7] See M. Hewstone, *Understanding Attitudes to the European Community* (Cambridge, Cambridge University Press, 1986), especially 31–2.
[8] See S. Ashford and N. Timms, *What Europe Thinks: A Study of Western European Values* (Aldershot, Dartmouth, 1992).

willingness-to-fight figure.[9] Ashford and Timms conclude their assessment of the survey as follows:

National culture and opinion in Europe remain robustly diverse in spite of the increasingly close political and economic ties which bind EEC member countries. . . . If present trends continue, the Europe of the foreseeable future is most likely to be a conglomerate of highly individual nation-states cemented by a common resource-management strategy but separated by different domestic concerns and aspirations.[10]

Since the EU is currently the strongest of the supra-national organizations, its failure to displace inherited national allegiances is surely of some significance. If no trans-European national identity has yet emerged, the prospects for a North American identity, a pan-Arab identity, or an East Asian identity (to mention some of those more frequently canvassed) must remain extremely dim. It seems that at present established national identities are more likely to be challenged from below—by Basques, Flemings, Scots, and others like them elsewhere in the world—than eroded from above by people coming to identify themselves with large heterogeneous entities like Europe.

All of this discussion presupposes that national identities continue to matter for political purposes. I have argued at length in this book that a shared national identity is the precondition for achieving political aims such as social justice and deliberative democracy, but this argument has been challenged on the ground that people need only acknowledge an allegiance to a common set of institutions to make aims such as these realizable. Constitutional loyalty can take the place of older and thicker national identities, with the advantage that one can sidestep the difficult issue of reconciling public and private culture discussed in the last chapter. The public culture can become narrowly political, taking the form of 'constitutional patriotism', in

---

[9] See S. Ashford and N. Timms, *What Europe Thinks: A Study of Western European Values* (Aldershot, Dartmouth, 1992), 89–91. In absolute terms, four-fifths of Europeans remain 'proud' of their country, and more than a third remain 'very proud'; 43% declare themselves willing to fight on its behalf. It might be said that a decade is too short a period to measure changes in underlying values; however, in other areas, most notably in relation to sexual morality (attitudes to homosexuality, abortion, etc.), there are quite noticeable shifts between 1981 and 1990.

[10] Ibid. 112.

the phrase used by Habermas and others.[11] This would also allow an easy extension of political identity to European or some other level, since if one can be patriotic about the constitution of a particular state, one can presumably also be patriotic about a federal constitution such as the EU might one day come to have. Habermas sees such a development as both welcome and feasible.

I believe, however, that we should be sceptical about 'constitutional patriotism' as a substitute for nationality of the more familiar sort. It is important not to confuse the idea that a constitution can be valuable as an explicit statement of a nation's political principles, or the idea that the *enacting* of a formal constitution can be an historic act that plays a very significant role in national history (as in the American case), with the claim that constitutional loyalty alone can serve as a substitute for national identity. A constitution usually contains a statement of principles and a delineation of the institutions that will enact them. The principles themselves are likely to be general in form, more or less the common currency of liberal democracies. Subscribing to them marks you out as a liberal rather than a fascist or an anarchist, but it does not provide the kind of political identity that nationality provides. In particular, it does not explain why the boundaries of the political community should fall here rather than there; nor does it give you any sense of the historical identity of the community, the links that bind present-day politics to decisions made and actions performed in the past.

To what extent is this a loss? It might be said that, so long as political boundaries are *de facto* settled, there is no problem in thinking of my fellow-citizens simply as those who subscribe along with me to constitution X. But to say this is to beg the question, for what settles boundaries is precisely a shared sense of nationality, where this embraces much more than allegiance to a constitution. We saw in the last chapter that, even in the case of the United States, where constitutional allegiance plays perhaps its most prominent role in defining national identity, there are also important historical and cultural elements in that identity. It is easy to lose sight of these elements just because the membership of the political community is taken for granted.

[11] See J. Habermas, 'Citizenship and National Identity: Some Reflections on the Future of Europe', *Praxis International*, 12 (1992–3), 1–19.

Besides setting boundaries to the political community, national identity also gives us an historical location, particularly in socially and geographically fluid societies where older sources of identity such as those of family and neighbourhood are weakened. Clearly, these more restricted identities still matter a good deal to some people, as is evidenced by the enthusiasm at present for tracing one's ancestry and reconstructing the histories of towns and villages. But a national identity gives us a much more ambitious account of our place in the world. It assigns us to a large collective unit, and tells us a great deal about the historic achievements and failures of that unit. It allows us to see the world around us as something we have built— for national identity is expressed in all kinds of physical and institutional forms, whether it is the war memorial in our village or the jury on which we are called to serve.

It might be said in reply that this ambition to understand our place in the world in terms of a single historical subject—the British people, for instance—acting over long periods of time is nothing but an illusion. The world we inhabit is the result of all kinds of chance and contingency, and trying to make sense of it by invoking some shared and overarching identity is simply misleading. We have seen in Chapter 2 that national identities are mutable, and to that degree it is clearly wrong to see ourselves as simply continuing the work of, say, our Victorian ancestors. But on the other hand, to say that there is no connection is to risk getting ourselves completely wrong, for it overlooks the impact that those ancestors continue to make on us, not least through the institutions that they created and that persist today, exerting influences on us of which we may not always be aware. As David Cannadine has written, in response to 'post-modern' critics of the idea of national history,

The majority of people in Europe still live their lives in the context of their national community, and continue to view their past and future in that political framework. Nations may indeed be inventions. But like the wheel, or the internal combustion engine, they are endowed, once invented, with a real, palpable existence which is not just to be found in the subjective perceptions of their citizens, but is embodied in laws, languages, customs, institutions—and history.[12]

---

[12] D. Cannadine, 'Penguin Island Story', *Times Literary Supplement*, no. 4693 (12 March 1993), 4.

One may of course challenge the idea that people need to have the kind of social map that a national identity provides—that they need to understand their social world as the precipitate of a course of events in which their forebears have acted in certain distinctive ways, upheld certain values. Many people seem not to need such a map; they are happy to think of themselves simply as individuals who happen to be working in this job, consuming these goods, married to this partner, and so on. Questions such as 'What kind of society am I living in, and how has it come to be the way that it is?' don't matter to them. Along with this goes a view of the world as a kind of giant supermarket in which different goods and services are on offer in different places, and in which it is perfectly reasonable for individuals to gravitate to whatever place offers them the best package. On this view, national ties should count for nothing except perhaps in so far as they affect the range of cultural goods on offer in a particular place. For reasons that will be apparent, I regard such an outlook as pathological. A society in which everyone held such views would be unable to sustain itself—it could not call on its members' loyalty when under attack, for instance—and so in the long run it could not provide the conditions under which they could pursue their personal visions of the good life in security. In that sense, we must either embrace a national identity and the obligations and commitments that go along with it, or free-ride on the backs of other people who do.

II

So far I have been challenging the idea that nationality is inexorably in decline (in the West at least) and also the idea that we can get along without it so long as we have something like 'constitutional patriotism' in its place. But I do not want to deny that national identities and the claims they make on us have become more problematic in recent years. People are both less sure of what it means to be French or Swedish, and less sure about how far it is morally acceptable to acknowledge and act upon such identities. In most places diffidence has replaced the confidence of earlier years. I shall try to illustrate this point by looking in some detail at British national identity where the decline in confidence is particularly marked. This necessitates an historical approach, for present-day beliefs and attitudes can be understood only by reference to what has gone before—indeed, the main problem of British national identity today is that the understanding of that identity which has emerged over the past centuries seems no longer appropriate to today's world. Hence we have the curious juxtaposition, in contemporary Britain, of a strong belief in the country's distinctness, together with a great deal of confusion about what that distinct identity consists in. This puzzle can be unravelled only by looking at it historically.

I owe a great debt here to Linda Colley's recent attempt to trace the origins of present-day British identity in the eighteenth and early nineteenth centuries.[13] Her thesis is that a genuinely national identity did indeed have to be forged in these years, in particular to bring the Scots and the Welsh into a framework that they could share with the English. The first component of this identity was Protestantism. Britons saw themselves as inhabiting an island illuminated by true religion under threat from the forces of darkness, represented above all by Catholicism. Connected to this was a belief in the superiority of British political arrangements, conferring liberty on British subjects, in contrast to the absolutism that prevailed elsewhere. The main enemy was of course France—Catholic, and governed in a way that seemed despotic to the British. Indeed, Colley's major claim is that British identity was formed and consolidated in the century-long struggle against the French, culminating in the Napoleonic wars, when unprecedented numbers of British men were enrolled in militias and volunteer forces to protect the country against invasion. Military success against the French, the winning of imperial possessions at their expense, and the collapse of the French Revolution into dictatorship were taken as confirmation of a British identity that embodied the root principles of liberalism: Protestantism, limited government, free commerce overseas.

Colley's analysis is a salutary reminder that national identities are very often formed in opposition to some specific other nation which is seen as posing a threat, and whose qualities are regarded as diametrically opposed to those of one's own country. She also reminds

---

[13] L. Colley, *Britons: Forging the Nation 1707–1837* (New Haven, Yale University Press, 1992). I lay stress here on *British*. Most commentators would trace the origins of *English* national identity back to an earlier period, perhaps to the Elizabethan age; see e.g. Greenfeld, *Nationalism*, ch. 1.

us of the part played by war, or the threat of war, in consolidating these identities.

Her analysis is also interesting for the elements she omits, or consigns to a minor role, but which have more recently often been seen as central to British identity. One of these is monarchy. In this formative period, Britons were of course supportive of the ruling Hanoverian dynasty, but mainly in contrast to what lay waiting in the wings—the Jacobites, carriers of Catholicism and absolutism. As persons, British kings from George I onwards—with the partial exception of George III—were regarded with indifference or contempt. The nadir was reached in the case of George IV—'widely denounced and mercilessly ridiculed'—whose relationship to his estranged wife Caroline might provide an interesting point of comparison with the present difficulties of the royal family. The monarch's job, in these years, was to uphold the constitution and protect the laws; provided he did that, his personal character and behaviour were largely irrelevant. The idea of the monarch as symbolizing the essential values of the nation came much later: the images of monarchy that we have inherited—the rituals and pageantry of coronations, royal weddings, and jubilees—originate in the late Victorian period and were perfected in the early years of this century.[14] Along with this went the idea that the monarchy, as repository of national ideals of family life and so forth, must be protected from adverse comment and scandal. What I am suggesting, in other words, is that the ideal of limited, constitutional monarchy has deeper roots in the British consciousness than the personal cult of monarchy, which appeared relatively late in the day.

Its appearance may be connected with a second aspect of national identity whose importance may also be exaggerated, namely the idea of empire. The question is not about the physical existence of the empire, but about how the British understood it, what they took themselves to be doing when painting large sections of the globe red. Generalizing broadly, we can say that in the early period of imperial expansion the underlying idea was to transmit to other parts of the world the principles that made up British identity itself—Protestantism, constitutional government, free commerce. The great

[14] See D. Cannadine, 'The British Monarchy *c*.1820–1977', in E. Hobsbawm and T. Ranger (eds.), *The Invention of Tradition* (Cambridge, Cambridge University Press, 1983).

shock to this self-understanding came with the revolt of the American colonies, and it is interesting to see how reluctant British public opinion was to engage in a war against colonists who themselves upheld the principles in question.[15] Later, in the second phase of imperial expansion, a different idea emerged: empire as the rule of the civilized peoples over the uncivilized who were not yet fit to govern themselves. Here, then, the mission was not to transmit British principles *in toto*, but to supply a partial version—good administration, impartial justice—in the expectation that sooner or later the barbarians would be fit for self-government.[16] As I suggested above, along with this image of the mother country governing its unruly offspring from afar went the idea of the monarch as an imperial figure receiving tribute from the local satraps, a picture vividly brought to life in the grand ceremonial occasions of the late Victorian and Edwardian eras and present even as late as the coronation of Elizabeth II.[17]

The question remains how deeply this second image of empire penetrated into the British national identity. Did Britons come to see it as an essential part of who they were that they should shoulder the white man's burden and carry the law to those lesser breeds presently without it? This may perhaps have been the sustaining ideology of that relatively small section of the upper-middle class who made careers out of imperial administration, but for the bulk of the population the colonial empire remained a somewhat remote entity. In so far as they thought about the empire at all, their attention was more likely to focus on the 'White Dominions' to which relatives might have emigrated, and which were later to supply troops to fight alongside the British in two world wars. 'The showy high imperialism of the late nineteenth century can be demonstrated to have been superficial and ephemeral in its impact', writes one recent commentator.[18]

Having now suggested that the cult of monarchy and 'high' impe-

[15] Colley, *Britons*, 132–45.

[16] We can find this view of imperialism expressed in, for instance, J. S. Mill, *Considerations on Representative Government*, chs. 4 and 18 in J. S. Mill, *Utilitarianism; On Liberty; Representative Government*, ed. H. B. Acton (London, Dent, 1972).

[17] Cannadine, 'British Monarchy'.

[18] P. J. Marshall, 'No Fatal Impact?' *Times Literary Supplement*, no. 4693 (12 March 1993), 10.

rialism were late and perhaps relatively transient grafts on to an older idea of British identity, I want to consider briefly how long-lasting was the impact of the Protestantism which we saw to be an essential ingredient in the original formation of British nationality. It is fairly clear that anti-Catholicism survived in popular culture for some while after it ceased to be an official doctrine of the state. When Catholic emancipation acts were proposed in the 1820s, petitions opposing them poured in from all quarters of the country, not only from the cities where there was a significant Irish Catholic population, but from tiny villages where no Catholic had ever been seen. According to Colley, 'the evidence suggests that many ordinary Britons who signed anti-Catholic petitions in 1828–9 saw themselves, quite consciously, as being part of a native tradition of resistance to Catholicism which stretched back for centuries and which seemed, indeed, to be timeless.'[19] Although the traditional Guy Fawkes night events proved capable of carrying different meanings at different times, their original anti-Catholic significance could always be resurrected, as it was in 1850 following the re-establishment of a Catholic hierarchy in Britain.[20] According to Flora Thompson's account of life in an Oxfordshire village in the 1880s:

On Catholicism at large, the Lark Rise people looked with contemptuous intolerance, for they regarded it as a kind of heathenism, and what excuse could there be for that in a Christian country? When, early in life, the end house children asked what Roman Catholics were, they were told they were 'folks as pray to images', and further enquiries elicited the information that they also worshipped the Pope, a bad old man, some said in league with the Devil. . . . People who openly said they had no use for religion themselves became quite heated when the Catholics were mentioned.[21]

These attitudes have no doubt weakened with the further passing of time (except of course in the case of the Protestants of Ulster), but Thompson's last sentence may help us understand the precise sense in which religious tolerance is now part of British national identity. It is, one might say, a specifically *Protestant* form of tolerance, which

---

[19] Colley, *Britons*, 330.

[20] D. Cressy, 'The Fifth of November Remembered', in R. Porter (ed.), *The Myths of the English* (Cambridge, Polity Press, 1992).

[21] F. Thompson, *Lark Rise to Candleford* (London, Oxford University Press, 1945), 210.

looks rather differently on religions that have their basis in individual experience and conviction as against those that involve deference to hierarchical authority. Faced with manifestations of the latter, the latent Protestantism of the British, even in those who no longer subscribe to any formal religion at all, is likely to surface. Catholics have probably now crossed the borderline of respectability, but Muslims in particular are liable to encounter greater resistance, mainly I think because the images of Islam that are projected through the media involve Ayatollahs apparently controlling large masses of adoring believers—the very thing that is most likely to raise the hackles of a Protestant culture.

If a lingering, very often non-religious, Protestantism is one component of current British identity, the other components have taken a severe bruising in the post-war period, to the point where many Britons may wonder whether there is anything distinctly valuable left in a British identity at all. The erosion of British identity has at least the following three aspects.

1. As we have seen, an important part of British identity at the time of its original formation was the idea that the institutions and culture of Britain would lead to commercial and trading success. There is some question as to whether manufacturing and commerce as activities were ever as highly valued as other modes of life—the life of the country gentleman, for instance.[22] Nevertheless, as far as the nation was concerned, success in overseas trade particularly was an important confirmation of the virtues of the British way of life. Britain's relatively dismal economic performance in the post-war period has therefore come as a severe blow to this self-image—to be overtaken economically by, for example, Italy suggests that something is seriously wrong with the basic institutions that have been handed down as component parts of British identity.

2. Whereas once it was possible to regard Britain's constitutional arrangements as more or less uniquely valuable, in a European context particularly this is no longer possible. Many other countries have established stable forms of liberal democracy, and by comparison with the formal constitutional arrangements of these states—with bills of rights, constitutional courts, and so forth—British

---

[22] This is the thesis of M. J. Wiener, *English Culture and the Decline of the Industrial Spirit 1850–1980* (Cambridge, Cambridge University Press, 1981).

institutions have come to seem outmoded and unenlightened. Readers of Dickens may recall Mr Podsnap's eulogy of the British constitution:

'We Englishmen are Very Proud of our Constitution, Sir. It Was Bestowed Upon Us by Providence. No Other Country is so Favoured as This Country.' . . .
  'And *other* countries,' said the foreign gentleman. 'They do how?'
  'They do, Sir,' returned Mr. Podsnap, gravely shaking his head; 'they do—I am sorry to be obliged to say it—*as* they do. . . . This island was Blest, Sir, to the Direct Exclusion of such Other Countries as—as there may happen to be.'[23]

No one could possibly hold such Podsnappian attitudes in Britain today. Whereas Americans may look upon their constitution with steady reverence, and Germans, seeking for a new identity that puts the Nazi period firmly in the past, readily embrace the idea of 'constitutional patriotism', no one can regard the British constitution as anything other than a ramshackle contrivance badly in need of radical renewal. We might still think that the constitutional arrangements of the country testify to British uniqueness, but they can hardly be looked on as a source of national pride.

3. One of the formative experiences in the life of people of my generation has been Britain's withdrawal from its overseas empire. I argued earlier that late Victorian high imperialism was superimposed on a more liberal view that the aim of imperial expansion was to allow free government on the British model to take root elsewhere in the world. As the empire came to an end, the prevailing view was that Britain would withdraw freely from its overseas possessions, bequeathing to them the parliamentary institutions that had ensured Britain's own success. As everyone knows, with a few exceptions this view proved to be wildly optimistic. The institutions quickly collapsed, to be replaced in some cases by military rule and in others by one-party government; the imperial borders themselves were frequently condemned as arbitrary impositions of the colonial power. What, then, had the whole imperial venture amounted to? If its purpose was not to export 'civilization' and free institutions to places that lacked these benefits, what could justify it? The ending of

[23] C. Dickens, *Our Mutual Friend* (London, Hazel, Watson and Viney, n.d.), 118–19.

empire—not so much the formal hand-over of power as what happened thereafter—called into question a very long-standing set of beliefs about Britain's role in the world, and indeed about the intrinsic value of British institutions themselves.

If we take these three points together, we can see that the post-war experience of people in Britain has directly undermined the main elements out of which British identity was originally constructed. This accounts for the confused feelings that many experience when asked what it means to them to be British. On the one hand, there is a strong sense that the British do have a separate identity, and that this matters a good deal; on the other hand, it is far from clear what this separate identity is supposed to consist in.

In this situation it is tempting to take refuge in what I shall call 'cultural Englishness'. By this I mean the set of private characteristics and ways of doing things that are thought to be typically English: such things as drinking tea and patronizing fish and chip shops, having an enthusiasm for gardening, a love of the countryside, and so forth—each person will have his or her own list. There is nothing wrong with cultural Englishness, but it is not the same as a British national identity, and to conflate the two is to put a private set of cultural values in place of a public understanding of the terms on which we are going to carry on our collective life. As we have seen, to have a national identity is to take part in a continuing process of collective self-definition which is expressed in essentially public ways—in political institutions, in the policies of a government, and so forth. If we try to make a private set of cultural values stand in for a shared public identity, we commit two kinds of mistakes. On the one hand, we have nowhere to look for guidance in directing our public life: saying that the British love animals and country pubs is no use at all if what we have to decide is whether to privatize the welfare state or ratify the Maastricht treaty. On the other hand, we make national identity depend on a private culture which may not be universally shared across the society. If we say that you are not genuinely British unless you enjoy gardening and watching cricket, then we immediately erect barriers in the face of all those who happen not to value these things. Indeed, as we saw in the last chapter, it may precisely be the members of the ethnic minorities who do not conform to 'cultural Englishness' who have the most to gain from a definition of national identity which sees it as a public phenomenon transcending private cultural differences.[24]

Another problem with 'cultural Englishness' is that it overlooks the existence of the Scots, the Welsh, and the Northern Irish.[25] Whatever British identity means to them, it cannot be that. It is quite often argued that these are separate nations, so that, rather than thinking in terms of British national identity at all, we should think of Britain as a multinational state in which common political institutions hold together communities with separate identities.[26] This view seems to me to misrepresent both the past and the present relationship between the Scots and the other national minorities and Britain as a whole. I noted earlier that a specifically *British* identity was first forged precisely to aid the integration of these communities—an integration that was favoured by élite groups on both sides for different reasons. There then followed more than two centuries in which the destinies of England, Scotland, Wales, and Ulster have been woven together politically, militarily, and in other ways—the Scots especially playing a central part in imperial expansion.[27] It is precisely this shared historical experience, together with a very substantial level of cultural interchange, that has sustained a sense of common nationality alongside an equally powerful sense of difference. When asked today about their identity, most Scots will describe themselves both as Scottish and as British, though when asked to assign priority between these identities, the majority will

---

[24] On this point see the persuasive argument in T. Modood, 'Establishment, Multiculturalism and British Citizenship', *Political Quarterly*, 65 (1994), 64–5.

[25] The Northern Irish raise special problems when British national identity is being discussed, and since I could not hope to do justice to these problems I shall simply set them to one side.

[26] This view can be found, for instance, in B. Crick, 'The English and the British', in B. Crick (ed.), *National Identities* (Oxford, Blackwell, 1991).

[27] As a pamphlet entitled *The Oppressed English*, published in 1917, noted:

Today a Scot is leading the British army in France [Field Marshall Douglas Haig], another is commanding the British grand fleet at sea [Admiral David Beatty], while a third directs the Imperial General Staff at home [Sir William Robertson]. The Lord Chancellor is a Scot [Viscount Finlay]; so are the Chancellor of the Exchequer and the Foreign Secretary [Bonar Law and Arthur Balfour]. The Prime Minister is a Welshman [David Lloyd George], and the First Lord of the Admiralty is an Irishman [Lord Carson]. (cited in Colley, *Britons*, 163–4)

emphasize their Scottishness.[28] There is no good word to describe the position of communities such as these: 'nations' is misleading for the reasons just given, but 'ethnic groups' is wrong too, for it overlooks the territorial element in the identity, and also, in the case of the Scots especially, the persistence of institutions—such as separate legal and education systems—that make the identity a semi-political one.

Although these national minorities are not properly described as ethnic groups, they may serve as a helpful example when considering what ought to be the relationship between ethnicity proper and nationality. For they serve as a vivid reminder of the fact that there are many distinct and equally legitimate ways of 'being British'.[29] To be a Scot in Britain is to share a common identity, but at the same time to have a powerful sense of the cultural distinctness of the group to which you belong, a distinctness that finds expression through public media such as television and newspapers. Right-wing would-be defenders of the nation who stress the homogeneity of the British people proper (in contrast to the immigrant communities)[30] overlook the deep-seated pluralism that has always been a characteristic of Britain as a nation. Why should it be less legitimate to be Chinese and British or Jamaican and British than to be Welsh and British?

The question we must still ask, however, is what British nationality actually consists in once we allow that there are many culturally distinct ways of being British. Others who have followed parallel lines of argument to that set out here have reached the conclusion

[28] See e.g. J. Brand, J. Mitchell, and P. Surridge, 'Identity and the Vote: Class and Nationality in Scotland', in D. Denver *et al.* (eds.), *British Elections and Parties Yearbook 1993* (Hemel Hempstead, Harvester Wheatsheaf, 1993). The preference given to Scottish identity does not necessarily mean that this identity will carry more weight when practical choices have to be made. It is a richer and 'thicker' identity, conjuring up images of the Scottish countryside and so forth, whereas British identity is understood in a thinner, more political, sense; it is not surprising that an open question should call the thicker identity to mind.

[29] Parekh expresses this idea well: 'So-called "Britishness" is the core which different individuals and groups appropriate differently and around which they frame their different identities. . . . Even as we all speak English but in our own different ways and accents, the Indians, the Pakistanis, the Afro-Caribbeans, the Scots, the English and the rest can all be British in their own unique ways' ('Britain and the Social Logic of Pluralism', in G. Andrews (ed.), *Citizenship* (London, Lawrence and Wishart, 1991), 74–5).

[30] See the references in Ch. 5, S. II.

hat what is needed is essentially a conception of British *citizenship* rather than nationality, where this is understood in terms of sub-cription to a set of political principles: tolerance, respect for law, belief in the procedures of parliamentary democracy, and so forth.[31] These principles should undoubtedly feature centrally in any story about what it means to be British today, and as I shall suggest shortly it would be very helpful to have them formally inscribed in a consti-tutional document. It does not, however, seem that these principles, which after all are the common currency of liberal democracies everywhere, can by themselves bear the load that would otherwise be carried by a national identity. As I have already argued, a national identity helps to locate us in the world; it must tell us who we are, where we have come from, what we have done. It must then involve an essentially historical understanding in which the present genera-tion are seen as heirs to a tradition which they then pass on to their successors. Of course the story is continually being rewritten; each generation revises the past as it comes to terms with the problems of the present. None the less, there is a sense in which the past always constrains the present: present identities are built out of the materi-als that are handed down, not started from scratch. (This was the point that I was trying to make when I referred earlier to the resid-ual Protestantism in British political culture.) The abstract principles we now subscribe to do not hang in a void. They are expressions of a political culture which has developed in the course of centuries

[31] For instance, John Gray writes:

> Because of our history and institutions, political allegiance for us today cannot be founded in ethnicity or nationality. It may, and should, invoke a shared sense of Britishness, where this means a sense of fair play, of equality before the law, and a spirit of tolerance and compromise on matters about which we have deep dif-ferences (*A Conservative Disposition*, London, Centre for Policy Studies, 1991, 20).

Bhikhu Parekh writes:

> Nationhood is not at all a practical ideal for [modern states]. Nor is it a desirable ideal, for the glory of the modern State consists in creating a non-natural or non-biological basis of unity and uniting people with nothing in common save the State itself. Further what characterises Britain as a civilised society is its liberal tradition of tolerance and respect for individuals and groups holding different beliefs. ('The "New Right" and the Politics of Nationhood', in *The New Right: Image and Reality*, London, Runnymede Trust, 1986, 42)

Parekh seems, however, to have modified his view somewhat in 'Britain and the Social Logic of Pluralism'.

during which different understandings of British identity have jostled with one another for recognition.

III

Before asking what might be done to revitalize British national identity, let us step back for a moment and ask how far the problems just outlined are unique to the British case or, on the other hand, are common to Western liberal democracies. The first factor identified—relative economic decline—does seem to be distinctively if not uniquely British. Few countries have experienced such a rapid erosion of economic superiority and of the political hegemony that follows a step or two behind. (Americans now fear something similar, but as yet this is an anxiety rather than a demonstrable fact.) But if we consider the other two factors I highlighted—loss of belief in constitutional superiority, and loss of belief in the imperial mission—these do seem to have their analogues in other countries. First of all, it is harder for the citizens of any liberal democracy to regard their political achievements as distinctive and peculiar. This is partly because the constitutional arrangements of the liberal democracies have tended over time to converge—despite differences of detail, all have universal suffrage, multi-party systems, constitutional protection of individual rights, and so forth[32]—and partly because distinct national projects, such as the Scandinavian version of social citizenship, or the French attempt to protect the national language and culture, are harder to sustain when the economy becomes increasingly internationalized.[33] So if asked, 'What is it that we do publicly that people in other democracies don't do? What *distinguishes* us as a political community?' it is more difficult to find an answer.

We should also recall here the way in which war and the threat of war helped originally to consolidate national identities, and take note of the fact that liberal democracies have succeeded so far in

[32] I do not mean to deny that the institutional differences that remain are very important if we want to understand how the various political systems work in practice. The point is rather that half a century ago it was plausible to make strong comparative evaluations of different countries' constitutional arrangements, whereas among the liberal democracies this is no longer the case.

[33] See D. Schnapper, 'The Debate on Immigration and the Crisis of National Identity', *West European Politics*, 17 (1994), 127–39, for the view that recent political developments have raised challenges to national identities throughout Europe.

maintaining peace among themselves. If a distinct national identity emanates partly from hostility to some Other or Others, then this can be sustained today only by projecting backwards and supposing that other people still have the characteristics that made them enemies in the past. (Germans are still closet fascists, the French are always out to knife the British in the back, and other such improbable ideas.)

Second, although the citizens of liberal democracies can and do compare their institutions favourably with those of authoritarian regimes, they no longer think of themselves as having a civilizing mission in the sense of having a right or an obligation to impose liberal institutions on societies that lack them. This is partly in deference to the doctrine of national self-determination, but partly because we have lost confidence in the idea that liberal democracy is in a universal sense a better or higher form of government. Instead, we tend to think that societies acquire the forms of government that suit them best, so that, although we are strongly attached to the institutions of liberal democracy ourselves, we have ceased to think of them as something in which we can take pride: they are not so much an achievement as what comes naturally to you when you live in an economically advanced society. In a post-imperial age, we tend to acquiesce in a certain kind of relativism, which does not obliterate the distinction between liberal democracies and authoritarian regimes, but does prevent us from seeing ourselves as the custodians of a unique political treasure. Like Mr Podsnap, we still say of other countries that, regretfully, they do *as* they do, but we no longer think that we have been blessed to the direct exclusion of everywhere else.

Thus, although the British may be unusual in the extent to which a long-established national identity has been disrupted by events in the post-war period, some of the same forces have been at work elsewhere, and we should not be surprised to find that people generally have become less clear about what their national identity amounts to, even if (as we saw earlier in the European case) the identity itself—reflected, for instance in people's expressed pride in their country—remains strong.

What, then, is to be done? Some may feel that the erosion of national identities is a trend to be welcomed rather than regretted, and that, at least within the ambit of the Western democracies, people should be encouraged to adopt a diffuse personal identity as

members of an enlarged civil society—what I earlier described somewhat disparagingly as a view of the world as a giant supermarket. In
a European context one would move freely between countries, living in one, working in another, holidaying in a third, having one's
children educated in a fourth, and so on—enjoying, in fact, the best
that each place has to offer. Appealing as this outlook and mode of
life may sound, I think that there are reasons to remain sceptical. It
presupposes continuing internal and external stability—it assumes
that the process of establishing liberal democratic institutions is irre-
versible, and also that relations between the liberal democracies continue to be friendly—whereas in the face of political crisis people
whose allegiances were fragmented in this way would lack the
deeper resources of a common historical identity. More immediately,
the cultural supermarket view fails to address the question what
holds a society together, and what is the source of the obligations
that we owe to one another—obligations of the sort that are manifested in social security schemes and public provision for citizens'
needs. It seems to me a corollary of a view of the world in which each
operates solely as a free chooser within the constraints of a diffuse
civil society that everyone must provide for themselves through private insurance and so forth. What then happens to minorities who
for one reason or another are less well equipped to take advantage of
the opportunities of the giant supermarket? Who has the responsibility to provide for them?

We cannot, then, simply welcome or be indifferent to the problems of nationality that the British case illustrates. There is no realistic alternative to the long-standing project of nation-building, but it
must now be carried out in circumstances where national identities
have to compete with a wider range of other potential objects of loyalty. This means, first of all, that if we want people to acquire secure
national identities, we must become more self-conscious about what
those national identities are actually going to consist in—what will
be distinctive about belonging to this nation rather than that.
Nationality can no longer remain a diffuse, taken-for-granted cultural matrix, something one acquires simply by living in a place,
breathing the air, being exposed to particular ways of doing things.
In this respect, older nations like Britain have much to learn from
newer nations like the United States, where nation-building as a
deliberate practice has a long pedigree and as a result there exists a

much clearer sense of what it means to make people into Americans. There needs to be an explicit public debate about the character of national identity, and especially about the ways in which an historically transmitted identity (such as plainly exists in the British case) must adapt to new circumstances, especially to increasing cultural pluralism. How, to take a specific instance, should the French tradition of republican and secular education (which as we saw in the last chapter was central to the creation of French national identity) respond to the demand of some Islamic students that they should be allowed to wear special items of dress such as headscarves in schools?[34] Questions such as these should not be brushed under the carpet or resolved through some administrative compromise, but should become the occasion for a public debate on where the boundaries between private culture and the public culture that is integral to nationality should be drawn.

In so far as national identity can be expressed in terms of political principles, it is important that these should be explicitly set down to serve as a point of reference for the future. The most obvious vehicle for this is a written constitution. Constitutions are not and should not be immutable, but they are relatively stable, and apart from their procedural functions they serve to articulate the basic principles according to which a society's political life is going to be conducted. In the British case, the absence of a written constitution has come over time to contribute to the crisis in national identity, as I argued above. So long as that identity could be linked to long-established institutions such as the monarchy, the Church of England, and the Houses of Parliament—institutions that operated according to conventions well-known among the political class at least—it was possible for the nation's Podsnaps to take pride in the constitution, despite its elusive quality. But now the operative principles have become simply mysterious. To questions such as 'How are governments to be formed when no single party has a majority in the Commons?' 'When should referendums be held and what authority do they have?' 'What is the legitimate political role of the Church of England?' 'What does the heir to the throne have to do to

---

[34] This has become a fiercely controversial issue in France, provoking powerful restatements of the republican ideal from intellectuals of both the Left and the Right.

disqualify himself from the succession?' there is no agreed answer. What is needed is a constitutional settlement that embodies and codifies the principles of such past constitutional documents as Britain possesses—the 1689 Bill of Rights and so forth—while adapting them to the contemporary world. This would need to cover, among other things, the role of the monarchy, the position of the established Church, the separate rights of the component parts of the United Kingdom, as well as the rights and liberties of citizens generally. Britain might here draw inspiration from the Canadian case, where, against the background of a somewhat similar political tradition, the enactment in 1982 of the Constitution Act, and especially the Canadian Charter of Rights and Freedoms, has quickly come to play a central role in Canadian identity.

The third element in a revived project of nation-building must be civic education as a means of transmitting the redefined and constitutionally embodied national identity to the incoming generation. But once again, this has to be done in a way that is sensitive to the realities of cultural pluralism. Cultural minorities should not be seen merely as the recipients of an identity, but must be expected to play their part in redefining it for the future. It is important, therefore, that they should have access to the raw materials of the debate. As I argued in the last chapter, from the point of view of education this means that we must accept the idea of a core curriculum, in the sense of a body of material to which every child is exposed in subjects such as history and politics. This view that cultural groups should be encouraged simply to absorb the historical experience and way of life of their particular group is indefensible. To attempt to isolate groups in this way would be to deprive them of the opportunity to participate in the continuous redefinition of national identity. If you want to persuade the majority of the British to change their view of themselves, you must first know what view they now hold, and this demands knowledge of their culture, history, and practices. Equally, however, the core curriculum must be presented in such a way that it leaves open the possibility of differing interpretations, and there should be scope to emphasize or de-emphasize material according to the needs of particular groups of children. Thus, Scottish children should learn British history, but should focus particularly on developments in Scotland, and the same general principle should apply to ethnic groups who will want to highlight their struggle to establish themselves in British society, and the changes in British political culture that have ensued.[35]

How, precisely, civic education should be carried out will depend on the national traditions of each country and the ways in which minority cultures converge with or diverge from the mainstream culture. I cannot say more here about, for example, religious education, because I do not believe that there is a universally correct answer to be found: one country may rightfully insist on a purely secular public education, while another may allow schools sponsored by religious groups to give religious instruction alongside the core curriculum. I have focused on the British case because it seems to illustrate particularly well the problems involved in adapting a strong historic national identity to meet the demands of citizenship in the contemporary world, but the particular solutions that might work for Britain cannot be exported wholesale. At a more general level, however, the main elements in the revitalization of nationality will be the same everywhere: an open debate about national identity and its redefinition to accommodate cultural and territorial minorities; the constitutional embodiment of the resulting principles; and the transmission of national identity through a civic education with a unitary core but a periphery that is flexible enough to serve the needs of minorities.

I have argued in this chapter that national identities and loyalties

[35] In this respect I do not think that the recommendations of the National Curriculum History Working Group can be faulted. First, the proposed curriculum gives central place to the development of freedom and democracy in Britain and aims to instil in pupils the attitudes of mind that support such achievements: 'respect for people of other cultures and from other backgrounds; an informed curiosity about the wider world; an understanding of how rights and liberties develop and how they may be threatened; some comprehension of what individuals can do within society and under the rule of law' (National Curriculum History Working Group, *Final Report*, London, HMSO, 1990, 184–5). Second, due weight is given to the pluralism of British society throughout its history: 'although they have much in common, individuals also have different inheritances specific to country, region, ethnic groupings, religion, gender and social class. We do not believe that school history can be so finely-tuned as to accommodate all of this range all the time, but it must make pupils aware of the richness and variety of British culture and its historical origins' (p. 17). Third, core units in British history are balanced against optional units in which pupils might, for instance, study 'Islamic civilization up to the early 16th C.' or 'India from the Mughal empire to the coming of the British'. These provisions signal a desire to do justice to the diversity of ethnic and other cultural identities in Britain, while at the same time drawing all groups towards a common understanding of national identity.

have not been declining (in liberal democracies) in the way that many commentators suggest. The issue (illustrated by the British case) is not so much one of a quantitative weakening of nationality as of growing uncertainty about the cultural values and political principles that distinguish one nation from the next. Because I am sceptical about the proposed replacements—the idea that people should acquire transnational political identities such as 'citizen of Europe', or that they should regard themselves simply as part of an amorphous civil society that crosses national borders—I have suggested that the project of nation-building, pursued so energetically in most liberal states in the eighteenth and nineteenth centuries, must be carried forward in a way that takes account of revitalized ethnic, regional, and other such identities. It remains to pull the threads of the argument together and to say a little more about how embracing the principle of nationality I have been defending should change our political outlook.

CHAPTER 7

Conclusion

My intention in this book has been to propose a way of thinking about nationalism and nationality. As I said at the beginning, people who in a broad sense would count themselves as liberals often find it difficult to know how to react to the demands made by nationalists in the contemporary world, or indeed how to come to terms with their own sense of belonging to an historic national community.[1] The questions I have mainly been addressing are these: Are nations themselves imaginary beings, whose apparent solidity depends upon a set of false beliefs about what has happened in the past and about what we have in common in the present? If nations are not merely imaginary, what practical demands do they make on us? Are we justified in recognizing and acting upon special obligations to our compatriots, and how can this be squared with our sense that we owe an equal respect to every human being regardless of nationality? What justifies nations in demanding political autonomy, and how should we react when some territorial minority group calls for the redrawing of political boundaries? More generally, how far should we go to protect national identities in the face of contemporary multiculturalism?

What I have tried to offer, in answering these questions, is a discriminating defence of nationality. I have attempted to show how we

---

[1] Here is just one example of the ambivalence I am describing:

Today is Armistice Day and the fiftieth anniversary of the end of the First World War. I listen to the ceremony on the radio, and as I type this I hear the guns rumbling across the park for the start of the Two Minutes' Silence. I find the ceremony ridiculous and hypocritical, and yet it brings a lump to my throat. Why? (Alan Bennett, *Writing Home*, London, Faber and Faber, 1994, 259).

can acknowledge the claims of national identity without succumbing to an unthinking nationalism which simply tells us to follow the feelings of our blood wherever they may lead us. The horrors that continue to be inflicted by this latter kind of nationalism are too well known to need further elaboration. Many have responded by seeking to extirpate the idea of nationhood entirely, replacing it with the kind of internationalist humanism expressed by H. G. Wells whose epigram I quoted in the Introduction, and perhaps best symbolized by the invention of Esperanto. These attempts seem to me misguided, for two main reasons. The first is simply that the majority of people are too deeply attached to their inherited national identities to make their obliteration an intelligible goal. People value the rich cultural inheritance that membership of a nation can bring them; and they want to see continuity between their own lives and the lives of their ancestors. The idea that they should regard their nationality merely as a historic accident, an identity to be sloughed off in favour of humanity at large, carries little appeal. If national identities are distasteful, or have distasteful aspects, it seems more reasonable to work from within, to get people to reassess what they have inherited, come to a new understanding of what it means to be German or Canadian, than to dismiss such identities from an external standpoint. Premature reports of the death of nationality have abounded in the twentieth century, and those who deliver them have constantly been caught off guard by the actual course of political events.

The second reason for not taking the cosmopolitanism of an H. G. Wells to heart is that nationality has served and continues to serve a number of important purposes, when judged by values that most liberals will want to uphold. I do not wish to claim either that national identities are a perennial feature of human life or that the functions they perform could never in any circumstances be served by other means. As we saw in Chapter 2, there is indeed something distinctively modern about our idea of nationhood, even though it builds upon ideas about the tribal divisions of the human species that can be traced much further back in time. Nationality, one might say, is the *appropriate* form of solidarity for societies that are mobile—so that clan and village can no longer serve as the primary forms of community—and egalitarian—so that people are no longer bound together by vertical ties to overlords and dependants. As the main focus of collective loyalty in societies of this kind, it serves the pur-

poses that I have outlined in earlier chapters: it provides the where-
withal for a common culture against whose background people can
make more individual decisions about how to lead their lives; it provides the setting in which ideas of social justice can be pursued, particularly ideas that require us to treat our individual talents as to
some degree a 'common asset', to use Rawls's phrase; and it helps to
foster the mutual understanding and trust that makes democratic citizenship possible. I have tried to spell out the arguments behind
these claims, and I have also suggested that in many liberal writers
the assumption of common nationality goes unnoticed because it is
taken for granted. Political philosophers will simply begin an argument about how 'society' or 'the political community' should organize itself—which principles of equality it should follow, for
instance—without laying out the assumptions they are making
about the kind of community in which the principles will be applied.
This is perfectly legitimate in so far as the audience are assumed to
be citizens of a reasonably well functioning nation-state; it becomes
illegitimate when the argument is developed in such a way as to
undermine this very assumption.[2]

But nationality, we have seen, is currently under attack. Alongside
the cosmopolitanism which was probably as popular among intellectuals seventy years ago as it is today, we have the impact of multiculturalism internally and the world economy externally. If societies
are becoming more culturally fragmented, while at the same time
they are increasingly exposed to the homogenizing cultural effects of
the global market, then it seems that national identities can be preserved only by increasingly illiberal means. Ethnic minorities have
to be turned into Frenchmen or Britons, while the French and the
British themselves have to be protected against alien influences by,

---

[2] I am thinking here of two possibilities. One is the case where a principle is
defended in a way that presupposes a common nationality, but is then used to justify policies which if implemented would destroy that very national community. (I
believe radical versions of multiculturalism exemplify this pattern.) The other is
where a principle defended in this way is then applied globally, without asking
whether the background assumptions still hold. So, for instance, someone might
argue in defence of Rawls's difference principle ('Social and economic inequalities
are to be arranged to the greatest advantage of the worst off members of society')
by assuming that the individuals to whom it will apply are bound together in a
scheme of social co-operation, and then, having established the principle as a principle of justice, claim that it was arbitrary to allow it to operate only within national
borders.

for instance, overriding their desire to watch American films and television programmes. In these circumstances the cause of nationality begins to look reactionary. The progressive response is to celebrate diversity, bolster ethnic pride, and encourage people to pick and choose among the array of cultural identities that a global culture makes accessible. Just as Marx looked forward to a future in which we would hunt in the morning, fish in the afternoon, and criticize after dinner, so the new cosmopolitanism holds up before us an image in which we might explore our Celtic roots on Monday, spend Tuesday celebrating the Buddha's birthday in our neighbourhood temple, on Wednesday join in a Greenpeace demonstration against international whaling, and take part on Thursday in a critical discussion of British imperialism.

This is a teasing description, obviously (as to an extent was Marx's), but I think it gestures at what is attractive about multicultural cosmopolitanism. (All of the activities described are interesting ones, more so than hunting and fishing.) What are the corresponding problems? The first is that the quest for cultural diversity may turn out to be self-defeating, because as cultures become more accessible to outsiders they also begin to lose their depth and their distinctive character. This is illustrated by the well-known paradox of travel, that, as more people are able to travel further afield, their presence dilutes the local cultures which must adapt to receive them, so that the main charm of travel—the promise of change, of encountering the strange and exotic—is lost. To find places where people's lives remain untouched by the global metropolitan culture, the traveller is forced to seek out the remotest corners of the earth. In an analogous way, cultures that are sustained only on a part-time basis, and not by people who are deeply immersed in them, are to that extent unsatisfying.

I am reluctant to push this argument too far, because it quickly degenerates into a dispute about the extent to which people really need the kind of encompassing culture that nation-states have traditionally provided, or on the other hand can be satisfied by the smorgasbord of cultural experiences that the cosmopolitan offers to replace it. The second argument cuts deeper. The appeal of cultural pluralism as I have described it depends on the assumption that everyone has equal access to the cultural opportunities on offer, and has the secure financial status that enables them to take advantage of these opportunities. But this is put in question by the very processes that are said to be dissolving national identities. If people's economic position depends increasingly on their position in the global market, then this is likely to lead to increasing polarization within the liberal democracies between an élite of highly skilled professionals and a non-élite of low-paid unskilled workers and the unemployed. The benefits of the global culture will be confined very largely to the élite, who can buy high culture at home (seats at the opera and so forth) and travel around to sample the surviving indigenous cultures abroad. The non-élite will have to put up with a lowest-common-denominator mass culture exemplified by Disney, McDonalds, and Australian soap operas. In other words, if national identities are indeed being eroded, what is likely to take their place is not rich cultural pluralism for everyone, but the world market as the distributor of cultural resources. And this will be bad news for the non-élite, on two counts. First, they will no longer have ready access to a rich common culture of the kind that is still available in most European and other Western states through publicly funded television stations, museums and art galleries, educational programmes, and the like. Second, their economic position will increasingly be determined by the workings of the global market, as national solidarity declines and people are no longer willing to allow redistributive policies to interfere with economic competitiveness.

It would be wrong to suggest that defenders of cultural cosmopolitanism are unaware of this point. They would undoubtedly wish to argue for the redistribution of resources along with the equal recognition of cultures. Their failure is not a failure of sympathy but a failure to look realistically at the conditions under which the polarizing effects of the global market can be mitigated. The welfare state—and indeed, programmes to protect minority rights—have always been *national* projects, justified on the basis that members of a community must protect one another and guarantee one another equal respect. If national identities begin to dissolve, ordinary people will have less reason to be active citizens, and political élites will have a freer hand in dismantling those institutions that currently counteract the global market to some degree.

If we are persuaded by these reasons to accept the principle of nationality I have been defending, how should it affect our political thinking? Let us be clear that the principle does not provide us with a complete political philosophy. No one is simply a nationalist and nothing else: she may be a liberal nationalist, a socialist nationalist, a conservative nationalist, or a nationalist of some other kind. The principle of nationality acts to modify these outlooks, conditioning the way in which other principles such as liberty and equality are used to support practical recommendations. But taking the principle by itself for a moment, what are its main practical implications for ethics and politics? I shall try to provide a summary statement.

Political communities should as far as possible be organized in such a way that their members share a common national identity, which binds them together in the face of their many diverse private and group identities. The drawing of political boundaries should therefore not be seen as a matter of sheer contingency. If a state's existing borders house two communities whose national identities are clearly distinct, then there will normally be good reason to allow the two communities to separate politically, as Norway and Sweden did in 1905 and the Czech Republic and Slovakia have done more recently. Equally, where current borders serve to divide a national community, as the two halves of Germany were divided before 1990, there will usually be a good case for dismantling the borders and creating a large state. (I shall come back shortly to the reasons why the 'normally' and 'usually' are needed here.) However, the link between state and nation must run in both directions. If a state houses a minority who for one reason or another do not feel themselves to be fully part of the national community, but who do not want or cannot realistically hope to form a nation-state of their own, then national identity must be transformed in such a way that they can be included. The aim is that every citizen should think of himself as sharing a national identity with the others, where, as I argued in Chapter 2, this means belonging to a community that is constituted by shared belief and mutual commitment, that extends over historical time, that acts collectively as its members determine, that has an identifiable homeland, and that possesses a distinct public culture that marks it off from its neighbours.

Since in saying this I am clearly denying that citizenship must have an exclusive ethnic basis, it may appear that I am advocating what others have called 'civic nationalism'.[3] This label is, however, a

[3] See e.g. A. D. Smith, *National Identity* (Harmondsworth, Penguin, 1991) or M. Ignatieff, *Blood and Belonging: Journeys into the New Nationalism* (London, Vintage, 1994).

source of possible confusion. Civic nationalism may amount to the view that nationality as traditionally understood should be set aside in favour of an idea of common citizenship. States should be composed of equal citizens whose ties to one another are purely 'civic' in the sense that each acknowledges the authority of a common set of laws and political institutions.

One version of this view is the 'constitutional patriotism' discussed in the last chapter. It seeks to bracket off questions about shared history and common culture and to claim that the basis on which citizens associate can be purely political. As should by now be clear, I reject civic nationalism in this form. I have argued that the national identities that support common citizenship must be thicker than 'constitutional patriotism' implies. If we are attempting to reform national identity so that it becomes accessible to all citizens, we do this not by discarding everything except constitutional principles, but by adapting the inherited culture to make room for minority communities. Thus, rather than abandoning the teaching of national history in schools, we establish a common curriculum which gives due weight to the place that these communities have occupied in the making of the nation. If religion has played a large part in constituting national identity, we do not turn our backs on it by enacting purely secular policies, but try to strike a balance between the claims of the community's historic faith and the claims of dissenters. (We support religious toleration and, although we allow the established church to keep some of its privileges, we ensure that there are no professions or jobs open only to its members.) In the matter of language policy, we do not opt for neutrality or *laissez-faire*, but instead decide which language or languages are going to be the national ones, and then ensure that every citizen learns these as her first or second language—a policy that is also compatible with protecting the languages spoken by ethnic minorities if the communities in question desire this.

The principle of nationality defended here is reiterative in Michael Walzer's sense.[4] That is, in advancing the claims of our own national community to security and self-determination, we also recognize that other communities may make equally legitimate claims on their own behalf. The overall aim is a world in which different peoples can

[4] M. Walzer, 'Nation and Universe', in G. B. Petersen (ed.), *The Tanner Lectures on Human Values*, xi (Salt Lake City, University of Utah Press, 1990).

pursue their own national projects in a spirit of friendly rivalry, but in which none attempts to control, exploit, or undermine any of the others. Besides the barriers this erects to overt or covert imperialism it also creates a general obligation to ensure that nation-states have adequate resources to remain economically viable. As I argued in Chapter 4, there are serious objections to the idea that each nation should enjoy *equal* resources; but these do not apply to the much weaker demand that each should be given access, directly or through trade, to resources that are sufficient to make self-determination a reality.

What does reiteration tell us about the cases in which national self determination in its full sense is not a realistic possibility—cases of dispersed national minorities, or communities too small to be genuinely autonomous? It tells us to find the second-best solution. I suggested in Chapter 4 that the secessionist demands of national minorities should sometimes be resisted on the ground that secession would create two bi-national states in place of one, an outcome that might be less desirable than the *status quo ante*. In these cases there is no arrangement that grants everyone national self determination, and an acceptable solution may require elaborate constitutional engineering.

Consider the case of Northern Ireland, where two communities sufficiently intermingled that they cannot easily be separated by border redrawing, identify primarily with two different nation states. If it is possible to govern this society in a way that both communities regard as legitimate,[5] it can only be through some division of powers between the British government, the Irish government and a devolved authority in Ulster itself whose powers are shared between the two communities. Each community gets partial self determination, or, more importantly perhaps, protection against its future's being wholly decided by the *other* community. Since full self-determination all round is an impossibility for the foreseeable future, the principle of nationality favours the compromise solution while remaining neutral as between British rule and Irish rule if this should fail.

The principle of nationality requires us to respect others' claims to

---

[5] A question that remains unresolved at the time of writing, despite some progress in reconciling the two national governments and the two communities in Northern Ireland itself.

national self-determination, but as the argument of Chapter 3 showed, it does not require us to treat foreigners and compatriots equally in all respects. We owe obligations to compatriots that are more extensive than those that we owe to outsiders, and institutions that discharge those obligations, such as the welfare state, are justified despite their restriction within national boundaries. I suggested that our universal obligations were best understood in terms of basic human rights, but that even here we should recognize that the *primary* obligation to respect these rights lies with co-nationals. Internationally, our first task is to persuade and if necessary induce political communities to respect the basic rights of their members, before intervening directly to enforce rights when no other course of action remains open.

How far should we be concerned, morally speaking, about global inequality? If we look at comparative living standards in rich and poor countries, for example at the Sweden–Somalia contrast that I instanced on p. 63, we are bound to find the comparisons disturbing. The inequalities we find would be morally intolerable within a single country, so why not when the comparison is made across borders? What is intolerable in the international case is not the inequality as such, but the low standard of living of the average Somali, which is kept low by human causes.[6] How we should react depends on what those causes are. If it is the result of our interference, or of an exploitative pattern of exchange which has grown up historically, then we are responsible and should aid the Somalis as a matter of justice. If it is a result of mistaken policies or domestic turmoil within Somalia itself, then our response must be more nuanced. The aim must be to create in Somalia a well functioning political community (or political communities, if divisions turn out to be too deep for a common sense of nationality to emerge) which can implement those policies that the Somalis themselves regard as just. Outsiders may

---

[6] I do not in general accept the view (advanced for example by Joseph Raz in *The Morality of Freedom*, Oxford, Clarendon Press, 1986) that equality has no value in its own right, and that inequalities are objectionable only in so far as the worse off are deprived in an absolute sense. (See my article 'Equality after Raz' in S. Caney and A. Williams, *Joseph Raz's Political Philosophy*, forthcoming.) Within nations, as well as within smaller communities, equality may have a value that is not reducible to the avoidance of deprivation and suffering. At a global level, by contrast, the Raz doctrine holds, and will continue to hold until such time as a world community exists in reality and not just in aspiration.

have some role in bringing this about, although usually it will be an oblique one. Certainly we must not impose the distributive pattern that we favour in place of the Somalis' own understanding of their mutual obligations.

I do not wish to defend the present pattern of global inequality, which undoubtedly bears the marks of past exploitation, and the continuing vulnerability of many developing countries to economic decisions taken by the Western states. At the same time, some degree of inequality is inevitable, and not unjust, because it is the direct consequence of a system where independent nations pursue the policies that reflect their own cultural values. No one thinks it an injustice that Germans now have a higher standard of living than Britons, because this is primarily the consequence of political decisions and cultural values in the two countries during the present century. (Particular subgroups within either country might have a legitimate grievance if they could show that their voices were not heard when decisions were reached.) In reacting to a case like that of Somalia, we should focus less on the inequality between their living standards and ours, and more on the ways in which their basic rights are being violated, who is responsible for the violations, and who has both the material means and the moral standing to intervene effectively to put a stop to them.[7]

To return now to questions of domestic politics, we can perhaps best appreciate the difference that the principle of nationality makes by asking how far it requires us to transmute liberal political ideals. (I use 'liberal' here in a broad sense to embrace a spectrum of political thinking that runs from liberal conservatives to democratic socialists.) We have noted already that 'liberal nationalism' is not a contradiction in terms: there can be liberal nationalists as well as nationalists of other kinds. Historically, too, the cause of national self-determination and the cause of political liberalism have often gone hand-in-hand, as they did in the person of the Italian nationalist Mazzini. So clearly, it is a mistake to start out thinking of liberalism and nationalism as opposing ideologies or value-systems. But how easily can they be conjoined?[8]

The main difficulty we face in answering this question is the pro-

---

[7] For a good brief exploration of the issues here, see M. Walzer, 'The Politics of Rescue', *Dissent*, 42(1) (Winter, 1995), 35–41.

[8] For the view that such a conjunction is possible, see Y. Tamir, *Liberal Nationalism* (Princeton, Princeton University Press, 1993).

tean nature of liberalism itself. The core political principles of liberalism may be fairly easy to state—toleration and free speech, the rule of law, government by consent of the governed, and so forth—but the justifying theories offered in support of these principles are extremely varied in character. I shall suggest that we are more likely to find divergences between liberalism and nationality at the level of justifying theory than at the level of practical policies, though even this will depend on the kind of liberalism that is in question. Some liberals—for instance J. S. Mill, whose views I have cited at several points—would agree with many of the arguments offered here in defence of nationality.

In this respect, liberalism *v.* nationalism may be a specific instance of what is frequently now regarded as a more general contest between liberals and communitarians.[9] It turns out that, if there is a contest here at all, it occurs at the level of justifying theory rather than at the level of political principle: most 'communitarians' adopt recognizably liberal political positions.[10] This is not to say that the justifying theory makes no difference at all. Liberalism-on-communitarian-foundations will diverge from liberalism-on-individualistic-foundations over certain practical issues. So it is, as we shall shortly see, with liberalism modified to take account of the principle of nationality.

Let me indicate four places at which liberals and nationalists may find themselves adopting opposing standpoints.

1. Liberals, who place a high value on individual autonomy, may be drawn towards what I called in Chapter 2 the radical chooser picture of the self. This is the idea that we should choose our values and goals, our identities and affiliations, by distancing ourselves from all those that we currently have, surveying a wide range of options, and making an individual choice. All our commitments, in other words,

---

[9] For a helpful introduction, see S. Mulhall and A. Swift, *Liberals and Communitarians* (Oxford, Blackwell, 1992); for a critique, see S. Caney, 'Liberalism and Communitarianism: A Misconceived Debate', *Political Studies*, 40 (1992), 273–89.

[10] At least two of the usual suspects in the communitarian lineup have expressly dismissed the idea that there is any simple contrast between liberalism and communitarianism; see M. Walzer, 'The Communitarian Critique of Liberalism', *Political Theory*, 18 (1990), 6–23, and C. Taylor, 'Cross-Purposes: The Liberal–Communitarian Debate', in N. Rosenblum (ed.), *Liberalism and the Moral Life* (Cambridge, Mass., Harvard University Press, 1989).

are open to review, and they become genuinely ours only after an act of choice on our part. In contrast, the nationalist will want to insist that our membership of a national community is not open to choice in this way, and that the public culture which the community embodies forms an unchosen background against which more specific private cultural decisions can be made.

2. Liberals, for somewhat similar reasons, may be drawn towards the idea that social and political institutions are legitimate only when each person gives, or at least can give, them his rational consent. This idea is expressed, for instance, in the contractual theory of the state, according to which the state's authority depends upon each individual citizen registering her consent through a social contract. The nationalist, in contrast, views the question in less individualistic terms; political institutions are legitimate when they serve to express the will of the national community, which requires that the interests and beliefs of each member should be represented, but not that there should be individual consent to institutions or policies. This difference in underlying view may lead to differences on the question of political secession, where, as we saw in Chapter 4, a liberal who sees the state as a voluntary association resting on consent will argue that any group that wishes to secede is prima facie entitled to do so. For a nationalist, the question is whether secession will promote or hinder the cause of national self-determination, which involves looking at political identities in the two states that secession would create, and not simply at the wishes of individuals.

3. Liberals are inclined to see little intrinsic value in public life and political participation. They attach most value to individuals pursuing their aims in private or in voluntary association with others. The aim of politics is to provide the conditions under which these subpolitical activities can be carried out successfully. The liberal citizen, therefore, is a bearer of rights and an observer of rules, someone who becomes active only to protect the constitution or to secure his interests. Nationalists, by contrast, are likely to attach intrinsic value to public life, and to adopt a republican view of citizenship, according to which the citizen should be actively engaged at some level in political debate and decision-making.[11] This follows from a view of national identity as something that is gradually but continuously

[11] This contrast is developed in my paper 'Citizenship and Pluralism', *Political Studies*, 43 (1995), 432–50.

remade through open discussion, and from the idea of national self-determination, which cannot be genuinely *national* unless all social groups are actively participating in the making of public policy.

4. Liberals are inclined, explicitly or implicitly, to favour a policy of cultural neutrality. They expect each person to choose his or her plan of life, either as an individual or as part of a cultural group, and that choice, having been made, must be respected. The state should respect personal choices by tolerating all plans of life that do not impinge on the lives of others, and more broadly by giving each equal recognition—so for instance, it should not permit one particular religion to be promoted at the expense of others through the education system. Nationalists, though perhaps favouring neutrality on some cultural questions, are committed to non-neutrality where the national culture itself is at stake. In other words, where some cultural feature—a landscape, a musical tradition, a language—has become a component part of national identity, it is justifiable to discriminate in its favour if the need arises. This might mean devoting resources to its protection, giving it a place in the school curriculum, and so forth. The justification is that a national culture gives the society its distinct identity, but may be unintentionally eroded in a cultural free-for-all. And, although I have distanced myself clearly from the view that a fixed version of national identity is to be inculcated in the rising generation, and favoured instead the view that sees such identities as open to continuing reinterpretation, I have defended a civic education that presents to students the political principles on which their society operates, and traces the historical process whereby those principles have come into play.

Liberals and nationalists will find themselves somewhat at odds over issues such as these. It does not follow, however, that nationality is an essentially illiberal idea. What it does mean is that the principle of nationality makes a difference to the way we think about a wide range of issues—citizenship, minority rights, education, the promotion of cultures, constitutions, political boundaries, duties beyond borders, and many more. Embracing the principle, we may still want to be liberals (or social democrats, or socialists . . .) but our assumptions have shifted. My aim in this book has been to spell these assumptions out as clearly as I can and to see where they lead us morally and politically.

BIBLIOGRAPHY

Acton, Lord, 'Nationality', in *The History of Freedom and Other Essays*, (ed.) J. N. Figgis (London, Macmillan, 1907).

Anderson, B., *Imagined Communities*, rev. edn. (London, Verso, 1991).

Archard, D., 'Myths, Lies and Historical Truth: A Defence of Nationalism', *Political Studies*, 43 (1995), 472–81.

Ashford, S. and Timms, N., *What Europe Thinks: A Study of Western European Values* (Aldershot, Dartmouth, 1992).

Baldwin, T., 'The Territorial State', in H. Gross and R. Harrison (eds.), *Jurisprudence: Cambridge Essays* (Oxford, Clarendon Press, 1992).

Barry, B., 'Self-Government Revisited', in D. Miller and L. Siedentop (eds.), *The Nature of Political Theory* (Oxford, Clarendon Press, 1983).

—— *Democracy, Power and Justice* (Oxford, Clarendon Press, 1989).

—— and Goodin, R. E. (eds.), *Free Movement: Ethical Issues in the Transnational Migration of People and Money* (Hemel Hempstead, Harvester Wheatsheaf, 1992).

Beitz, C., *Political Theory and International Relations* (Princeton, Princeton University Press, 1979).

—— 'Cosmopolitan Ideals and National Sentiment', *Journal of Philosophy*, 80 (1983), 591–600.

—— 'Sovereignty and Morality in International Affairs', in D. Held (ed.), *Political Theory Today* (Cambridge, Polity Press, 1991).

Bell, D., *Communitarianism and its Critics* (Oxford, Clarendon Press, 1993).

Bellah, R. *et al.*, *Habits of the Heart* (Berkeley, University of California Press, 1985).

Benn, S., *A Theory of Freedom* (Cambridge, Cambridge University Press, 1988).

Benner, E., *Marx and Engels on Nationalism and National Identity: A Reappraisal* (D.Phil. thesis, University of Oxford, 1992).

Bennett, A., *Writing Home* (London, Faber and Faber, 1994).

Beran, H., 'A Liberal Theory of Secession', *Political Studies*, 32 (1984), 21–31.

—— 'More Theory of Secession: A Response to Birch', *Political Studies*, 36 (1988), 316–23.

Berlin, I., 'Two Concepts of Liberty', in *Four Essays on Liberty* (Oxford, Oxford University Press, 1969).

Berlin, I., 'Nationalism: Past Neglect and Present Power', in H. Hardy (ed.), *Against the Current* (Oxford, Oxford University Press, 1981).

Birch, A. H., 'Another Liberal Theory of Secession', *Political Studies*, 32 (1984), 596–602.

—— *Nationalism and National Integration* (London, Unwin Hyman, 1989).

Brand, J., Mitchell, J. and Surridge, P., 'Identity and the Vote: Class and Nationality in Scotland', in D. Denver *et al.* (eds.), *British Elections and Parties Yearbook 1993* (Hemel Hempstead, Harvester Wheatsheaf, 1993).

Brierly, J. L., *The Law of Nations*, 6th edn. (Oxford, Clarendon Press, 1963).

Brubaker, R., *Citizenship and Nationhood in France and Germany* (Cambridge, Mass., Harvard University Press, 1992).

Buchanan, A., *Secession* (Boulder, Colo., Westview Press, 1991).

Caney, S., 'Liberalism and Communitarianism: A Misconceived Debate', *Political Studies*, 40 (1992), 273–89.

Cannadine, D., 'The British Monarchy c.1820–1977', in E. Hobsbawm and T. Ranger (eds.), *The Invention of Tradition* (Cambridge, Cambridge University Press, 1983).

—— 'Penguin Island Story', *Times Literary Supplement*, no. 4693 (12 March 1993), 4–5.

Casey, J., 'Tradition and Authority', in M. Cowling (ed.), *Conservative Essays* (London, Cassell, 1978).

—— 'One Nation: The Politics of Race', *Salisbury Review*, 1 (1982), 23–8.

Cohen, J., 'Deliberation and Democratic Legitimacy', in A. Hamlin and P. Pettit (eds.), *The Good Polity* (Oxford, Blackwell, 1989).

Cohen, L. J., *Broken Bonds: The Disintegration of Yugoslavia* (Boulder, Colo., Westview Press, 1993).

Colley, L., *Britons: Forging the Nation 1707–1837* (New Haven, Yale University Press, 1992).

Connolly, W. E., *Identity/Difference* (Ithaca, NY, Cornell University Press, 1991).

Cottingham, J., 'Ethics and Impartiality', *Philosophical Studies*, 43 (1983), 83–99.

Cressy, D., 'The Fifth of November Remembered', in R. Porter (ed.), *The Myths of the English* (Cambridge, Polity Press, 1992).

Crewe, I., 'Has the Electorate become Thatcherite?' in R. Skidelsky (ed.), *Thatcherism* (Oxford, Blackwell, 1989).

Crick, B., 'The English and the British', in B. Crick (ed.), *National Identities* (Oxford, Blackwell, 1991).

Davis, S. M. and Schwartz, M. D., *Children's Rights and the Law* (Lexington, Mass., D. C. Heath, 1987).

Defoe, D., *The True-Born Englishman*, in *Works*, v (London, Bell and Daldy, 1871).

Dicey, A. V. and Rait, R. S., *Thoughts on the Union between England and Scotland* (London, Macmillan, 1920).

Dickens, C., *Our Mutual Friend* (London, Hazel, Watson and Viney, n.d.).

Dryzek, J., *Discursive Democracy* (Cambridge, Cambridge University Press, 1990).

Dukas, H. and Hoffman, B., *Albert Einstein: The Human Side* (Princeton, Princeton University Press, 1979).

Fichte, J. G., *Addresses to the German Nation* (Chicago, Open Court, 1922).

Fleras, A. and Elliott, J. L., *The 'Nations Within': Aboriginal–State Relations in Canada, the United States, and New Zealand* (Toronto, Oxford University Press, 1992).

Foot, P., *The Politics of Harold Wilson* (Harmondsworth, Penguin, 1968).

Forsyth, M., *Unions of States: The Theory and Practice of Confederation* (Leicester, Leicester University Press, 1981).

Gellner, E., *Nations and Nationalism* (Oxford, Blackwell, 1983).

Gewirth, A., 'Ethical Universalism and Particularism', *Journal of Philosophy*, 85 (1988), 283–302.

Glazer, N. and Moynihan, D. P. (eds.), *Ethnicity: Theory and Experience* (Cambridge, Mass., Harvard University Press, 1975).

Gleason, P., 'American Identity and Americanization', in S. Thernstrom (ed.), *The Harvard Encyclopaedia of American Ethnic Groups* (Cambridge, Mass., Harvard University Press, 1980).

Goodin, R. E., *Protecting the Vulnerable* (Chicago, University of Chicago Press, 1985).

—— 'What Is So Special About Our Fellow Countrymen?' *Ethics*, 98 (1987–8), 663–86.

Gorovitz, S., 'Bigotry, Loyalty, and Malnutrition', in P. G. Brown and H. Shue (eds.), *Food Policy* (New York, Free Press, 1977).

Gray, J., *A Conservative Disposition* (London, Centre for Policy Studies, 1991).

Greenfeld, L., *Nationalism: Five Roads to Modernity* (Cambridge, Mass., Harvard University Press, 1992).

Habermas, J., 'Citizenship and National Identity: Some Reflections on the Future of Europe', *Praxis International*, 12 (1992–3), 1–19.

Hannum, H., *Autonomy, Sovereignty and Self-Determination: The Accommodation of Conflicting Rights* (Philadelphia, University of Pennsylvania Press, 1990).

Harles, J., *Politics in the Lifeboat: Immigrants and the American Democratic Order* (Boulder, Colo., Westview Press, 1993).

200 *Bibliography*

Harman, N., *Dunkirk: The Necessary Myth* (London, Hodder and Stoughton, 1980).

Harrington, M., 'Loyalties: Dual and Divided', in S. Thernstrom (ed.), *The Harvard Encyclopaedia of American Ethnic Groups* (Cambridge, Mass., Harvard University Press, 1980).

Hart, H. L. A., 'Are There any Natural Rights?' in A. Quinton (ed.), *Political Philosophy* (Oxford, Oxford University Press, 1967).

Hayek, F. A., *The Road to Serfdom* (London, Routledge, 1944).

—— *Law, Legislation and Liberty*, ii, *The Mirage of Social Justice* (London, Routledge and Kegan Paul, 1976).

—— 'The Atavism of Social Justice', in *New Studies in Philosophy, Politics, Economics and the History of Ideas* (London, Routledge and Kegan Paul, 1978).

Hewstone, M., *Understanding Attitudes to the European Community* (Cambridge, Cambridge University Press, 1986).

Hill, C., 'The Norman Yoke', in *Puritanism and Revolution* (London, Mercury, 1962).

Hinsley, F. H., *Sovereignty*, 2nd edn. (Cambridge, Cambridge University Press, 1986).

Hobsbawm, E. J., *Nations and Nationalism since 1780* (Cambridge, Cambridge University Press, 1990).

Horowitz, D., 'Ethnic Identity', in N. Glazer and D. P. Moynihan (eds.), *Ethnicity: Theory and Experience* (Cambridge, Mass., Harvard University Press, 1975).

—— *Ethnic Groups in Conflict* (Berkeley, University of California Press, 1985).

Horton, J., 'Liberalism, Multiculturalism and Toleration', in J. Horton (ed.), *Liberalism, Multiculturalism and Toleration* (London, Macmillan, 1993).

Hume, D., *A Treatise of Human Nature*, (ed.) L. A. Selby-Bigge, rev. P. H. Nidditch (Oxford, Clarendon Press, 1978).

—— 'Of National Characters', in *Essays Moral, Political, and Literary*, (ed.) E. Miller (Indianapolis, Liberty Classics, 1985).

Ignatieff, M., *Blood and Belonging: Journeys into the New Nationalism* (London, Vintage, 1994).

Kamenka, E., 'Political Nationalism: The Evolution of the Idea', in E. Kamenka (ed.), *Nationalism: The Nature and Evolution of an Idea* (London, Edward Arnold, 1976).

Kearney, R. N., 'Ethnic Conflict and the Tamil Separatist Movement in Sri Lanka', *Asian Survey*, 25 (1985), 898–917.

Kedourie, E., *Nationalism* (London, Hutchinson, 1966).

Kirzner, I., *Discovery, Capitalism, and Distributive Justice* (Oxford, Blackwell, 1989).

Klosko, G., *The Principle of Fairness and Political Obligation* (Lanham, Md., Rowman and Littlefield, 1992).

Kohn, H., *The Idea of Nationalism* (New York, Macmillan, 1944).

—— *Nationalism and Liberty: The Swiss example* (London, Allen and Unwin, 1956).

Kukathas, C., 'Are There Any Cultural Rights?' *Political Theory*, 20 (1992), 105–39.

Kymlicka, W., *Liberalism, Community and Culture* (Oxford, Clarendon Press, 1989).

—— *Multicultural Citizenship* (Oxford, Clarendon Press, 1995).

Levinson, S., *Constitutional Faith* (Princeton, Princeton University Press, 1988).

Lunn, E., *Prophet of Community: The Romantic Socialism of Gustav Landauer* (Berkeley, University of California Press, 1973).

MacCormick, N., 'Nation and Nationalism', in *Legal Right and Social Democracy* (Oxford, Clarendon Press, 1982).

MacIntyre, A., 'The Magic in the Pronoun "My"', *Ethics*, 94 (1983–4), 113–25.

—— *Is Patriotism a Virtue?*, Lindley Lecture (University of Kansas, 1984).

Manin, B., 'On Legitimacy and Political Deliberation', *Political Theory*, 15 (1987), 338–68.

Margalit, A. and Raz, J., 'National Self-Determination', *Journal of Philosophy*, 87 (1990), 439–61.

Marshall, P. J., 'No Fatal Impact?' *Times Literary Supplement*, no. 4693 (12 March 1993), 8–10.

Mill, J. S., *Utilitarianism; On Liberty; Representative Government*, (ed.) H. B. Acton (London, Dent, 1972).

Miller, D., 'Market Neutrality and the Failure of Co-operatives', *British Journal of Political Science*, 11 (1981), 309–29.

—— *Philosophy and Ideology in Hume's Political Thought* (Oxford, Clarendon Press, 1981).

—— 'In What Sense Must Socialism be Communitarian?' *Social Philosophy and Policy*, 6 (1988–9), 51–73.

—— '"Autonomous" *v.* "Autarchic" Persons', *Government and Opposition*, 24 (1989), 255–8.

—— *Market, State and Community* (Oxford, Clarendon Press, 1989).

—— 'Equality', in G. M. K. Hunt (ed.), *Philosophy and Politics* (Cambridge, Cambridge University Press, 1990).

—— (ed.), *Liberty* (Oxford, Oxford University Press, 1991).

—— 'Deliberative Democracy and Social Choice', *Political Studies*, Special Issue, 40 (1992), 54–67.

—— 'Public Goods without the State', *Critical Review*, 7 (1993), 505–23.

Miller, D., 'Citizenship and Pluralism', *Political Studies*, 43 (1995), 432–50.
—— 'Equality after Raz', in S. Caney and A. Williams, *Joseph Raz's Political Philosophy* (forthcoming).
Minogue, K., *Nationalism* (London, Batsford, 1967).
Modood, T., 'Establishment, Multiculturalism and British Citizenship', *Political Quarterly*, 65 (1994), 53–73.
Mulhall, S. and Swift, A., *Liberals and Communitarians* (Oxford, Blackwell, 1992).
Nagel, T., *Equality and Partiality* (New York, Oxford University Press, 1991).
Nathanson, S., *Patriotism, Morality and Peace* (Lanham, Md., Rowman and Littlefield, 1993).
National Curriculum History Working Group, *Final Report* (London, HMSO, 1990).
Nickel, J. W., 'Rawls on Political Community and Principles of Justice', *Law and Philosophy*, 9 (1990), 205–16.
Oldenquist, A., 'Loyalties', *Journal of Philosophy*, 79 (1982), 173–93.
Orwell, G., *The Road to Wigan Pier* (Harmondsworth, Penguin, 1962).
—— 'The English People', in *The Collected Essays, Journalism and Letters of George Orwell*, iii, (ed.) S. Orwell and I. Angus (Harmondsworth, Penguin, 1970).
—— 'The Lion and the Unicorn', in *The Collected Essays, Journalism and Letters of George Orwell*, ii, (ed.) S. Orwell and I. Angus (Harmondsworth, Penguin, 1970).
Oxford English Dictionary (Clarendon Press, Oxford, 1989).
Palmer, R. R., 'French Nationalism before the Revolution', *Journal of the History of Ideas*, 1 (1940), 95–111.
Parekh, B., 'The "New Right" and the Politics of Nationhood', in *The New Right: Image and Reality* (London, Runnymede Trust, 1986).
—— 'Britain and the Social Logic of Pluralism', in G. Andrews (ed.), *Citizenship* (London, Lawrence and Wishart, 1991).
Plamenatz, J. P., *On Alien Rule and Self-Government* (London, Longmans, 1960).
—— 'Two Types of Nationalism', in E. Kamenka (ed.), *Nationalism: The Nature and Evolution of an Idea* (London, Edward Arnold, 1976).
Pocock, J. G. A., *The Ancient Constitution and the Feudal Law* (Cambridge, Cambridge University Press, 1957).
Quirk, R., 'Language and Nationhood', in C. MacLean (ed.), *The Crown and the Thistle* (Edinburgh, Scottish Academic Press, 1979).
Rawls, J., 'Legal Obligation and the Duty of Fair Play', in S. Hook (ed.), *Law and Philosophy* (New York, New York University Press, 1964).
—— *A Theory of Justice* (Cambridge, Mass., Harvard University Press, 1971).

—— *Political Liberalism* (New York, Columbia University Press, 1993).

Raz, J., *The Morality of Freedom* (Oxford, Clarendon Press, 1986).

—— 'Multiculturalism: A Liberal Perspective', *Dissent*, 41(1) (Winter 1994), 67–79.

Renan, E., 'What is a Nation?' in A. Zimmern (ed.), *Modern Political Doctrines* (London, Oxford University Press, 1939).

Rodal, B., 'The Canadian Conundrum: Two Concepts of Nationhood', in U. Ra'anan, M. Mesner, K. Armes, and K. Martin, *State and Nation in Multi-Ethnic Societies* (Manchester, Manchester University Press, 1991).

Runblom, H. and Roth, H. I., *The Multicultural Baltic Region*, i (Uppsala, Baltic University Secretariat, 1993).

Sacks, J., *The Persistence of Faith* (London, Weidenfeld and Nicolson, 1991).

Sandel, M., *Liberalism and the Limits of Justice* (Cambridge, Cambridge University Press, 1982).

Sartre, J. P., *Existentialism and Humanism* (London, Methuen, 1948).

Schama, S., *The Embarrassment of Riches* (London, Fontana, 1991).

Schlesinger, A. M. Jr, *The Disuniting of America* (New York, W. W. Norton, 1992).

Schnapper, D., 'The Debate on Immigration and the Crisis of National Identity', *West European Politics*, 17 (1994), 127–39.

Scruton, R., *The Meaning of Conservatism* (Harmondsworth, Penguin, 1980).

—— 'In Defence of the Nation', in *The Philosopher on Dover Beach* (Manchester, Carcanet, 1990).

Sen, A., *Poverty and Famines: An Essay on Entitlement and Deprivation* (Oxford, Clarendon Press, 1981).

Seton-Watson, H., *Nations and States* (London, Methuen, 1977).

Shue, H., *Basic Rights: Subsistence, Affluence and American Foreign Policy* (Princeton, Princeton University Press, 1980).

—— 'Mediating Duties', *Ethics*, 98 (1987–8), 687–704.

Sidgwick, H., *The Elements of Politics*, 2nd edn. (London, Macmillan, 1897).

—— *The Methods of Ethics*, 7th edn. (London, Macmillan, 1963).

Sieyès, E. J., *What Is the Third Estate?* (London, Pall Mall Press, 1963).

Singer, P., 'Reconsidering the Famine Relief Argument', in P. G. Brown and H. Shue (eds.), *Food Policy* (New York, Free Press, 1977).

Smith, A. D., *The Ethnic Origins of Nations* (Oxford, Blackwell, 1986).

—— *National Identity* (Harmondsworth, Penguin, 1991).

Sunstein, C. R., 'Beyond the Republican Revival', *Yale Law Journal*, 97 (1988), 1539–89.

Tamir, Y., *Liberal Nationalism* (Princeton, Princeton University Press, 1993).

Taylor, C., 'Cross-Purposes: The Liberal–Communitarian Debate', in N. Rosenblum (ed.), *Liberalism and the Moral Life* (Cambridge, Mass., Harvard University Press, 1989).

—— *Multiculturalism and 'The Politics of Recognition'*, (ed.) A. Gutmann (Princeton, Princeton University Press, 1992).

—— 'Shared and Divergent Values', in G. Laforest (ed.), *Reconciling the Solitudes* (Montreal, McGill-Queen's University Press, 1993).

—— 'Can Liberalism be Communitarian?' *Critical Review*, 8 (1994), 257–62.

Thompson, F., *Lark Rise to Candleford* (London, Oxford University Press, 1945).

Tolstoy, L., 'On Patriotism', in *Essays and Letters* (London, Henry Frowde, 1903).

Trudeau, P., 'Quebec and the Constitutional Problem', in *Federalism and the French Canadians* (Toronto, Macmillan, 1968).

Van Dyke, V., 'The Individual, the State and Ethnic Communities in Political Theory', *World Politics*, 29 (1976–7), 343–69.

Van Gunsteren, H., 'Admission to Citizenship', *Ethics*, 98 (1987–8), 731–41.

Waldron, J., 'Minority Cultures and the Cosmopolitan Alternative', *University of Michigan Journal of Law Reform*, 25 (1991–2), 751–93.

Walzer, M., *Spheres of Justice* (Oxford, Martin Robertson, 1983).

—— *The Company of Critics* (London, Peter Halban, 1989).

—— 'Nation and Universe', in G. B. Petersen (ed.), *The Tanner Lectures on Human Values*, xi (Salt Lake City, University of Utah Press, 1990).

—— 'The Communitarian Critique of Liberalism', *Political Theory*, 18 (1990), 6–23.

—— 'What Does It Mean to Be an "American"?' *Social Research*, 57 (1990), 591–614.

—— 'The Politics of Rescue', *Dissent*, 42(1) (Winter 1995), 35–41.

Ward, C., 'The Limits of "Liberal Republicanism": Why Group-Based Remedies and Republican Citizenship Don't Mix', *Columbia Law Review*, 91 (1991), 581–607.

Weber, E., *Peasants into Frenchmen* (London, Chatto and Windus, 1979).

Weber, M., 'Politics as a Vocation', in H. H. Gerth and C. W. Mills (eds.), *From Max Weber* (London, Routledge and Kegan Paul, 1970).

Wiener, M. J., *English Culture and the Decline of the Industrial Spirit 1850–1980* (Cambridge, Cambridge University Press, 1981).

Williams, B., 'Persons, Character and Morality', in *Moral Luck* (Cambridge, Cambridge University Press, 1981).

—— *Ethics and the Limits of Philosophy* (London, Fontana, 1985).

Wilterdink, N., 'An Examination of European and National Identity', *Archives Européennes de Sociologie*, 34 (1993), 119–36.

Wittgenstein, L., *Philosophical Investigations* (Oxford, Blackwell, 1963).

World Tables 1993 (Baltimore, Johns Hopkins University Press, 1993).

Young, I. M., *Justice and the Politics of Difference* (Princeton, Princeton University Press, 1990).

Young-Bruehl, E., *Hannah Arendt: For Love of the World* (New Haven, Yale University Press, 1982).

INDEX